PACKWOOD

Mark Kirchmeier

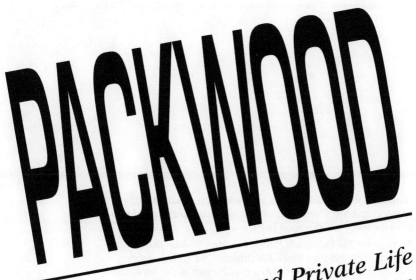

PACKWOOD

*The Public and Private Life
from Acclaim to Outrage*

HarperCollins*West*
A Division of HarperCollins*Publishers*

HarperCollinsWest and Mark Kirchmeier, in association with the Rainforest Action Network, will facilitate the planting of two trees for every one tree used in the manufacture of this book.

FIRST EDITION

Library of Congress Cataloging-in-Publication Data
Kirchmeier, Mark.
    Packwood : the public and private life from acclaim to outrage / Mark Kirchmeier. — 1st ed.
        p. cm.
    ISBN 0-06-258549-5 (cloth : alk. paper)
    1. Packwood, Bob. 2. Legislators—United States—Biography.
3. United States. Congress. Senate—Biography. I. Title.
E840.8.P33K57 1994
328.73'092—dc20
[B]
                                                94-21234
                                                CIP

95 96 97 98 99 RRD(H) 10 9 8 7 6 5 4 3 2 1

This edition is printed on acid-free paper that meets the American National Standards Institute Z39.48 Standard.

CONTENTS

To Jane Hagan

ACKNOWLEDGMENTS

More than two hundred interviews went into the making of this book. Senator Robert Packwood declined to be one of those interviewed, although close friends of his provided invaluable insights and anecdotes. Interviews were almost entirely on the record. A few individuals did not want their names used, and one of them is quoted under a pseudonym. Bill Donahue, a contributor to *People* magazine, and Jill Smith, former *Willamette Week* political reporter, helped in completing interviews, particularly those on Packwood's early years and his family.

Previously published reporting by news organizations, including the *Washington Post, Los Angeles Times, New York Times, Wall Street Journal,* the *Oregonian,* the Associated Press, and *Newsweek,* supplemented my work.

The reporting of Tom Bates was indispensable, particularly his October 1979 *Oregon Magazine* profile, and later the *Los Angeles Times Sunday Magazine* and the *Oregonian* articles.

Peter J. Boyer published an insightful profile in April 1994 for the *New Yorker,* which revealed key information. I interviewed Trip Gabriel, the author of the *New York Times Sunday Magazine* article on Packwood. In Washington, D.C., *Roll Call* staff writer Glenn Simpson produced several excellent stories on the Senate Ethics Committee; Linda Kramer of *People*'s Washington bureau provided interviews and access to many of her notes. My debt to these people is large.

I was also aided by published pieces from a number of journalists, including Helen Dewar of the *Post;* Scott Sonner of the Associated Press's Washington bureau; Rose Ellen O'Connor, Steve Duin, Jeff Mapes, Jim Long, Dee Lane, Steve Mayes, and others from the *Oregonian;* Terry McDermott for a 1986 *Seattle Times* magazine profile; Jim Redden, Jr.'s, September 1985 *Willamette Week* profile; Brent Walth and Karen McCowan of the Eugene *Register-Guard;* the Salem *Statesman Journal,* and Medford *Mail Tribune.*

Congressional Quarterly, National Journal, Politics in America, and the *Almanac of American Politics* all provided details about either Packwood's career or the sexual misconduct investigation. Stories on the 1986 Tax Reform Act by Anne Swardson and Dale Russakoff were central to chapter 10.

Pertinent books included *Showdown at Gucci Gulch,* by *Wall Street Journal* writers Jeff Birnbaum and Alan Murray; *Capitol Games,* by Timothy Phelps and Helen Winternitz; *Nightmare: The Underside of the Nixon Years,* by J. Anthony Lukas; *Sexual Harassment of Working Women,* by Catharine A. MacKinnon; and the United Nations International Labor Organization reports.

This book would not have been completed without the support of University of Portland vice president for university relations Anthony DiSpigno, and the priceless encouragement of John Soisson, director of public relations. The aforementioned Tom Bates, a former *Los Angeles Times Sunday Magazine* editor, now of the *Oregonian,* provided invaluable editing advice. I am indebted for manuscript suggestions by media critic Robert Fulford, a University of Portland journalism professor, and Elizabeth Moss of Washington, D.C.; Brian Doyle, *University of Portland Magazine* editor, provided writing refinements. They all share in the book's successes. The failings are mine alone.

Ann Harroun, Tony Barnes, and Christine Fundak, the latter on her off-hours, provided research and checked stray facts. In the book's initial phases, Steve Forrester of the *Daily Asto-*

rian provided helpful material through interviews and his *Northwest Newsletter.* Bill Redden of *PDXS,* Gary Malecha, Ronald Buel, Win McCormack, and former colleague G. Pascall "Gregg" Zachary, now of the *Wall Street Journal,* gave editing advice. Charlotte Voorde provided her Hoosier hospitality and a memorable dinner during my stay in Washington, D.C. Thanks to Jo Laughlin for turning me over to Charlotte.

Cathy Cheney performed yeoman's duty. Gannett writer/editor John Ferris lent assistance. Susan Orlean of the *New Yorker* helped unlock a key interview. I am also appreciative to Timothy Egan, of the *New York Times,* for a private comment that had much to do with the book's completion.

I am deeply obliged to the careful tenders of the reference sections at the Library of Congress, the Reagan, Carter, and Nixon presidential libraries, the University of Portland, the Multnomah County Library, the Western States Center, the Investigative Reporters and Editors Library in Columbia, Missouri, and Alden Moberg of the Oregon State Library.

My agent, Diana Finch, of the Ellen Levine Literary Agency, gave encouragement during the inevitable delays. My gratitude to the patience and hard work of HarperCollins*West* editors Joann Moschella, Naomi Lucks, Karin Mullen, and Lisa Zuniga-Carlsen.

Thanks to my parents, Helen Kirchmeier and the late Fred Kirchmeier, for passing on their love of history and government. And, most importantly, I am grateful for the editing and special encouragement of my wife, Jane Hagan. I won't always need Jane's blue pencil. I will always need her love.

Mark Kirchmeier

PROLOGUE

Who is Bob Packwood? This twenty-seven-year veteran of the Senate, respected by many Americans for his strong, independent stands on a variety of issues, from women's rights to tax reform, is nothing if not complex.

He's a longtime Republican senator who's known as a maverick, regularly voting against his party on such issues as abortion, civil rights, and Israel-Arab conflicts.

He writes sentimental notes to people and loves watching sweet, uplifting movies such as *It's a Wonderful Life* and *Easter Parade,* yet he tells reporters that he prefers the moody and psychologically dark *Lawrence of Arabia.*

He's a highly competitive sportsman who never quits. "Bob *detests* losing," says his longtime friend CBS news anchor Dan Rather. One Senate colleague, Rhode Island Senator John Chafee, says that Packwood's hypertenacity even applies to his squash game. "You can never count him out. When [you're ahead] fourteen to eleven, don't relax." Pennsylvania Senator Arlen Specter once left the court with a bone fracture after one of Packwood's wide backswings connected with his face.

He enjoys speaking to large audiences and shines in pressure-cooker debates, yet freezes when faced with simple one-to-one xii interactions. He enjoys sailing, but only when he's at the helm of a one-man Laser. An introvert in the quintessential extrovert's profession, Packwood projects an odd sense of distance, as if there were an impenetrable space around him. As a member of his family once said, "This is not a warm and fuzzy person."

He has worked for many years with America's great monied interests, but he has little concern with personal financial gain. "He takes pride in calling himself 'one of the Senate's poorest members,'" says one reporter. And few doubt Packwood's sincerity. He has never gone in for sweetheart stock arrangements or taken advantage of cushy investment deals from contributors and lobbyists. He has lived on his salary and, when they were still legal, honoraria. He buys his suits off the rack and drove an unpretentious Plymouth Voyager for many years. He drinks draft beer and pours his wine out of a box.

He enjoyed the reputation of a happy family man and champion of women's rights, yet now he stands accused of having always been a sleazy womanizer.

Few Americans have more starkly personified an issue than Packwood now has in becoming a nationwide symbol for sexual misconduct. This story literally altered the nation: the rate of sexual harassment claims rose in direct proportion to Packwood disclosures. The effects of these disclosures have ripped through the lives of women, agency administrators, attorneys, politicians, executives, managers—not only in the United States, but in Canada, the United Kingdom, Japan, and elsewhere.

As of this writing, the U.S. Senate and the Justice Department have not decided on Packwood's innocence or guilt. But this much is clear: Packwood has already lost the esteem of the country, and the hundreds of thousands of women who admired his pro-feminist leadership.

This book tries to discover why his downfall happened, and why this figure of political achievement, soaring intellect, and capacity for decency, so often chose a manipulative and cynical path. His story is largely one of the failure of cynicism, and of the age-old struggle between power and ethics.

1

It was October 1991, and veteran Oregon Senator Bob Packwood's reelection bid was shaping up to be a tough one: after twenty-four successful years in the Senate, he was up against a sick economy and an electorate that was tired of seeing his face. Married for twenty-six years, he had divorced his wife, Georgie, the year before. In the past, this Republican had triumphed over image problems by masterfully manipulating national issues and outcampaigning weak opponents. But in Democratic Representative Les AuCoin, the incumbent senator found himself up against someone who might actually beat him.

AuCoin, who had won election to Congress in 1974, the Watergate reform year, had risen steadily to become an environmental and pro-choice leader. Younger and more telegenic than Packwood, he appealed to the same suburban, female, and blue-collar constituencies that the fifty-nine-year-old Packwood needed to retain his seat. As those voters comparison shopped, the senator's popularity dipped dangerously low.

Waning support gave Packwood a jolt. The difficult races were supposed to be over after nearly a quarter-century in the Senate. After all, no American male politician championed

4   women's rights more; few Republican senators equaled his record on labor; and none matched his expertise on health-care reform. Yet here he was, struggling to maintain the lead.

Packwood had never really had a career outside politics, and the prospect filled him with loathing. So, brilliantly and with renewed energy, he prepared for his 1992 reelection campaign. He worked innumerable fund-raising dinners in Los Angeles, New York, San Francisco, Chicago, Boston, St. Louis, Detroit, and Louisville, Kentucky, and he salted away the contributions. His goal of $7.5 million in campaign funds rivaled sums collected by candidates in neighboring California, a state with ten times the population of Oregon.

The senator's mastery as a strategist came to the fore as he constructed, sometimes street by street, the state's most sophisticated campaign machine. He planned an advanced-technology telephone bank that would send his message to every Oregon voter during a single weekend. And for this race, he even improved on nature with cosmetic surgery for his drooping eyelids.

After surgery, Packwood refused to take even a short convalescence lying down. While recuperating at the southwest Portland home of his closest friend, Jack Faust, Packwood ordered boxes of material about AuCoin delivered to his room. He worked his way through everything from legislative bills to news releases and press clippings, searching for AuCoin's soft spots.

His diligence paid off when he discovered AuCoin's financial base rested with labor unions. That October, AuCoin had won a key endorsement from the Oregon American Federation of Labor-Congress of Industrial Organizations (AFL-CIO), which meant that each of Oregon's numerous member unions could give their maximum contribution—$10,000—to the candidate. Determined not to let that happen, Packwood picked up the phone to call some old friends.

When weeks had passed and AuCoin's campaign still hadn't received any AFL-CIO money, the Democrats began to get a little worried. Oregon AFL-CIO president Irv Fletcher called the union's national treasurer in Washington, D.C., trying to get the money flowing through the pipeline, but to no avail. Finally, he asked national AFL-CIO political director John Perkins point-blank: "Where's the check?"

"We're not releasing *your* money to AuCoin," Perkins informed him.

Stunned, Fletcher learned that Packwood had managed to slip in and cut a deal with AFL-CIO national president Lane Kirkland. The Republican senator knew how desperately labor wanted legislation passed that would prohibit companies from permanently replacing strikers. Since 1981, when President Ronald Reagan abruptly fired thousands of striking air traffic controllers, big business had followed that example and displaced tens of thousands of striking workers. Although the House of Representatives had already passed a labor bill to support the rights of such workers, Senate legislation dangled just beyond the union's reach—a few votes short of approval.

Packwood sold the AFL-CIO a watered-down version of the labor bill that might lure the additional four or five conservative votes needed for passage. In return, Kirkland agreed to obstruct AuCoin's fund-raising efforts until the Senate voted on the legislation in mid-1992.

The AFL-CIO and Packwood were now joined at the hip, and the union's hapless loyal friend, AuCoin, was powerless to fight this betrayal. Many Oregon workers were angry when they learned what the national union had done to AuCoin, and a rebellion erupted at the spring 1992 state AFL-CIO convention when longshoremen maneuvered for votes to condemn the Packwood compromise. A Packwood supporter in the building trades union leaked news of the rebellion to Tom Donahue, Kirkland's right-hand man in Washington, D.C. But the union stuck to the Packwood deal. "And holy shit," Fletcher said, "Donahue called and just chewed my ass for screwing up their Packwood agreement."

Although the union-Packwood arrangement survived the convention protest, the senator ultimately failed to obtain the conservative support he had promised Kirkland in return for his betrayal of AuCoin. The opponents of the bill, led by Republican senators Orrin Hatch of Utah, Bob Dole of Kansas,

6 and Jesse Helms of North Carolina, helped filibuster the measure to defeat in June 1991.

After having allowed Packwood to spin him around for months, a red-faced Lane Kirkland had gained nothing in exchange for obstructing the Oregon unions. The consequences for AuCoin were devastating: the candidate lost out on an estimated $150,000 in hard and soft money when he most needed it.

That spring, more powerful ammunition against AuCoin fell into Packwood's hands. A March 1992 audit of the U.S. House of Representatives Bank revealed AuCoin to be one of 130 lawmakers who had been overdrawing checks. He had made eighty-one overdrafts for a total of $61,000 over several years. Up until that point, AuCoin had been the favorite to defeat environmentalist Harry Lonsdale in the May 1992 Democratic Senate primary; but now, in the midst of the overdrawn check embarrassment, all bets were off. Since Packwood preferred to face the lightly regarded Lonsdale in the general election rather than AuCoin, he tried to manipulate the Democratic primary by purchasing his own television commercials—aimed at Democratic voters—pillorying AuCoin for his overdrawn checks. In the uproar, voters cared little that the congressional bank had held the checks and that AuCoin had made deposits to cover them.

AuCoin's eight-point lead over Lonsdale withered as primary day approached. Both Packwood and Lonsdale targeted him with a barrage of attack ads; Oregonians had seldom seen a politician portrayed so negatively. The primary cliff-hanger forced the embattled Democratic congressmember to empty the $2 million war chest he was saving to use against Packwood.

After a humiliating recount gave him a microscopic victory margin of just 330 votes (out of more than 360,000 cast), AuCoin staggered into the campaign against Packwood with neither his confidence nor his clean-government reputation intact.

The bottled-up AFL-CIO money hamstrung efforts to prepare for the general election. "We wanted to start reserving television time and rent campaigns but couldn't while the labor money was tied up," an AuCoin campaign aide said.

Even though Packwood was facing a weakened opponent, another potential problem arose that threatened to tip the race in AuCoin's favor. The conservative religious right-wing group Oregon Citizens Alliance (OCA) often created havoc for the state's Republicans. OCA leader Al Mobley prepared his own independent candidacy to protest Packwood's pro-choice and liberal social views. Mobley, who had similarly poisoned chances for pro-choice GOP gubernatorial nominee Dave Frohnmayer in 1990, threatened to siphon away Packwood votes, thereby potentially resuscitating AuCoin.

To evade this threat, Packwood masterminded another deal. In August, Texas Senator Phil Gramm invited OCA leaders to Washington, D.C., to hammer out an agreement: Packwood would not oppose the OCA's centerpiece issue, an anti-gay rights initiative, in exchange for Mobley's vow to bow out of the Senate race. The Republicans sweetened the pot by having Arizona Senator John McCain help the financially strapped OCA with a fund-raiser.

Oregon Republican party Chairman Craig Berkman later said that he and Elaine Franklin, Packwood's campaign manager, personally negotiated that bargain so that Packwood could have passed a lie detector test saying he did not make the arrangement himself. After Mobley's filing deadline expired in late August, Packwood reneged on the deal and announced his opposition to the anti-gay rights measure.

With Mobley out of his way, Packwood was running at full speed. He entered the fall campaign with nearly $3 million in his coffers compared to AuCoin's anemic $220,000, and he had a double-digit lead in the polls. He had skillfully turned the tables in the toughest race of his career but feared a scandal that was about to blow his world apart.

———

On 22 April 1992, Packwood aide Cathy Miles* was eating lunch with a friend, a former staffer for *Common Cause* magazine, at a Union Station cafe in Washington, D.C. As Miles took a sip of her drink, the conversation suddenly turned serious.

———

* Not her real name.

8   "I need to tell you," her friend confided, "that the magazine's former editor Florence Graves is writing a story accusing Senator Packwood of sexual harassment. Will you talk with her?"

Miles put down her glass, cleared her throat, and explained that she supported Packwood and would not cooperate. Later that afternoon she approached Packwood to warn him of the imminent danger.

"You have a problem," she said. "Former *Common Cause* editor Florence Graves is trying to write a story accusing you of sexual harassment."

Packwood said, "My God . . . What would sexual harassment be?"

"Well," replied Miles, "remember how you acted that time in the office?" She was referring to a time when the senator had suddenly kissed her, an encounter that left her in tears.

"Oh."

"That could be sexual harassment."

Packwood's mind was in gear now. "Yeah . . . "

"I'm loyal to you," Miles told him, "but if you have acted that way with other women, you could have a problem if they talk to Florence Graves."

The senator immediately asked Elaine Franklin to come into the office. The tough-as-nails campaign manager scowled as Miles reiterated the news.

The next day Packwood asked staff members to gather the names of every one of the several hundred women who had worked for him. Thus began an all-out effort to bury the story until after Packwood's November reelection bid and, he hoped, forever.

———

On the surface, Florence Graves didn't seem to be much of a threat: she was working as a freelancer, with no advance cash, no budget, and no certainty of finding a publisher. But Graves was a tenacious, shoe-leather journalist who had a keen interest in women's issues. Growing up in Waco, Texas, she had learned to recognize and deplore the injustices of segregation.

The white establishment had seemed oblivious to unfair conditions, and Graves concluded years later that some men were similarly blind to the indignities that women suffered. She took an activist approach to journalism, using the press to expose social problems.

Graves had been involved in journalism since high school, when she had edited the school newspaper. After working as an editorial page editor for the *Daily Texan* at the University of Texas in Austin, she finished her education at the University of Arizona Graduate School of Journalism. In the mid-1970s, she became managing editor of *Tucson Magazine,* where she displayed a talent for investigative reporting. Graves enlivened the lifestyle magazine with stories on the mid-1970s land development scandals that erupted in the aftermath of the murder of *Arizona Republic* crime reporter Don Bolles.

She parlayed her experience into a brief stint editing the *Washington Journalism Review* in Washington, D.C. She was particularly proud of a 1978 article alleging that CBS News withheld news film from the U.S. House of Representatives special committee investigating the assassination of President John F. Kennedy.

Graves differed from many members of the Washington media who seemed afflicted with a terminal sense of their own importance. She disarmed people with her friendly Lone Star accent, and her mid-forties blonde appearance reminded some people of Meryl Streep. She was soon hired to help establish the muckraking magazine *Common Cause,* for which she wrote and edited stories that led to more than a dozen congressional hearings and probes. One, accusing military contractors of charging millions of dollars in lobbying expenses to taxpayers, prodded the Reagan administration to crack down on such practices. Another, alleging shoddy regulation of the controversial sweetener Nutrasweet, led to hearings at the Food and Drug Administration.

After years in the Washington media scene, Graves began to feel that personal change must precede political change. She moved to Boston to become editor and associate publisher of *New Age Journal,* where she ran reflective pieces from Bill

10 Moyers, M. Scott Peck, and Alice Walker on the connections between politics, psychology, and spirituality.

By 1989 her job had become too managerial, and she decided to return to freelance writing and publishing. In the fall of 1991, while researching a prospectus for a new women's issues magazine, she became transfixed by the televised national debate involving a young Oklahoma lawyer named Anita Hill.

Hill's accusations of sexual harassment against her former boss, Supreme Court nominee Clarence Thomas, rang bells for Graves, who knew what many women coped with in Washington, D.C. And while Graves had no quarrel with flirting or office romance, she saw harassment as something entirely different. She believed that harassment was more than a man's sexual affront to a woman: it was a phenomenon that disempowered and silenced women, undermining their confidence and performance, and diminishing their value in the workplace.

To better understand the mind of the sexual harasser, she invested countless hours interviewing psychologists. She agreed with Harvard University psychologist Judith Jordon's analysis: "It's a way of saying, 'You may have an important job. You may think you're smart. But I still have power in this situation. And one of the ways I can exercise my power is by making you feel uncomfortable.'"

Graves believed that rebellious women were often discredited and silenced. The Hill-Thomas hearings seemed to validate that, as the judge's supporters dismissed his accuser as "delusional," "fantasizing," "a man-hater," and "a vengeful woman who combed *The Exorcist* looking for details to concoct her story."

After the Senate voted 52 to 48 to confirm Thomas, Graves anxiously waited for a major news organization to write what seemed to be the obvious follow-up—a story scrutinizing Congress on sexual harassment patterns.

By late March 1992 no major publication had produced such a piece, so Florence Graves decided to do it herself. She approached *Vanity Fair* with a proposal, which they accepted. As she delved into her research, she maintained a distinction between consensual philandering and unwanted sexual advances in the workplace, focusing on the latter. Over and over again Graves's sources kept singling out Bob Packwood, and the stories jibed with what Graves had heard of Packwood during her time at *Common Cause*.

The notion that the outspoken, pro-feminist Packwood habitually made unwanted sexual advances was stunning. Feminists had revered Packwood as their champion ever since he introduced the first pro-abortion bill in the Senate in 1970. He had risked his political neck against presidents Nixon, Ford, Carter, and Reagan to advance abortion rights, and he had become the leading Republican advocate for the Equal Rights Amendment and its extension. He had written groundbreaking proposals on child care, pregnancy leave, and insurance industry reform to end discrimination against women.

Could this man really be guilty of sexually harassing the very women who formed his base of support? Graves started checking the story, making calls from her suburban Boston home. She had many sources in Washington, but Oregon was foreign territory. In fact, she knew just one person in the entire state—Mark Zusman, editor of Portland's *Willamette Week* newspaper. In 1985 Zusman had asked reporter Teresa Riordan to check into rumors that the senator regularly made passes at women and had had numerous extramarital partners. Frustrated Oregon reporters could not confirm the allegations, and the project was shelved. Now Zusman was happy to provide Graves with a crucial source, political consultant Julie Myers Williamson of Portland.

When Graves telephoned Williamson, she heard an amazing story. Williamson had begun her political career as a twenty-eight-year-old aide during Packwood's successful 1968 Senate race, and in January 1969 he invited her to join his Portland office staff. Her tasks included planning dinners at which the senator could entertain reporters when he visited from Washington, D.C. These dinners were exclusively for Packwood and reporters—staff members were never invited. So she was thrilled when he asked her to attend one such affair at Burt Lee's restaurant in downtown Portland in February. Excited

12 at the prospect, she telephoned her husband, Doug Myers, and declared, "We're going out to dinner with Packwood!"

"But I was so dumb. As soon as I entered the restaurant and I saw Packwood's annoyed look, I knew that I'd goofed by bringing Doug." The lawmaker seated Julie next to him and sat Doug clear at the other end of the table; repeatedly, he put his hand on her knee, forcing her to keep brushing it off. After dinner, the group retired to the cocktail lounge, where Packwood sat beside Julie and Doug in a secluded, high-backed booth. When Doug excused himself to use the men's room, her boss leaned over and kissed her. The five-foot-one woman struggled to shove the 175-pound senator aside until her husband returned.

She attributed Packwood's advances to the steady stream of liquor he had consumed that night. Hoping for no further problems, she kept the incident quiet.

Packwood returned to the Portland office that spring. As he made his rounds, he saw Myers talking on the telephone—alone. Packwood sneaked up behind her and kissed her on the neck. Myers, shocked and surprised, spun around and warned: "Don't ever do that again."

She put down the receiver and walked into an adjacent room, but the senator followed. He cornered her, pulling her blonde ponytail and standing on her toes.

Packwood was not behaving like a person who was shy, drunk, or innocently unsophisticated. He was simply a bully. "He reached his hand up my skirt to try to pull my underpants down. I struggled to free my feet. I freed one and began kicking him hard on the shins. That made him stop," Myers remembered.

"Not today, but someday," Packwood responded.

That night Myers told her husband what had happened, and was crushed when he refused to believe her. Years later, she recognized that moment as a turning point in their relationship, which ended in divorce.

Despite her husband's disbelief, Myers lodged a complaint with Packwood's office director, Bill Mayer, and aide Roy Sampsel. The two men sympathized but shrugged, "That's just the way Bob is."

That made Myers even more angry. She confronted Pack- 13
wood about a week later, on their way to a Girl Scout event.
"What was supposed to happen next? Were we just going to
lie down on the rug? Like animals in the zoo?"

"I guess you're the type that wants a motel," Packwood
replied.

That same evening she went to the apartment of friend and
fellow staffer Ann Elias to tell her about the attack. A few weeks
later, Julie Myers quit her staff job.

Early in March 1992, another reporter smelled a story here.
The *Seattle Times* had reported charges that former Democratic
Senator Brock Adams of Washington had harassed and even
drugged several women in order to have sex with them. Adams
admitted knowing at least one of the women, but denied the
charges. Steve Duin, a columnist for Portland's *Oregonian*, wondered if any Oregon women had been harassed by male politicians. He reached for a well-thumbed card in his Rolodex, that
of political consultant Julie Myers Williamson. She agreed to
speak with him on the condition that he not identify her in print.

Although Williamson valued the interest by reporters, she
remained torn about letting them use her name. Six years earlier she had considered revealing her story by signing an affidavit for a Packwood biographer. But since then her political
consulting business had grown, and having her name splashed
in the headlines could alienate Republicans who were potential
clients. She had deep emotional barriers to overcome, too. But
the Clarence Thomas–Anita Hill hearings, which had concluded
a few months earlier, were a turning point for Williamson. Her
submerged anger at Packwood gradually began to surface.

"When a majority of senators didn't believe Anita Hill, it
made me angry," she said, "and then depressed." The hearings
awakened memories of shame inflicted by a supposedly honorable public figure. She had given up a coveted Senate job and
salary because of his advances. Depression led her into a purga-
tive journey.

14   "When I returned to work after the [Hill-Thomas] hearings, other women—women I barely knew—shared their own harassment experiences with me. I saw that I was not alone. And I saw that while the world could deny one person's story, it could not deny the stories of the many."

On 8 March 1992, Duin wrote a column describing an incident in which an unnamed Oregon politician stood on the toes of an unnamed woman, pulled her hair, and tried to take off her clothes.

The next morning Williamson picked up her ringing phone and heard these healing words:

"Julie, this is the dope who didn't believe you in 1969."

It was Doug Myers, her ex-husband. He had recognized her story in Duin's column and was calling to apologize.

"But Doug, why didn't you believe me *then?*" she asked.

"I didn't want to believe it," he explained sheepishly, "because I would have had to punch out a U.S. senator."

But Doug Myers may not have been the only person who had read that column.

In May 1992 Packwood loyalist and former aide Ann Elias telephoned Williamson. The two women had not spoken to each other in a long time. Elias opened with small talk about the election recount between Les AuCoin and Harry Lonsdale for the Democratic nomination. Although Williamson supported AuCoin, she did not have any details about the recount. She became suspicious when Elias asked abruptly:

"Whatever happened with you and [Packwood] that time, anyway?"

Williamson, taken aback, explained that Packwood tried to forcibly kiss her and rip off her underwear.

"Who else did you tell?" Elias asked.

"Bill Mayer and Roy Sampsel," Williamson answered.

"Do you think it will ever come out [in the press]?" Elias continued.

"I've never kept it a secret. And I think as a result of the Anita Hill hearing it may come out . . ."

Elias now dropped the pretense and began asking Williamson leading questions about her personal life.

"That," Williamson said, "was like an ice cube down my back." She refused to answer questions, and the silences grew longer. Finally Elias concluded, "Is there anything you're not telling me?"

Shocked, Williamson hung up on her former friend. She turned to her husband and said, "Charlie, I think I've just been threatened."

After her disturbing conversation with Elias, Williamson agreed to help Graves on every background fact that she could. But she remained fearful and withheld what Graves wanted most: permission to use her name in print.

––––––

Meanwhile, Packwood was on the offensive. He had directed campaign manager Elaine Franklin to launch a full-blown strategy to thwart the story.

Franklin was Packwood's alter ego. The senator's ex-wife and most of his staff believed that Franklin was his lover, but Franklin denied that. The daughter of a British Royal Air Force sergeant, she was something of a drill sergeant herself, and often as tough as she had to be to get the job done. She had risen through the ranks quickly, joining Packwood's staff as a volunteer in his 1980 reelection bid and becoming his chief of staff in 1986.

The counterattack must have been a bitter task for her. Cathy Miles and others close to the senator believed that Franklin had warned Packwood sternly about his behavior in 1990, and that he had promised to stop his drinking and philandering if she would direct his 1992 reelection campaign. The incident rate seemed to cool after that, but one effort at self-reform was not enough.

If Florence Graves could show a pattern of misconduct over the preceding twenty years, people would pay attention and maybe even consider changing their votes. The powerful senator could be dislodged from his long-held seat of power.

The key elements of the plan to stymie Graves were to keep former Packwood aides from talking, to prevent Graves from getting a publisher, and to distract the media by claiming that

16 Les AuCoin had spawned the allegations. Franklin telephoned former aides, urging them not to talk with Graves or the *Oregonian*'s writer Holley Gilbert, now assigned to track Duin's lead. This potentially Pulitzer Prize–winning story now literally kissed the *Oregonian* on the lips.

In early March the newspaper's Washington correspondent, Roberta Ulrich, stopped by Packwood's office for an interview. As was his end-of-the day custom, Packwood offered her a glass of wine from the box he kept in his cooler, and the senator had a drink himself. As Ulrich prepared to leave, she received the shock of her career. Packwood stood up from his desk and, in view of a female aide in the room, strode over and tried to kiss the sixty-four-year-old reporter on the lips.

Ulrich told editors about the incident, but internal rivalries and jealousies in the newsroom had frozen the free flow of information. The *Oregonian* botched what could have been a national scoop. Packwood, unaware of the newspaper's internal difficulties, gave the story a second wind by complaining to the publisher that Holley Gilbert had "harassed" female aides with phone calls. Nonetheless, the story died that spring when the newspaper failed to flush out any rumors of sexual advances.

But fear of what might happen continued to eat away at Packwood and Franklin. In May, Cathy Miles, who had been the first to warn them of Graves's activity, called the Portland office where Franklin was working. Office manager Karen Belding took the call, saying: "I don't know what you told her, but it's incredible. Elaine is constantly on the telephone trying to contain this story."

By now Miles felt torn between her natural inclination to always stick with one's boss, and concern over what she suspected Franklin was covering up. The chief of staff also seemed to punish and isolate Miles for originally bearing the bad news of the Graves investigation.

And the Franklin calls continued. She made at least four calls to *Vanity Fair* editors to attack the piece and try to get it killed, even though she had never spoken to Graves about its content. Graves now asked her mid-level editors to guarantee legal protection in writing in case Packwood sued. The liberal magazine overseen by editor in chief Tina Brown, one of the 17 most powerful women in publishing, refused.

It looked like Graves was out of luck. Determined to see her project through, she shopped the idea to several other national magazines, including *Ladies Home Journal*, but they all refused—chiefly for legal reasons. Now, with no publisher, no money, and little hope of finishing the story before Packwood's reelection in November, it looked like Packwood would triumph once again.

2

In July, Graves shared her disappointment with friends at an Association of Alternative Journalism conference in Seattle. After she returned to Boston, Graves and her husband left for a trip to Maine. As they drove, Graves reflected on her dilemma for hours. Finally, she turned to her husband and suddenly said, "Sam, I can't know what I know about Bob Packwood and not do anything about it. It may cost thousands of dollars. But I need to write this story."

Graves decided to propose the story to the *Washington Post*, even though she feared that they wouldn't want to run a free-lancer's piece on such an important topic. Upon her return to Boston, Graves began a barrage of telephone calls to investigate Packwood's behavior, hoping to document the charges so well that the *Post* could not turn her down. Graves watched nervously as the unpaid expenses piled up, trying to ignore the little voice that told her she might be wasting her time.

With each call the journalist found information that began to form a telling pattern. Packwood often directed his advances toward young women in entry-level slots who were emotionally and financially vulnerable. Many, after run-ins with Packwood, reacted with shame, self-doubt, and most important, silence.

They feared retaliation even after leaving Packwood's employ, especially those who were still working in Washington, D.C.

But Williamson was different. Older, stronger, and more financially secure now than when she had worked for Packwood, she stood out as one of the women most likely to go on the record with a compelling tale.

Graves contacted her in August to line up another interview. Williamson said she was leaving for a family reunion in New Hampshire, so Graves offered to drive up there for a few minutes of Williamson's time.

The two women respected each other immediately and talked for three hours. Williamson finally had to break off the conversation, only because her family had been standing by her car waiting to leave. Still fearful, Williamson agreed to go on record with her story if Graves could establish a pattern by persuading at least three other women to do the same. Graves now worked at full throttle to convince others to step forward.

By late September she had enough hard evidence and promising leads to contact the *Post*. Her documentation impressed executive editor Leonard Downie, Jr., successor to famed editor Ben Bradlee. Downie placed Graves on special contract to complete the article, and the *Post* guaranteed legal protection. Her editors emphasized the necessity of getting Williamson and others on the record; they would not run a late-election story that relied on anonymous sources.

Downie assigned skilled investigative reporter Charles Shepard to help Graves produce the story before the November general election. Shepard had won a Pulitzer Prize in 1988 for his investigation of televangelists Jim and Tammy Bakker.

Graves had begun her work in April, hoping that *Vanity Fair* would run the story by late summer. It was now early October, just four weeks to the election, and witnesses were beginning to question if the story would reach the voters in time, if ever.

The reporters now focused on women who might join Williamson in going on the record, including former Packwood aide Paige Wagers of Fairfax County, Virginia; Jean McMahon of Philadelphia, who had applied for a job on his staff; and former intern Maura Roche of Portland.

It was 1976. As Senator Bob Packwood walked into his office through a throng of screaming abortion foes thrashing him over the head with long-stemmed roses, twenty-two-year-old aide Paige Wagers followed behind. She admired how unflappable the senator remained, and she felt proud of his refusal to buckle under pressure to take the GOP's stand on abortion. Wagers still couldn't believe her own good fortune; fresh out of college, she had lucked into a job on Capitol Hill.

Delicate and soft-spoken, Wagers had grown up in Baltimore, where her father was a veterinarian and her mother was a toxicologist/genealogist. After graduating from St. Paul's School for Girls, she attended Lafayette University in Pennsylvania. In 1975, diploma in hand, she decided to join her older sister in Washington, D.C., and find a job on Capitol Hill. The position as mail clerk on Packwood's staff only paid about $11,000, but Wagers said she enjoyed reading letters "to get to know the issues." She liked her office pals, and the entire staff often went out together. As she got to know people around the Senate, she heard rumors about womanizing and "that the word was, 'Put out or get out.'. . . There were a lot of women who did, some who thought they couldn't say no, and some who perhaps didn't want to," she told writer Linda Kramer.

As mail clerk, she was at the bottom of the staff hierarchy, so she was surprised when Packwood invited her into his office one day to play bridge with two top aides. Soon after the game was finished, the senator buzzed her on the interoffice phone and asked her to return.

After she entered the office, Packwood locked the doors. Suddenly he embraced her, running his fingers through her hair and forcefully kissing her on the lips. Wagers said he told her how much he liked her wholesome good looks.

"I could feel my skin crawl," Wagers said. "I was paralyzed and trying to push him away." She was able to talk her way out of his office. "I never dreamt he would do that to me. He was my boss, and he was married, and it never should have happened."

A colleague later told her that other female aides had had similar experiences and advised her never to enter his office alone. Wagers ignored two more invitations from Packwood and left her job within a few months.

She stayed on Capitol Hill, where she worked for then–Vice President Nelson Rockefeller, Democratic Senator Ernest Hollings of South Carolina, and the Jimmy Carter White House Council of Wage and Price Stability. In 1981 she joined the Labor Department as a legislative assistant on employment and training. Her job required her to discuss those issues with members of Congress, and one day, while passing through the subterranean corridors of the Capitol, she came face-to-face with Packwood. The lawmaker seemed interested in her Labor Department job, and Wagers felt proud that she could talk at a higher level with her former boss.

As they walked along a corridor, Packwood said he wanted to hear about her work. "He stopped at an unmarked office and said, 'Step in, and we'll finish this conversation.'" He locked the door behind him, grabbed her hair, kissed her, and pushed some pillows off a sofa.

"I resisted," Wagers remembers, "but he had a tight grip, and I pushed him away until he stopped. I didn't want to call for help because I felt no one would believe me, and he'd suggest it was my idea. I felt completely bereft, a feeling of absolute betrayal. I kept saying to myself, 'How could you be so stupid?' but then I realized it was not my fault."

Once again, Wagers confided in coworkers, only to be reminded that she—not Packwood—would most likely suffer if she blew the whistle. Disheartened, Wagers left the Labor Department job, which was becoming increasingly frustrating, to make a fresh start outside of politics.

Graves and Shepard confirmed her account with five people whom Wagers had told of the two incidents shortly after they occurred.

Jean McMahon applied for a job in Packwood's Portland office in 1976, when she was about thirty. The senator arranged for McMahon, then working as an editor at the Oregon Department of Higher Education in Salem, to meet him in his

22 motel room during a visit to that city. There, she said, the two discussed drafting a speech for him.

Over the following weeks, Packwood phoned her several times to check on her progress with the speech. He asked her to meet him again, this time in a motel sixty miles away on the Oregon coast.

Once she arrived at the motel, however, Packwood showed no interest in the speech. "Instead, he came after me, sexually. I ran, but he chased me around the table in the motel room, grabbed me, and kissed me against my will. I was able to get loose and fled the room. There didn't seem to be any way to calm him down and get him back to what I thought we were going to do," she told the *Post* reporters.

"The feeling I remember is of him trying to get power over me, both physically and psychologically," McMahon said. She contacted Packwood's staff about the speech she was presumably still drafting, but they told her they had no knowledge of it.

Graves and Shepard contacted McMahon's husband (who had been her boyfriend at the time), and he confirmed that she had told him about Packwood's actions soon afterward. They further verified that she confided in a Portland friend about the incident.

———

As a twenty-two-year-old college intern, Maura Roche was assigned to watch videotape on abortion issues in Packwood's inner office one evening in 1989. The senator, who was working late on a budget bill, had just walked through the outer offices offering his staff wine, when he entered the room where Roche sat. After the videotape ended, he pulled out a binder and began reading sexually explicit jokes to her, she told Graves and Shepard.

"I couldn't believe it . . . I didn't know what I should do. I just sat there and took it," Roche said. Finally, she excused herself from the room. Reflecting on the incident, she remembers the explicit jokes as "very degrading to women."

Wagers, McMahon, and Roche still dreaded going public and feared the attendant loss of privacy. Wagers had even been too embarrassed to tell her husband. They all shuddered at the specter of an ordeal like the one endured by Anita Hill. Wagers explained that because she had been alone with Packwood at the time of his come-on, there was no way to prove it. "You're vulnerable. You're totally out on a limb." And as a Republican, Wagers refused to go on the record before the November election, which would make her story ballast for the Democrats.

———

Florence Graves was closer than ever to her goal of a published exposé, and she was not about to give up. She pleaded with her witnesses, arguing, "This is not an issue about Republicans and Democrats. It's about ethics and morality. If women don't speak out about this subject, nothing will ever change. You do what you must do. But if you see a way, we need you."

Pressure to complete a story before the election intensified daily, revealing differences in style between Shepard and Graves. The tall, quiet, bespectacled Shepard worked diligently, as he would on any important piece. But Graves, feeling a sense of injustice, was driven by the need to see this story through to the end.

Graves's soft Texas accent grew insistent when talking with women who she sensed may have withheld pivotal information. "We have to stop this conspiracy of silence," she told former Packwood aide Marsha Dubrow. Shepard became a complement to his partner's intensity, the softer sell of the reportorial team.

As the election approached, an inspiration came: Why not let these women meet anonymously, in three-way calls, so they could support and encourage each other? Graves arranged calls to still-hesitant women, and for the confident Williamson to talk to them. Williamson never knew to whom she was speaking, but as she shared her experiences some of the other women began opening up about theirs. Many were emboldened and empowered when they learned that others had undergone the same trials.

The momentum was gaining just as Packwood launched his most comprehensive attacks to date on the witnesses, and on the newspaper that had pledged to tell their stories. Cathy Miles had left Packwood's staff that summer to work for the

24 federal government in Portland. Graves tried to reach her for
months, but Miles felt guilty about tipping off Packwood to the
pending story and was embarrassed to tell Graves that she had
done that, so Shepard tried, reached Miles, and invited her
to join the patch calls with some of the other women. But
Miles remained torn. Even though she knew the senator was
capable of manipulating people—and the rumors that he acted
inappropriately with other women genuinely disturbed her—
she had never really seen that side of him. Miles suspected
some of the women alleging harassment had a partisan bias
against Packwood.

The Packwood Miles mostly knew was gentle, reflective, and
surprisingly vulnerable around women. She liked the man who
sang Sinatra songs, adored Frank Capra's film *It's a Wonderful
Life*, and gave sentimental gifts, a man she cared for and loved
almost as if he were her father. She had once written him a
Christmas card encouraging him to view *It's a Wonderful Life*
not as a movie, but as an example of how to live his own life,
according to a source. Packwood penned a warm and tender
note thanking her. He sometimes counseled Miles on family issues and even fostered her spiritual self. Once, when Miles admitted that she never thought about religion, Packwood
declared, "My God, that's terrible, you don't wonder about religion? You don't wonder about God?"

But there was no disputing that Packwood had a dark side,
too. She hated the way he used Elaine Franklin as a tool to
abuse and intimidate people, and personally warned him that
he should not treat others as chess pieces. She abhorred the
senator's rudeness, recalling that when she introduced him to
her parents—modest folk from a small Northwest town—he
shook their hands and praised their daughter, saying, "Your
daughter is great. She'll tell me to fuck off." Miles's mother was
offended and never liked Packwood after that.

However, Miles's loyalty to Packwood prevailed, and she declined to talk with Shepard. The *Post* reporter persisted, even
calling Miles's fiancé in an unsuccessful attempt to convince
him to persuade her. But that pressure paled in comparison
to what Miles faced next.

According to a source, Miles had hoped to enjoy her federal Columbus Day holiday by unwinding at her Portland area home. Then Elaine Franklin called. Her former boss skipped the pleasantries. In her sharp British accent, she got right to the point:

Franklin: Have you talked with Charlie Shepard?
Miles: No, I have not.
Franklin: I want to know who . . . you told about the incident with the senator [when Packwood kissed Miles].
Miles: I won't tell you.

A long silence followed.

Franklin: What are you doing home today?
Miles: Columbus Day is a federal holiday.
Franklin: [sarcastically] It must be nice to have a federal job.

Miles put down the receiver as a sickening realization washed over her: Franklin could try to get her fired.

On 14 October, two days later, Franklin called again, this time at the office where Miles worked in downtown Portland. Franklin called three times, but Miles refused to take the calls. On the fourth try, Franklin told the receptionist, "You tell her to get out of that goddamned meeting and take this call." Miles took the call.

Franklin: This time, I want the truth. Are you helping Charlie Shepard?
Miles: Elaine, I'm scared.
Franklin: You're scared! *How do you think the senator feels?*
Miles: Elaine, there's a big difference. I didn't do anything wrong.

Franklin had pushed her over the edge, and she hung up. Right away, Miles called Shepard at the *Washington Post* and said, "If you come to Portland, I will answer yes or no to whatever questions you have."

Graves and Shepard flew into Portland on 23 October, twelve days before the election. Miles shared her whole story

26   with them. She explained how she and the senator had several conversations in 1990 about their mutual interest in Frank Sinatra. According to a source, they had exchanged cassette recordings and occasional notes. After one such exchange, around October 1990, the senator penned a note: "Were you the girl I met under the clock at the Biltmore in New York in 1954?" The tone made her nervous. She told her husband, 'I think Packwood has a crush on me.'"

A few days later the senator and several aides, including Miles, gathered for drinks at Kelly's Irish Times bar on Capitol Hill, and Packwood struck up a conversation about labor politics. He boasted about how much AFL-CIO support he could wield against any Democrat in his 1992 reelection campaign. Then he invited Miles to stop by his office that evening so he could show her his records of labor allies. Another aide, Lindy Paull, also came.

Once inside the office, as they were momentarily alone, Packwood abruptly kissed her. She later told friends that she had left the room and building in tears. She remained on Packwood's staff for more than a year after this. No other incidents occurred, but the relationship became cooler, and her notes to him less frequent.

———

Election day drew near. On 23 October, the day Graves and Shepard arrived in town, they asked Packwood for an interview. The senator's staff put them off, citing his tight campaign schedule. But Packwood found time to call *Post* chairwoman Katherine Graham, complaining that her out-of-state newspaper might unfairly skew an Oregon election. Graham forwarded the message to Downie, who suggested that Packwood share his concerns with the *Post* reporters.

Meanwhile, Graves and Shepard pursued leads indicating that Packwood had made unwanted sexual advances to legions of women. In addition to Williamson, Wagers, McMahon, and Roche, they interviewed several more women, all former Packwood aides, volunteers, or lobbyists, who told of being fondled, grabbed, or forcibly kissed by Packwood. Some agreed to let the

Post print the incidents and reveal their names to Packwood, as long as their identities were not made known to the public.

Much of the Oregon media began hearing rumors about the *Post*'s investigation. As reporters called Packwood's office, Elaine Franklin labeled the inquiry an election-eve "witch-hunt" concocted by AuCoin.

AuCoin's press secretary, Rachel Gorlin, dismissed that charge when contacted by reporters. Yet Gorlin knew that such an explosive story could knock Packwood out of the race. She wanted to help the story along, but it was essential that AuCoin avoid being entangled in charges of dirty campaigning. So while AuCoin stayed out, his staff sent special instructions to Garin, Hart, the campaign's polling firm in Washington, D.C.

Each night beginning on 23 October, pollster Geoff Garin left his Cleveland Park home in the middle of the night to pick up an early edition of the *Washington Post* from the paper's office on Fifteenth Avenue. He then called AuCoin's office to tell them whether the Packwood story was running in the next day's paper.

He never saw the story, because Graves and Shepard had not yet been able to convince Packwood to answer the charges. The senator stalled for six days, but he knew he could not stonewall them indefinitely. If the *Post* merely ran a portion of the story without his response—or if someone leaked it—Packwood would probably lose the election. The senator needed to see the reporters to retain his last shred of control, and he finally agreed to an interview on Thursday, 29 October. To stay out of public view, Packwood suggested meeting at the Portland home of his press aide, Julia Brim.

At Brim's house, Graves and Shepard began laying out their allegations to Packwood, Franklin, and Jack Faust, the senator's friend, attorney, and close advisor. As both sides turned on their tape recorders, the reporters disclosed the names of Packwood's accusers, including Williamson, Miles, McMahon, Roche, and Wagers. They identified other women and detailed their complaints.

Packwood heard the charges and responded that he was not the kind of person who would make those sorts of advances. "I'm so hesitant of anything at all that I just, I don't

28 make approaches," he said. "It is simply not my nature, with men or women, to be forward."

The senator pointed out that he had a good record of hiring women for important positions. If his office was such an uncomfortable place, he asked, "Why do they come to work here?"

Asked to comment on Wagers's story, Packwood replied that there was "no event with Paige," either in 1976 or 1981. Packwood also said that he did not recall McMahon and did not use speechwriters.

Then the senator said he remembered neither Roche nor the incident she alleged. The former claim begged credulity. Roche's mother, Nancy Roche, was an erstwhile Packwood ally and prominent leader of Oregon's Women's Rights Coalition, and Maura's internship was at least an indirect product of her mother's working relationship with the senator.

Packwood remembered Cathy Miles very well but denied having kissed her. He and his staff later produced several statements attacking Miles's truthfulness. Packwood also provided copies of nine notes that she had written to him over two years, declaring that "somebody would not write these kinds of letters" if they were upset about his behavior.

Unbeknownst to all, Packwood had won in his attempt to stall the publication of the piece until after the election, because Downie had decided that it could not run unless Packwood confessed outright on the day he met with the reporters. Wisely, the editor didn't pass this information on to Graves and Shepard. The reporters told Packwood that the paper planned to run their story on Sunday, 1 November, and that they needed his final response by Friday, 30 October.

The senator now had something for the reporters. He said he needed to identify these particular women from among the 860 individuals who had worked for him over the years, and that his team required more time to gather information "to detract from the credibility" of the women as news sources. Attorney Jack Faust would "conduct an investigation" of the women named in the interview "to see if there may be motivations." Faust wanted time to "see if we can find prior inconsistent statements to judge their credibility." *Post* editors know the dangers of not rigorously checking out sources. At the newsroom, Graves had met editor Bob Woodward of Watergate fame. In that conversation she said this story might have a "Perry Mason" ending. Woodward disagreed with that, and now he seemed to be right. Packwood's tactics doomed any pre-election headlines. If he successfully discredited all of his accusers, he might kill the story permanently.

After the interview, the senator and Elaine Franklin flew to Bend, Oregon, for the next day's scheduled debate with Au-Coin. Packwood, facing the biggest crisis of his life, saw his advisors split into two camps. At least two advisors suggested that his response address the women's work history and possible political bias, reasoning that anything perceived as a "smear campaign" would backfire. But Franklin rejected that strategy. She called for a no-holds-barred effort, gathering derogatory information—even delving into their personal lives—to destroy the women's credibility.

"Packwood wasn't listening to anyone but Franklin," one source said. In Bend that evening the two spent hours arranging for acquaintances of Packwood's accusers to provide damaging statements about the women. Advisor Dave Barrows later told Miles that it was near this crucial juncture that "Elaine had won the battle for Bob's soul."

The battle plan Packwood agreed to that night dealt a harsh blow to his accusers. Four days before the election, on 29 October, Charlie Shepard called Cathy Miles at home. He said, "It's Charlie Shepard, please don't hang up. We taped the interview with Senator Packwood, and I'd like to play what he said about you." Then Miles heard these key excerpts:

Shepard: What about Miles?

Packwood: I don't want to talk about her.

Franklin: [interrupting] Oh, senator, you must.

After a pause, Packwood proceeded to say defamatory things about Miles's character, morals, and work performance.

30   According to a source, as Shepard finished playing the tape, Miles began sobbing, overwhelmed by feelings of betrayal. "I wanted to look [Packwood] in the eye and say, 'I told you about Florence Graves. I refused to help them. And I get repaid with Elaine Franklin's threats—and your trashing me to the *Washington Post*.'"

That same day, the *Oregonian*'s Jeff Mapes asked Packwood press aide Julia Brim about rumors that the *Post* was researching a story on sexual harassment.[1] According to Mapes, Brim claimed that AuCoin's camp had spread that false rumor. Mapes then posed the same question to Franklin, who also denied the story and blamed the AuCoin campaign.

Franklin later maintained that she did not lie to Mapes. According to Franklin, he asked only two questions: Had the *Post* interviewed the senator, and had the *Post* contacted the senator? Denying the first was easy; the reporters had not interviewed the senator—yet. They would that afternoon, but Mapes did not properly phrase the question, Franklin claimed. Franklin also said no to the second question, later explaining that the *Post* had truly not been in contact with Packwood; it had been in contact with her. At the time, Packwood had completed a television ad campaign accusing AuCoin of being a "study in hypocrisy" for his check overdrafts, pay raises, and votes. The new spot running against AuCoin ended with, "And tell us the truth."

By the time AuCoin and Packwood arrived in Bend for their Friday, 30 October, debate, the senator's lead had shrunk to less than five points and, as best as he knew, the lethal *Post* story was still to come. As AuCoin aide Gorlin entered the banquet room where the debate was to be held, the first person she saw was Eugene *Register-Guard* political writer Brent Walth, whose first words were: "Do you know what Florence Graves and Charles Shepard look like—and are they here today?"

The entire statewide media now knew of the *Post*'s investigation, but Packwood's retinue kept them at bay prior to the debate. AuCoin and Packwood addressed the audience from behind an elevated table. Agile and surefooted, Packwood had

---

1. David Sarasohn. 31 January 1993, *Oregonian.*

dominated his opponent in previous debates in Portland and Coos Bay, exuding the confidence of a senior attorney. But this time he looked tense and distracted. During the audience question-and-answer period, the candidates alternated standing to answer, but an edgy Packwood jumped up during AuCoin's turns. He looked like a marionette for the next twenty minutes.

At the conclusion of the debates, the reporters dashed straight for Packwood, ignoring AuCoin. The senator repeated that AuCoin's campaign was behind the *Post* rumor. KATU-TV (ABC) reporter Mark Hass pinned Packwood down, asking whether the *Post* was working on a sexual harassment story on him. Packwood—who had been interviewed by the *Post* the day before—said no.

After the debate, Packwood flew back to Portland—keeping his distance from the AuCoin entourage on the same flight— and checked into the downtown Red Lion Inn, where he apparently continued to solicit damaging statements on his accusers. At one point, Packwood telephoned Faust and asked the lawyer to receive a faxed statement at his own office because the fax at the senator's hotel was not private enough. According to the *Oregonian*, Faust received the fax and then drove to the hotel to deliver the document to Packwood.

On the Friday morning Packwood was preparing for his debate, and with the election only three days off, Graves and Shepard rose at 4 A.M. from their adjoining hotel rooms and began checking out Packwood's last-minute charges against the women. Graves viewed these charges as "mean-spirited"; she wanted to convince Downie that the *Post* owed it to the women, the voters, and the country to run the story on Sunday, so voters could decide whether to send Packwood back to office.

They worked without a break; but after a day of reporting and rewriting, they knew disappointment lay ahead. Packwood's delays and derogatory letters had worked. The next morning they agreed with their editor that the story was not ready to run—yet.

32   Graves and Shepard called the Packwood campaign office, apparently too late for the senator to turn off his misinformation machine. Three Packwood aides called Cathy Miles on Saturday and left messages claiming that Charlie Shepard had betrayed her and would expose her in Sunday's paper. They pleaded with her to call Packwood "for help," not knowing that Shepard had already played the tape showing Miles who her real enemies were. They even called Miles's husband in Washington, D.C., to tell him that a news story would expose his wife. He immediately telephoned Shepard with a blistering statement before the reporter could show him that Packwood's people had misled him.

Thus, on the eve of what would have been a preelection news bombshell, Graves and Shepard began the grim task of informing their witnesses that the story would not run. All the women were angry with the reporters, but Williamson was the most upset. After all, she had risked losing clients by letting Packwood know of her damning charges. She had anticipated that, in return, a story in the *Washington Post* would remove Packwood from power and render him unable to harm her. But now there would be no story.

Distraught, she grabbed her car keys and escaped from her northwest Portland home, speeding down Burnside Avenue and onto Interstate 5. She drove for thirty minutes before her fury subsided enough to stop at a rural telephone booth. She dialed her husband's law office.

"Charlie," she said, dissolving into tears, "they hung me out to dry."

Williamson drove aimlessly for several hours. When she finally returned home that evening, she was greeted by a surprise—a message blinking on her computer screen. She stepped closer and squinted her eyes in amazement. Charlie had composed a $10,000 full-page advertisement to run in the next day's *Sunday Oregonian*. The copy roughly read:

"I, Charlie Williamson, want the people of Oregon to know that the *Washington Post* reporters Florence Graves and Charles Shepard have gathered evidence that Senator Bob Packwood has made unwelcomed sexual advances to women including . . ."

Julie dialed her husband's office and gasped, "Charlie, did you really place that ad?!"

"No," he said, his voice sinking sadly, "It was too late to get in."

———

On Tuesday, 3 November, Packwood defeated AuCoin with only a 52 percent majority, in one of the closest Senate races in the nation. But he could not celebrate as long as the *Washington Post* reporters continued to hound him. The information that Packwood had promised the reporters on 29 October now began to pour in. Beginning Saturday, 31 October, and over the next nine days, Packwood showered the *Post*'s downtown office and editor Downie's home with at least eight faxes about Williamson, Miles, and others. The statements suggested some women were attracted to Packwood, might have invited his advances, or were untruthful.

Several statements, written by former and current staff, purported to describe the women's personal lives and sexual histories. Former Packwood aide Greg Dow had not heard from his old boss in ten years, but now he was being called on for a favor. According to the *Oregonian*, Packwood asked about a woman Dow had dated when he worked in the senator's office.

Packwood wanted Dow to write a statement detailing what he knew about the woman and her other boyfriends. Initially Dow did not want to comply, but he finally decided that the senator had a right to defend himself. He faxed a statement to Packwood. "I didn't feel comfortable in saying no," he said. "I mean, this is a guy who has done an awful lot for me."

Timothy Lee had worked for the senator for six months as a staff member on trucking deregulation—a cause that Packwood championed. After leaving the staff, Lee developed a freight brokerage business that was eventually worth more than $1 million. In 1992 he helped orchestrate a Packwood fundraiser featuring President George Bush that grossed about $500,000. The senator's campaign had paid Lee's company approximately $5,000 in connection with that event.

34 As Packwood told him about the *Post* inquiry, Lee became "outraged" to learn that his former girlfriend, Paige Wagers, had claimed such things. Lee provided the senator with a letter about his personal experiences with Wagers, which Packwood gratefully accepted.

Another statement came from Portland General Electric Corporation lobbyist Jill Eiland. She had been a Packwood aide, and her husband even worked for the senator's pollster, Bob Moore. Packwood personally approached former aide Terry Kay, a Salem attorney, but Kay declined to discuss his recollections with the senator.

Three then-current Packwood aides agreed to write statements: Josie Martin, Senate Finance Committee minority press secretary; Lindy Paull, committee deputy GOP staff chief; and press aide Julia Brim. Martin and Brim had recently switched from Packwood's Senate staff to his campaign staff.

Paull seemed the most reluctant, claiming her statement "did not contain any reference to anyone's past sexual conduct." But Brim plowed into it. Her blistering report attacked Miles's "professionalism, behavior in the office, and interaction with coworkers." Brim agreed to repeat that statement before the Senate Ethics Committee.

Finally, Ann Elias attacked Williamson in a statement. She later told a reporter that Williamson was a good friend and she believed that Packwood had "made a pass" at her.

Packwood even called ex–U.S. Representative John Miller for special help. The senator knew that one of the women had worked for the Seattle-area Republican, and he inquired about her employment and sexual reputation. Distressed, Miller declined to cooperate.

Packwood placed another desperate telephone call to Mark Long, a member of the same Portland law firm as Jack Faust. Packwood asked about a woman Long had known more than a decade earlier, when he worked for Packwood's office. The senator wanted to know if the woman had ever come on to him aggressively. According to Long's friends, the attorney answered no, joked his way out of the conversation, and would not lend his assistance.

Packwood continued making calls until at least 9 November, when he contacted Oregon abortion-rights advocate Mabsie Wallers to ask if National Abortion Rights Action League (NARAL) lobbyist Mary Heffernan, now accusing Packwood of sexual misconduct, had ever had a nervous breakdown. Another Packwood supporter, claiming to act on Elaine Franklin's behalf, called Portland television reporter Tim Hilliard to give derogatory information about Williamson's personal life, according to the *Oregonian*.

Graves and Shepard now prepared for the crucial second interview with Packwood, to be held in his Senate office on 17 November. Packwood had hired attorney James F. Fitzpatrick from the firm Arnold and Porter to assist him.

At the meeting, Florence Graves asked about the defamatory remarks against the women. Packwood backpedaled briefly, explaining that his aides had quickly assembled the statements because the *Post* had asked for a prompt response. "This was hardly something they had a long time to work on," he explained. "I sent them on to you roughly as we got them."

When Graves asked if the statements were designed to intimidate and silence the women, Fitzpatrick jumped in:

"You don't think some of those statements are relevant to the questions of whether there's an unwanted sexual advance?" he charged. And Packwood added, "If those [statements] impeach credibility—not the substance of the story—is that relevant?. . . It certainly is."

But Graves was prepared for that answer. The senator had dramatically asserted the relevance of prior sexual history, so Graves began interrogating him about his. She unloaded question after question—naming names—about Packwood's alleged consensual relationships with numerous female employees (on the taxpayer's payroll) during the years Packwood was married.

"I don't see the relevance of that," he snapped.

Graves responded, "If you say we must consider how the private sexual history of the accusers reflects on their character, the newspaper must also examine what *your* private sexual history says about *your* character."

36 Packwood did not want to open that door.

When she next heard from Packwood, Graves was at the offices of the *Post*. The senator sent a fax saying he would not dispute any of the allegations the women had made against him.

A triumphant Graves saw Bob Woodward nearby; she took the fax and waved it about her head and shouted, "Look, Bob, a Perry Mason ending!"

She called Packwood to confirm the statement. The subdued senator said he had never had any intention of publicly releasing the statements. "I don't intend to blow any of the women down," he said. "Those statements were for [the *Post*] to consider."

Post editor Downie decided to lead with the piece on Sunday, 22 November. Late Saturday night the national wire services were buzzing with the story as newspapers across the country began to pick it up. The headline read: PACKWOOD ACCUSED OF SEXUAL ADVANCES, ALLEGED BEHAVIOR PATTERN COUNTERS IMAGE.

On the day the papers hit the newsstands, ABC, NBC, and CBS opened their evening news broadcasts with the story. The *Post* piece documented incidents between Packwood and ten women over a twenty-year period, and listed five of them, including Williamson, McMahon, Wagers, Roche, and Heffernan, by name. The reporters also described the encounters of four other former aides, and another woman who could not be identified in print. The women include:

- A Packwood clerical employee who allowed the *Post* to identify her to the senator. One evening in 1982, Packwood invited her inside his inner office and expressed pride that the twenty-one-year-old was returning to college. She was surprised that he even knew her name. Packwood was drinking wine and offered her some. She declined but did agree to sit down and talk. Feeling uneasy, she stayed far away from his desk, refusing an invitation to come closer.

  Then, she said, "He walked over to me and pulled me out of the chair, put his arms around me, and tried to kiss me. He stuck his tongue into my mouth."

The former employee "squirmed" out of Packwood's grasp, left the office immediately, and hurried to her home on Capitol Hill, leaving behind her purse and coat, despite the winter cold. Two friends confirmed that she had told them about Packwood's advances shortly afterward.

"I was embarrassed, insulted, and feeling like an idiot . . . for ever thinking he thought I was important," she told the *Post*. After the incident, she avoided Packwood and left her job that spring. She did not file a formal complaint because, she thought, "I wasn't important enough for anybody to believe . . . I didn't know who to complain to, and he would probably just deny it, have me fired, and that's all I needed at that time."

When asked about the woman's story, Packwood said he did not remember her, although he later confirmed that she had worked for him.

- A former Packwood aide who did not allow her name to be used in print. Her original decision to remain quiet about an incident with the senator haunted her, and she later wrote a letter of encouragement to Anita Hill after the Clarence Thomas confirmation hearings. The letter praised Hill for having more courage than she did.

- A former Packwood aide who said she repeatedly rebuffed his sexual advances. She also said that the senator's actions jeopardized all he had stood for. The woman, who spoke only on condition that she not be identified, finally quit her job after Packwood did not alter his behavior.

The capitulatory statement that Packwood had faxed to Graves also appeared in the article:

I am very concerned about the reports in the *Washington Post*. I have always tried to be mindful and respectful of the wishes of others. The reports in the *Washington Post* indicate that I have not always succeeded at that.

If any of my comments or actions have indeed been unwelcome or if I have conducted myself in any way that has caused any individual discomfort or embarrassment, for that I am sincerely sorry.

My intentions were never to pressure, to offend, nor to make anyone feel uncomfortable, and I truly regret if that has occurred with anyone either on or off my staff. I will not make an issue of any specific allegation.

I have an outstanding record of hiring and promoting women and I am proud of that record. My offices, both in Oregon and Washington, D.C., have outstanding professional reputations and the atmosphere attracts bright and committed people.

Again, if over the years I have done or said anything that could now be interpreted as improper, I apologize for that. That was never my intention.

In the article, Jack Faust, Packwood's friend and advisor, acted as spin doctor to control the damage. The lawyer said that the senator "is admitting to some human flaws. . . . You have armies of politicians trying to dodge this and that. He's accepting responsibility."

The amount of material the *Post* presented meant that "denial is not credible," concluded Faust, an odd phrase implying that Packwood had surrendered for tactical rather than ethical reasons.

As the country reeled with the news, the anger of women erupted in a show of political power. Democratic Senators-elect Patty Murray of Washington, and Dianne Feinstein and Barbara Boxer of California, rose to support Packwood's accusers. Murray vowed to propose legislation to end the long-standing exemption of senators and congressmembers from the federal law prohibiting sexual harassment of government employees. "It's as if being able to harass women is a perk of their job," she said. "We don't accept that kind of behavior in the private sector. We shouldn't accept it in the U.S. Senate." Los Angeles attorney Gloria Allred filed a complaint asking the Senate Select Committee on Ethics to investigate Packwood for sexual misconduct.

The National Organization of Women (NOW), NARAL, and Oregon feminists—heretofore staunch Packwood supporters—now rejected him. They swore the issue would not die. Feminists, still bitter that the overwhelmingly male Senate had narrowly confirmed Clarence Thomas, suddenly had a powerful symbol of senatorial hypocrisy to show the country.

3

After the *Post* exposé broke, Julie Williamson received a telephone message at home. The frantic voice was Jack Faust, reacting to a Steve Duin column about his role in the smear campaign. "The story is bullshit. It's *all* bullshit. I was just the messenger boy. Call me at home."

When Williamson phoned him back, Faust told her how much—despite Packwood's charges—he respected her.

"Jack," she replied, "if you respected me so much, why did you help send the [smear] fax to the *Post*? I don't think you have deniability, Jack."

As Faust and other supporters scrambled to distance themselves from Packwood, the senator could not be found for comment.

An Associated Press editor called Washington bureau reporter Scott Sonner at home on Sunday morning, alerting him that a scandal had broken and directing him to locate Packwood for an interview. Sonner checked the senator's office. No answer. He then drove to Packwood's apartment at 3000 Woodley Avenue NW, near National Cathedral in Washington, D.C. No one came to the door, so Sonner parked his car outside. Although he feared neighbors might call the police, he staked

40   out the building into the night before concluding that Packwood had fled to another location.

Packwood had indeed eluded reporters and angry constituents. He mysteriously surfaced one week later at the Hazelden Institute, a widely respected addiction treatment center outside Minneapolis. Packwood's staff suggested to the press that alcohol abuse had influenced his behavior.

For nearly a week, Packwood underwent counseling and nightly bed checks at Hazelden. Although confidential, treatment includes interviews, group sessions, and lectures. Counselors analyze alcohol consumption, and physical, emotional, and psychological health. After the weeklong evaluation, the Hazelden assessment team would have diagnosed Packwood; however, he refused to submit to the full twenty-eight-day program.

Even from the confines of Hazelden, Packwood had the presence of mind to mount an offensive against feminist groups and to request his own ethics probe before they claimed sole credit. The ethics panel began its preliminary investigation on 1 December. Women's groups opened a two-front war by filing a separate complaint to the Senate Rules Committee asking to invalidate Packwood's reelection on the grounds that he lied to voters about the *Post* charges before the election.

Packwood flew from Minneapolis to Washington, D.C., on the day the preliminary investigation began. The *New York Times* ran a photo and story showing an ashen Packwood trudging through National Airport with Elaine Franklin. The senator refused to answer reporters' questions. He now hoped to lay the issue to rest by scheduling a televised news conference certain to attract national attention. But what would he say? Franklin began dropping hints, shaping the notion that Packwood was a victim of misunderstandings and changing mores.

The 10 December news conference loomed in front of Packwood as a defining moment. He was no doubt aware that crises also provide the opportunity for redemption. The beleaguered underdog recasting his image with a bravura speech is an American classic: Richard Nixon rescued himself with the "Checkers" speech; and a generation later, Lieutenant Colonel Oliver North, medals shimmering on his chest, turned the tables on his accusers.

Ever the confident orator, Packwood usually prevailed in exchanges with reporters. But he had never faced an examination like this. People wanted to hear a genuine apology, not a self-serving one. He had to acknowledge misleading the *Post* and the *Oregonian* before the election, and he needed to atone for the derogatory letters against the women. If he came clean at this juncture, he might minimize the damage.

Packwood retreated into secrecy for ten days to prepare for the news conference. Associated Press reporter Sonner persisted in his quest for an interview and saw Packwood in his office just one hour before the senator faced the press. "He looked horrible," Sonner said. Anticipating his ordeal, Packwood quietly vowed to speak from the heart about the charges.

As Packwood entered the Senate television studio, an explosion of klieg lights illuminated the room. Naturally thin, Packwood had lost ten pounds and looked gaunt. CNN broadcast the news conference live to the nation. After press aide Matt Evans introduced him, Packwood, visibly tense and uncomfortable, opened with a statement:

> At a time when public officials and institutions are correctly under scrutiny and when cynicism about people in public office is at an all-time high, there must be accountability and responsibility for official actions and conduct. I am here to take full responsibility for my conduct.

Packwood described his office as a "beacon of opportunity" for women and his "belief in women's rights and the political agenda of the women's movement as one of the cornerstones of my political career." He continued:

> But now all of my past record is clouded because of incidents in which my actions were unwelcome and offensive to the women involved.
>
> This is clear. My past actions were not just inappropriate. What I did was not just stupid or boorish. My actions were just plain wrong.

Packwood then digressed to explain the evolution of his convictions on women in the workplace:

> My childhood of the 1930s and 1940s was typical of the times. Male and female students were on separate tracks,

42 even in coeducational public schools. Boys took shop; girls took cooking. . . .

Through college and law school it was the same. . . . Even when I started to practice law in 1958, there was a major debate in law firms about whether women should be made partners.

A sea change occurred for me in 1960 when I was elected chairman of my county Republican central committee. It had a very gender-biased structure. The women on the committee, equally competent or, in many cases, more competent than the men, were nevertheless confined to subordinate roles, doing tasks traditionally assigned to women. . . . I moved these women into positions of authority and responsibility.

From that time forward, all of my political activities have been, for a lack of a better term, "gender neutral". . . .

In light of my commitment to women's issues and my deep belief that the workplace must be gender neutral, the current charges about my behavior trouble me in a profound way. I recognize now that my conduct was at variance with these beliefs—not because my convictions are not genuine, but because my conduct was not faithful to those convictions.

Although most of these incidents are a decade or two decades old, and no one's job was threatened, my conduct was wrong. I just didn't get it. I do now.

I said I was here to take full responsibility for my conduct, and I do so. The issue here is my conduct, and my conduct alone. I will not debate the recent accounts of my actions toward my staff and those who worked with my office. The important point is that my actions were unwelcome and insensitive. Those women were offended and I am truly sorry. . . .

Now let me make these assurances. I pledge to restructure, drastically and totally, my attitude and my professional relationships. If that requires professional counseling, I will seek it. I will guarantee that nothing like this will ever happen again.

Packwood concluded by promising to "cooperate fully with the Senate Ethics Committee to investigate and resolve this matter."

After a pause, reporters began the cross-examination. Within two minutes it became clear that Packwood's statement had flopped. He had insulted the audience by ignoring two key issues: Did he lie to the media? And did he smear the women's sexual histories?

The first questioner asked if his initial denial of the story had been simply a cover-up to stall until after the election.

Packwood replied that the *Post* reporters interviewed him late in the afternoon on the day before a debate with AuCoin 130 miles away in Bend. "I was not prepared for it. And for the first time, they mentioned charges I had never heard. They mentioned names I had never heard, and said, 'You have one day to respond.'"

This, of course, was untrue. His own staffer, Cathy Miles, had specifically informed Packwood of the impending story months before, on 22 April. Packwood had called the *Oregonian* in May to dispute the charges. His confidante Elaine Franklin had made numerous calls complaining about Florence Graves's investigative digging. And Graves had asked for an interview only the week before.

Packwood continued, "I thought to myself, 'I could not have done those things. I did not do those things.' I denied it to myself because I didn't believe it, and I denied it to my friends, and I denied it to the *Post*. . . ."

National Public Radio reporter Nina Totenberg now pressed Packwood about the information he had collected on his accusers.

Totenberg: You said you are taking responsibility for your conduct, but part of your conduct was the affidavits that you submitted to the *Post* casting questions on the character of the women who were making these allegations.

Now, I'm not asking you to discuss any of these affidavits in particular. Nonetheless, you submitted seventeen affidavits. And a number of these women have said in interviews that was worse than the original conduct, that they were being smeared. Why did you do that?

Packwood: I will say again, I am not going to discuss the issue at all as to how I have characterized their conduct.

44   I'm not going to get into it, and I'm not going to respond at all to the issue that you are raising.

Totenberg: Senator, you are not really taking responsibility for your own conduct if you won't discuss it.

Packwood fought off ten more questions about the scarlet letters. He also dropped the Hazelden alibi attributing his behavior to alcohol abuse. When asked if he had a drinking problem, he answered, "I don't—I don't think so. It's hard to ask a person who uses alcohol . . . but in any event, I am going to seek counseling and see further what the situation is."

But as he dropped that pretext, he suggested another one for misleading the *Post* and the *Oregonian*—personal denial.

Reporter: Senator, you say you realize now that your conduct was wrong, just plain wrong, but what did you think back then?. . . Did you think it was normal? Did you think that's just the way things are? Can you tell us what your state of mind was back then?

Packwood: No, I can't tell you what my state of mind was. When the *Washington Post* first came, I couldn't even believe I engaged in this kind of conduct. I couldn't believe that I would treat women this way when I felt so strongly about equality and fairness.

As the questioning continued relentlessly, Packwood's eyes grew angry. Icily, he vowed not to resign under "any circumstances," but as he was grilled about lying to the *Post,* his confidence faltered.

The national reporters had Packwood staggering. As the senator fumbled to answer a charge, press aide Evans stepped in to save him. He asked for a final question, singling out hometown television anchor Mike Donahue, hoping for friendlier treatment. Donahue asked if Packwood believed he was the victim of a "modern witch-hunt."

———

When the smoke cleared, few analysts gave Packwood acceptable marks. The *New York Times* editorialized: "His apology comes conveniently late. It would have counted for a lot more had Mr. Packwood reacted with such candor before the election, thus giving Oregon voters a chance to pass judgment on his misconduct. . . . Resignation would clear the air."

The thunderous disapproval shocked Packwood. "They were dumbstruck that it didn't go over," according to AP reporter Scott Sonner. The senator made ethical omissions and critical tactical errors. By trying to gag the women, Packwood had nullified the argument that he had done nothing wrong—and had nothing to be afraid of. And the senator had not realized how much reporters knew about the secret faxes to the *Post*.

Most egregiously, he did not—as he had promised Sonner—speak from the heart. In failing to show any sorrow for the people he hurt, this brilliant man overlooked an obvious truth. He had let pass the first—and best—opportunity to repent and thereby soften the hearts that were rapidly hardening against him.

His accusers believed Packwood's self-serving apology was worse than no apology at all. "If he really cared about making the women feel better, he'd resign so that the women wouldn't have to go through the Ethics Committee hearings," said Mary Heffernan. "An apology isn't enough. . . . It said you can do this as much as you want, and it's okay as long as you say you're sorry. Well, what if he had stolen money? Do we consider harassing women equally wrong?"

The *Post* disclosures now helped to identify other women with Packwood encounters. The 22 November story brought old memories to the surface for Gayle Rothrock of Olympia, Washington, who had taken a job as a receptionist for Senator Len Jordan (R-Idaho) after graduating from Mills College in 1969. That spring she went to Packwood's office to deliver some papers. Packwood introduced Rothrock, then twenty-three, to his wife Georgie, who was visiting the office. Georgie asked if Rothrock would babysit their children that night.

Rothrock agreed. That evening, as Packwood walked her to the car to drive her home, he forcibly kissed her. As the senator drove, he reached over and touched her legs several times. Rothrock said she kept talking to signal her lack of interest, and he stopped.

46   The incident helped sour Rothrock's views of a career on Capitol Hill, although she kept the story to herself for several years. Eventually, however, she told both her mother and a close friend.

After her time in Washington, Rothrock returned to the Northwest, earned a master's degree, and became a lobbyist in the Washington state legislature. When the *Post* disclosures came out, Rothrock recognized a name in the article, and tried calling the woman, whose husband then gave her the number to reach Florence Graves.

Rothrock told her story to Graves. She even sent a letter to Senator Slade Gorton (R-Washington) citing Packwood's conduct as an example of a larger problem of congressional indifference. The *Oregonian* got wind of that and published her story in mid-December.

Several of the other women now hired attorneys and Packwood loyalists hurled countercharges. Julie Myers Williamson slept fitfully each night, dreading the sound of the *Oregonian* hitting her porch at 4 A.M. "I'd step outside to see if I survived another day's news," she said.

Williamson had long ago planned an antique-shopping vacation in Washington, D.C., for December. While in D.C., she dined with Paige Wagers, who spoke of her self-hatred for letting Packwood victimize her twice. Williamson also accepted invitations on the East Coast to appear on *Larry King Live* and *Sally* to speak out against Packwood.

In response to the negative publicity, the senator's loyalists asked why Packwood should have to resign when Ted Kennedy was allowed to stay in office after the Palm Beach disgrace involving his nephew Willie. Key allies formed the Oregonians for a Fair Hearing to direct counterattacks. They painted a red target around a picture of Williamson. Pro-Packwood leader Jeanette Slepian denounced Williamson as a former Les AuCoin aide burying a partisan hatchet in the senator's reputation. Slepian, a New York attorney, claimed Williamson should make her charges under oath.

Williamson now prepared to do just that. Art Johnson, one of the state's top trial lawyers, took her case. As she began the two-hour drive to Eugene to see him on an icy day in January, she reflected on what intimate aspects of her life, dignity, and privacy she risked exposing. Williamson felt her eyes and face tic uncontrollably as she drove.

At Williamson's behest, the Ethics Committee agreed to permanently invoke the Rape Shield Law in questioning witnesses, forcing Packwood's attorneys to refrain from asking the women about past sexual activity. Packwood had to focus on the specific incidents he stood accused of. But the shield law contained a loophole. It only applied to sexual misconduct—not to charges that Packwood intimidated the women by sending derogatory statements to the *Post*. One woman ruefully explained, "If Packwood harassed you, he can't defend himself by calling you a slut. Your privacy is protected. But if he called you a slut in a private fax to the *Washington Post*, the Ethics Committee must examine the fax in which he called you a slut."

———

In his long senatorial career Packwood had usually returned to Oregon every three weeks, but he stayed cloistered in Washington for two months following the *Post* story. This only heightened the suspense of the inevitable face-off with his constituents. In late January he gingerly returned to the state, avoiding forums likely to draw protesters, and arranging a cocoon of friendly Farm Bureau, timber, and business audience receptions. But protesters burst into those meetings in Eugene, Corvallis, and Bend. And passions were further enflamed when Packwood, in essence, retracted his apology. He said his attorneys would cross-examine the women and a loyalist would testify against one of his accusers to the Ethics Committee.

The senator made his decision sound very reasonable. "All I'm asking is that in that [Ethics] forum, that those who have complained come forward," he said, "and that we have a chance to ask them questions."

His statements infuriated feminists. "He tried denial and that didn't work. He tried smearing his victims and that didn't work. He tried alcoholism and that didn't work, and now he's trying this," declared Virginia Burdick, of Oregonians for Ethical Representation, pushing the Senate Rules Committee complaint.

48   Packwood's retreat from his earlier apology was "outrageous and disgraceful," claimed Holly Pruett, executive director of Oregon's Coalition Against Domestic and Sexual Violence. "He started out by saying that he didn't get it. Then he said he did get it. Now he says the women are going to get it."

The stormy homecoming totally deteriorated as Packwood completed his tour in Portland on 29 January. Aides frantically rescheduled meetings to avoid protesters. The Portland Police Bureau assigned one hundred officers, including mounted police, to quell any violence.

Meanwhile, encouraged by the Rape Shield Law, more women stepped forth to tell their stories to Graves and Shepard. In a front-page story on 7 February, the *Post* revealed that including Rothrock, an additional thirteen women—aides, campaign volunteers, lobbyists, acquaintances, and virtual strangers—claimed that Packwood had made uninvited sexual advances, including touching and kissing. For example:

- Gena Hutton had watched the news conference from her home in Eugene and was so incensed by Packwood's performance that she was provoked to call the *Post*. Hutton had responded to a fund-raising letter signed by Gloria Steinem for Packwood's 1980 reelection. A Packwood aide subsequently recruited Hutton to serve as campaign chairwoman for Lane County, the state's second largest metropolitan area. Shortly afterward, Packwood called to arrange a meeting in Eugene to "get acquainted" and introduce Hutton to then-chief of staff Mimi Weyforth.

  Hutton met Packwood, Weyforth, and another aide at the restaurant at the Red Lion Inn. Hutton brought along photos of her two children, then ages ten and eight, and of her cat, because the senator "told me he wanted to know who I was."

  After dinner, Packwood walked Hutton to her car in the parking lot where, she said, he abruptly "turned and pulled me toward him and sensuously kissed me in a way that was very inappropriate." She said he tried to put his tongue in her mouth.

Even though Hutton "backed him off" and made it clear she had no interest in his advances, Packwood reportedly invited her several times to his motel room. "It was pretty clear what his intent was," she said.

Her initial reaction was that the senator had been drinking too much and that she had to protect him from being publicly embarrassed. She drove Packwood the short distance from the restaurant parking lot to his room at the same motel. Hutton said she declined his invitations to come inside by telling him she had "too much work to do the next day."

On the drive home, Hutton pulled off the road and burst into tears. Her emotions ranged from blaming herself to "feeling protective of Georgie [Packwood's then-wife]."

Campaign duties required Hutton to return to the Red Lion Inn the next day. As she entered the lobby, she saw Packwood sitting near the entrance. "We just stared at each other—there was a lot of intensity." Hutton recalls attempting to send the visual message that "I am done with this—and nothing more will be spoken about this."

Though troubled by the senator's actions, Hutton decided to honor her commitment to manage his campaign in Lane County. Packwood made no further sexual advances. About two months after the encounter, Hutton "gingerly approached" campaign manager Craig Smith. According to Hutton, Smith told her that Packwood had made similar advances to other women, and his staff had tried on numerous occasions to talk with him about his behavior.

Twelve years later, a shocked Hutton learned of the *Post*'s revelations in her hometown paper, the Eugene *Register-Guard*. "I started reading the story and just cried," she said. "And that was when the agonizing began—I thought, 'These women stepped forward, what will I do?'"

Hutton called the local women's hot line, and the counselors encouraged her to contact Florence Graves. She did not call immediately, held back by fear of intimidation and a desire to protect her family's privacy. "I knew

50 he was a formidable warrior and streetfighter," she said. Also, this lifelong Republican from rural Klamath Falls agonized over possibly damaging the career of a man whose political views she still greatly admired—particularly his support for abortion rights. Ultimately, however, she resolved that Packwood had "brought all this on himself," and decided to step forward.[2]

- Gillian Butler worked in 1980 as front-desk clerk at the Red Lion Inn in downtown Portland, where Packwood often stayed. One day, as the senator was checking out, Butler told him about a letter she had sent his office protesting the military draft. Packwood asked her to write again, promising to meet and discuss her views the next time he was in town.

  Butler, who was twenty-two and admittedly naive, was flattered. In a neat script, she wrote three painfully earnest pages analyzing "international aggression." Soon after, she says, Packwood invited her to discuss the subject over drinks. Confused about why he wanted to meet in a bar, she had invited her boyfriend as an escort. The senator's chosen meeting place had red, upholstered walls like a Las Vegas lounge, and when Packwood entered, Butler was amazed to see he was greeted like a regular.

  One day after that, according to Butler, Packwood unexpectedly leaned across the front desk of the Red Lion and kissed her on the lips. "I backed away and laughed it off," she says. "I was embarrassed, and I was trying to think what I could have done to make him think that was okay." On another occasion, the senator followed her into a luggage closet and kissed her on the lips. Butler swiftly backed out. "I started telling people he was sleazy after that," she says.

- Sharon Grant sought a job in Packwood's Washington office in 1969, when she was twenty-nine. Grant claims

---

2. Florence Graves and Charles Shepard. 7 February 1993, *Washington Post*. Karen McCowan. 2 December 1993, *Register-Guard*.

that during the interview, Packwood made it clear that he
wanted to spend the night with her, and she had to talk her
way out of his office. "He didn't know me at all, yet he felt
he could have what he wanted with impunity," she said.

- Lois Kincaid attended a fund-raiser at an Oregon ranch in
1971, when she was twenty-seven. She said that she had
never met Packwood, but when the two were alone in a
room he tried to embrace her "out of the blue and without
saying a thing." She stopped him. He "acted kind of confused and mumbled some kind of apology, like 'Excuse
me,' like it was inadvertent, which was pretty ridiculous
considering the size of the room," she said.

- A Packwood clerical employee, identified to the Senate
Ethics Committee, was twenty-one in 1982 when the senator invited her into his Capitol Hill office one evening
and offered her wine. She agreed to sit and talk but declined the drink. "He walked over to me, pulled me out of
the chair, and put his arm around me. He tried to kiss me.
He stuck his tongue in my mouth." The employee said she
squirmed away and left. She avoided Packwood in the
future and some months later quit her job.

- A onetime high school summer intern, who agreed to be
identified to Packwood but not named publicly, said that
while she worked as a driver for Packwood in 1982, the
senator unnerved her by saying several times that she was
pretty and poised and that he considered her a woman
despite her age.

In the fall of 1983, when she was a seventeen-year-old
senior, she asked Packwood for a written recommendation for a college application.

He agreed but insisted on personally delivering it to
her suburban Maryland home, arranging to come when
no one else would be there. Once inside, Packwood tried
to hug her. "He seemed a little heated," she said. After
being rebuffed and asked to leave, he "laid a juicy kiss on
my lips. I could feel the tongue coming." The teen pushed
Packwood away and escorted him to the front door. She

was "unbelievably shaken" and double-locked the door after he left.

- A Eugene woman, who agreed to be identified to Packwood but not named publicly, said that in 1985 while she was being considered for a campaign job, Packwood asked her to dance at a restaurant in Bend. He proceeded to kiss her on the neck and then, in her words, "his hands were all over my back, sides, and buttocks, and he made suggestive movements."

  After a political event later that year, she drove Packwood and Elaine Franklin, then a top aide, to their Eugene motel. Franklin got out of the car, but Packwood remained. Suddenly, she said, he kissed her. "It turned into a French kiss, and I said, 'I don't appreciate that,' and I pushed him away." When the woman then complained to Franklin and asked if putting up with such behavior would be part of her job responsibilities, she said Franklin asked for more details.

  According to the woman, Packwood called a week later to warn her to never again tell anyone about any problems she had with him. She was then offered the job, but turned it down. Franklin refused comment through an aide.

The total number of complaints soon exceeded the twenty-three accusers that the *Post* had reported. The *Oregonian* revealed that Packwood had tried to kiss their Washington correspondent, Roberta Ulrich. On 8 December, the newspaper also reported the story of Tiffany Work, who said that Packwood grabbed her buttocks while she worked as a hostess at a political gathering in Eugene in 1973.[3] She was thirteen at the time (though she had been dressed up for the occasion to look older).

According to Work, Packwood would not have known how young she was. "I wasn't even dating. . . ." she said. "I was so excited [about getting the job]. I got to wear a black dress and black panty hose. It was the first time I'd ever gotten to wear black panty hose," she told a reporter.

---

3. Dee Lane, 8 December 1992, *Oregonian*.

Work claimed that Packwood had put his hands on two 53 other teenagers at that event. One was seventeen at the time; the other was eighteen.

After the *Post* story of 7 February, Packwood did not even pretend to be apologetic. No dash to Hazelden. No news conference. His attorney, James Fitzpatrick, instead tersely told reporters that the Senate Ethics Committee was the "appropriate forum" to respond to the assertions. In a statement released through press aide Matt Evans, the senator specifically denied Work's accusation. "This is an outrageous lie," Packwood said. The fact that Work was underage at the time made Packwood's alleged sexual advances toward her illegal, not to mention even more distasteful, to constituents.

Packwood had drawn his line in the dust. His combativeness might save his Senate seat, but the imminent debate would surely make him a universal symbol of the sexual harasser, the embodiment of the classic male assumption that women are not to be taken seriously.

Congress now began to uncover the truth about the charges against Packwood as the Senate Ethics Committee launched the biggest sexual misconduct investigation in history. By January 1993, according to an ABC News/*Washington Post* poll, more than two out of three Americans knew about the Packwood charges. Voters from California to Kansas to Washington, D.C., were all asking the same question: What could have led Bob Packwood, champion of women's rights, pioneer of abortion rights, to make such egregious errors in judgment?

Part II

4

Young lobbyist John Lansing was jerked awake at 3 A.M. by the sound of a ringing phone. Fumbling to get the receiver to his ear, he heard the slurred, drunken voice of his partner, Fred Packwood.

"The goddamn police have put me in jail," Packwood said. "Get me out of here!"

Lansing dashed into the rainy night and got to the nearby Marion County jail as soon as he could. He stated his business and asked for his partner, but the jail clerk shook his head and answered, "There's no Fred Packwood here."

Perplexed, Lansing returned through the pelting rain to the hotel and fell asleep. One hour later, the telephone rang again. It was Packwood. "This time he was really cussing at me," said Lansing. "I told him that I had gone to the county jail, but Fred just got madder. 'You stupid _ _ _, I'm at the *city* jail!'"

Once again, Lansing headed out into the drenching night. He arrived sopping wet at the Salem city jail and inquired about his associate.

Yes, they had Fred Packwood in custody. And, no, they would not release him. They wanted bail money first.

"On what charges?" demanded Lansing. **57**

The desk clerk paused ominously and began reading from a lengthy rap sheet. A Salem policeman had reported seeing an intoxicated Packwood relieving himself on the state capitol lawn that night. When the officer approached him, the fifty-one-year-old lobbyist resisted arrest. After subduing Packwood, the lawman escorted him to the backseat of the patrol car. As the officer closed the rear door and began to enter the car, Packwood picked up a tire iron from the floor and took a boozy swing at him.

"And so the charges," the jail clerk intoned, "are alleged public drunkenness, indecent exposure, urinating on public property, resisting arrest, and assaulting an officer."

"My God," Lansing gasped. "You could put him away for twenty years on that."

"Yes," the jail clerk smiled. "We could have—many times."

Suddenly, Lansing realized that the drunk tank was almost a second mailing address for his partner. The desk clerk knew what to do next.

"He asked me how much money I was carrying on me," Lansing said. "And I remembered that I had just broken a $20 bill to buy cigarettes. As I began to explain that, the clerk interrupted to say, 'Just turn that over, and we'll let him go on bail.'"

———

U.S. Senator Robert W. Packwood's reputation for maverick individualism is the legacy of a troubled and brilliant political family that has influenced Oregon for a century. His father, Fred, was a chronic alcoholic and a highly respected Oregon lobbyist and tax analyst. His grandfather, Billy, was a successful lawyer who abandoned young Fred and his mother to join the gold rush in Alaska. His great-grandfather, William, who got his start in life as an army deserter, went on to become an entrepreneur and renowned judge who designed the seal of the State of Oregon. The story of what happened to make Bob Packwood what he is, a consummate politician whose personal problems have brought him to the brink of ruin, has its roots deep in his family's history.

The clan originated in colonial Virginia where during the 1700s a devastating James River flood near Richmond drowned virtually an entire family. The lone survivor was a child named Billy, whom boatsmen rescued from a drifting tree trunk and adopted as one of their own. The orphan was too young to know his last name, but he was not too young to make himself useful by hauling wood to camp. In recognition of the lad's industry, the men named him "Packwood."

While the truth of that story is lost in antiquity, it's clear that the family migrated to frontier Illinois, where Bob Packwood's great-grandfather, William Henderson Packwood, was born near Springfield in 1832. He spent his youth on a farm and as a teenager found work in Springfield as a store clerk. Walking to work in the morning, he regularly saw a young attorney named Abraham Lincoln taking the same route to his law office.

But a clerk's life did not satisfy Packwood. In 1848, during the Mexican-American War, the fifteen-year-old lied about his age and enlisted in a U.S. Army mounted rifle company. The youth was spared from charging the Halls of Montezuma when Congress decided that the United States also needed soldiers to protect settlers from Indians out West. Packwood's rifle company was dispatched to Northern California, where the young private discovered adventure far beyond army life.

In 1849 the gold rush began at Sutter's Mill, near Sacramento. Many unlettered farm boys like Packwood suddenly became fabulously rich. Some "Forty-Niners" earned one hundred times Packwood's puny two-dollar-a-month soldier's salary—one gold prospector's fortune eventually founded the Hearst newspaper chain.

Lured by the prospect of found money, Packwood ditched his blue army uniform for miner's overalls and headed for the Sierra Nevada goldfields. Desertion, of course, was not a new problem for the army, and military authorities knew just where to look. They promptly arrested Packwood, sentenced him to hard labor, and put him on a prison ship bound for the wild Oregon territory farther north. But before the ship made port, Packwood's luck changed: the ship crashed on the rocky southern

60 Oregon coast. The young fugitive swam ashore, picked up another gold pan, and eventually prospered in the appropriately
named town of Gold Beach.

Packwood prospered to such a degree, in fact, that he became
one of the remote Curry County's most affluent citizens. In 1857
he went to Salem to represent the county at the Oregon Constitutional Convention that led to Oregon becoming an antislavery
state near the eve of the Civil War. That experience opened a new
world for him, and he never returned to Curry County.

The enterprising young man was soon packing supplies
on horseback to mining camps throughout the state. He took
his earnings and explored opportunities in Baker City, an Oregon Trail outpost near the Idaho border that was surrounded
by snowcapped peaks studded with ponderosa pine. Luck was
still with him: no sooner had he wiped the trail dust from his
mouth than prospectors discovered gold near Baker City. The
nearby Blue Mountains yielded $20 million worth of the pre-
cious metal in just one sixty-two-day period in 1863, one of the
richest—and briefest—gold rushes in American history.

Packwood thrived here as a miner and a merchant, and
eventually he was selected as a judge. Despite his own brief career as a fugitive, he had few compunctions about capital punishment and hung several outlaws. The judge almost ended
up on the wrong side of the law himself once, after he dredged
a mining canal and simultaneously sold 100 percent interest to
more than one buyer.

But politics was the field in which Judge Packwood made a
lasting impact. He designed the state seal that Oregonians permanently adopted. As the Civil War approached, he joined antislavery forces coalescing under the new Republican party
banner, and he helped organize Abraham Lincoln's successful
1860 presidential campaign in Oregon.

In later years, Packwood became Baker City's assistant post-
master and served for decades, retiring in 1911. He lived to become the last survivor of the historic 1857 state Constitutional
Convention, and at age eighty-three he made a sentimental
journey to Salem, where he was honored by the 1915 Oregon
legislature.

Packwood and his wife, an Irish Catholic schoolteacher named Joanna O'Brien, began a family that continued the Packwood tradition of working in Oregon law and government. Their son, William H. "Billy" Packwood, Jr., became one of eastern Oregon's top trial lawyers. A son-in-law, John Rand, became a state senator and Oregon Supreme Court justice.

Following the lure of gold, as his father had, Billy abandoned both his family and his law practice in 1900 to join the Alaska gold rush. His wife and their five-year-old son, Fred, eventually settled three hundred miles away in Portland, one of America's largest cities west of the Missouri River. After the move she pointedly refused the Packwoods' request that Frederick be raised a Roman Catholic.

One day Fred developed a strange fever and a disturbing loss of motor control. Physicians broke the frightening news that he had infantile paralysis, and they prescribed orthopedic shoes. That day, the world changed for Fred. He could no longer engage in playground games, and by the time he entered Portland's Jefferson High School in 1909 he was on crutches. Feeling like an outcast, Fred retreated into the world of libraries and focused his energies on attaining knowledge. He developed a mind to match his father's, and in 1914 enrolled at the University of Oregon in Eugene. The isolated Packwood declined to even list his father on his application papers.

During his freshman year, a friendly coach, Bill Hayward, spotted Packwood and suggested that he try out for the wrestling team. Fred thought that Hayward had lost his mind, but the coach persisted, arguing that the sport might develop his muscles and relieve his dependence on crutches. Fred agreed to try. He never made the varsity squad, but wrestling did strengthen his legs. He was able to throw away the loathsome crutches and could now walk with leg braces. Although he was not as fast as other people, no one could walk farther.

Polio forced Fred to struggle to achieve what came naturally for many students, and this fostered his competitive drive. He strived to win student elections, scholarships, and the love of a Gamma Phi Beta sorority girl. Politics became a passion. This economics major won election to the student council in an era when peers took student government seriously. Many of the campus politicians later became state leaders, but few could match Fred Packwood in debates. "He loved arguing and was good at it," a schoolmate remembers.

Fred completed his undergraduate degree in 1918, when American involvement in World War I was reaching its climax. The army shipped most graduating seniors to France for the final offensive against the Germans, but polio kept Fred out of the fray.

The disease, however, ultimately affected more than just his legs. He had begun drinking heavily as a student to kill the physical pain. But in 1919, with the establishment of Prohibition, he switched from hard liquor to high-proof vanilla cooking extract. Alcoholism would dog him throughout his life.

The driven young man also completed law school in Eugene, and events in his personal life changed considerably. His mother had remarried and moved to California, and Billy had returned to Baker City after years in Alaska. Although Fred had his law degree, he took a schoolteaching job to be near his father. He enjoyed teaching, but when his father died in 1924 there was no longer any reason to delay his legal career. He moved to Portland in 1925 to become a lobbyist for a statewide business group.

———

Fred spent most of his time at the state capitol in Salem, where his intellect was quickly recognized. He published an independent daily bill digest trusted by politicians and the press corps because of Packwood's clear and unbiased bill descriptions.

One of the people who met him that year was Oregon legislative historian Cecil Edwards, who would share forty years with Fred Packwood. The new lobbyist was unmistakable, said Edwards. "You'd see Fred trudging down the capitol corridors with his crippled walk, skinny as hell, and with a sallow complexion."

Packwood had long since broken up with his University of Oregon girlfriend. He lacked success in courtship—the effects of his polio may have put women off, or perhaps his illness, which forced him inward, had stunted his social skills. Gladys Taft first met her future husband in 1925 at a Portland Progressive Club violin concert. Sixty years later this blunt, outspoken woman recalled her first impression of him as "boring and uninteresting." Her opinion never changed, she said, but— perhaps lacking other suitors—she dated him anyway.

The Tafts came from New England and spent a generation on the North Dakota prairie before arriving in Portland in 1921. Gladys was the oldest child in this family of Republican burghers. Gladys's great-grandfather named a son Ulysses S. Grant, after the Republican president, and her parents had considered naming her younger brother William Howard Taft, in honor of another White House resident.

Gladys, however, had stayed away from politics. She was a gifted musician, and her family encouraged her to study classical piano at the University of Minnesota, Oregon State University, and the Denver Conservatory of Music. "When I began dating Fred, I didn't know what his politics were—because I didn't know anything about politics," she said.

The couple married in June 1929. Instead of going on a honeymoon, Gladys spent the summer studying in Denver. She returned in the fall, shortly before the stock market crashed and the Great Depression enveloped the country. The hard times that followed aggravated tensions between the newlyweds. They lived in modest apartments on Portland's inner Northeast side for three years before the birth of their first child, Robert William Packwood, on 11 September 1932. His sister, Patricia, was born when Bob was five.

Packwood's relationship with his mother was strained from the start. "Bob was a very, very difficult birth," Gladys once said, and she apparently did nothing to ease things. According to Bob's schoolmate Jane Notson Gregg, Gladys Packwood was "a very unpleasant woman who'd say unpleasant things about Bob in front of him and other kids. . . . She seemed 'crabby' in ways other mothers were not." Nonetheless, he gave Gladys her family nickname when his first attempts to say "Mommy" came out as "Mindy."

64   As a young student at Fernwood Elementary School, Bob was difficult to manage. He acted up, disrupting the class and generally "doing things you did not do in that era," says Gregg. The rewards and incentives for good behavior that worked with other kids did not tempt Bob. Teachers graded students for "deportment," and children earned movie privileges for behaving themselves. Packwood later admitted that he had received only one movie privilege in his early grades.

One summer evening in 1942, Fred Packwood took his nine-year-old son to a minor league baseball game. The father, to his surprise, discovered that Bob could read nothing on the centerfield scoreboard. The family optometrist prescribed thick-lens glasses. In much the same way that crutches had transformed his father's life, Bob's glasses changed his.

Big for his age, Bob tried out for the Fernwood football team, despite his poor vision. He became a fine lineman, eagerly getting his licks in, but the eyeglasses proved to be a hindrance. Like his father before him, he withdrew socially and turned to the company of books.

The Packwoods bought their first home, a handsome Fernwood neighborhood Cape Cod, when Bob was ten. The two-story house at 3663 NE Stanton Street featured stately evergreen trees that towered over the backyard. The interior was sparsely outfitted, except for the three pianos—including a baby grand—that his mother seemed to treasure more than anything else.

Gladys, now called Mindy, taught piano lessons to neighborhood children, as well as to her son, for eight years. Mindy drilled students crisply and efficiently, and an arch of her eyebrows could send a chill through any ten-year-old who had not practiced. Students remembered her as aloof, methodical, and incessantly organized. "She wasn't the kind of teacher to hug you at the door," one recalled.

The material comforts at the Stanton Street house could not plaster over the difficulties between husband and wife. Mindy loved order, but Fred's inner demons made that impossible. Prohibition had not stopped Fred from drinking, and his alcoholic stupors and rages mortified her and the children. He and Mindy fought constantly. In one terrible incident, Bob saw his mother run to the kitchen drawer and pull out a long butcher knife to attack Fred with. Negotiating between his bellicose parents became Bob's first lesson in politics.

Mindy and Fred didn't show much affection for each other, and they were not overly loving to their children. At best, Fred might pat Bob on the head and note "Say, haven't you lost weight?" Mindy, who was closer to her daughter, hardly ever had a kind word for Bob at all.

Bob and his sister, Patricia, were drawn close by their shared experiences growing up in an explosive household, but they were different in nearly every way. The boy had inherited his mother's blonde features, stout cheekbones, strong jaw, and snub nose, and he also acquired her Midwestern accent with its long, flat vowel sounds and inflections. "Patsy" physically resembled her father, with her sharper features and dark hair. Bob kept his room in meticulous order, while his sister preferred to leave the contents of her bedroom in utter disarray. As Bob became progressively quieter and more studious, Patsy grew up to be a sociable and well-liked girl.

Both children were unarguably affected by their distant mother and unpredictable father. Patsy once warned a boyfriend that her father was often abusively drunk, and the constant anxiety may have contributed to her extroverted, nervous demeanor.

Conversely, her brother escaped into the world of tasks, often locking himself in his room to study for hours. Radio sets, model airplanes, and books provided a respite from the often unbearable tension between his parents. Reading fueled his growing curiosity for the world beyond Stanton Street.

The year Bob entered the fourth grade, the Japanese attacked Pearl Harbor. West Coast cities, including Portland, Los Angeles, San Francisco, and Seattle were blacked out for fear of Japanese air raids. Shortly afterward, Bob asked his father why two Japanese-American classmates had suddenly disappeared from school. Fred explained the Civilian Internment Law, which enabled the U.S. government to remove American citizens of Japanese ancestry from their homes, confiscate their

66 property, and intern them in camps, out of fear that they would be sympathetic with Japan. He warned his son that the arbitrary imprisonment of American citizens showed "just how wrong a government could be." Perhaps because of his polio, Fred empathized with minorities and underdogs.

Such exchanges became dinner table staples. It was hard for any Republican family to take much partisan pleasure in the military successes of Democratic President Franklin D. Roosevelt, and the Packwoods directed their praise toward Britain's liberal Tory Prime Minister Winston Churchill. Father and son discussed news of the war, and Bob's political education was under way.

———

Fred now regularly traveled to Salem to lobby the business interests of Columbia Empire Industries. He entertained dinner guests, including lobbyists, journalists, and politicians such as Republican Governor Earl Snell.

Bob wanted to be able to converse intelligently with the company, and he began to read newspaper editorials before turning to the comics page. "I was probably fifteen or sixteen before I realized that most of my friends or their families didn't commonly talk about government around the dinner table," he once said. He patrolled Stanton Street, newspaper in hand, asking adults about the goings-on in Salem. No longer a deportment problem, he now took his schoolbooks home and read them.

It wasn't easy for Bob to keep up with Fred, whose idea of light reading was curling up with a volume of the encyclopedia and reading it from cover to cover. Fred was also drawn to the writings of rationalist freethinkers such as Thomas Hobbes, John Locke, and Montesquieu. He was especially interested in de Tocqueville's essays on America, and underlined passages for his son's edification.

Fred drove Bob incessantly to analyze problems, and even Saturday night card games became contests of logic. On road trips he grilled his son with political, historical, and philosophical questions until the boy would at times burst into tears.

As a teenager Bob often came home from school anxious to tell his father about something he had learned. The issue could be as lofty as minority rights or as mundane as street potholes. Fred would generally quiz his son on the source of his information, then ask if he had checked the facts on the other side.

Fred sometimes extended the lesson by directing Bob to a tome such as Hobbes's *Leviathan,* which could utterly demolish the boy's hypothesis.

When Bob was in his teens, Fred revealed glimpses of his personal skepticism about certain Republican principles. For two decades Fred had lobbied for business interests, and he had compiled a scrapbook of big business inconsistencies. He showed Bob examples of proposed legislation that companies claimed they could not afford; yet when the bills became law, business somehow managed to survive. "Son, businessmen will always say they cannot afford it. They're not lying. But they cannot see beyond where they are."

———

In the fall of 1946 Packwood enrolled at the 1,800-student Grant High School, one of the most demanding public schools on the West Coast. *Pageant* magazine selected Grant as one of the top ten high schools in America. Packwood-era high achievers at Grant included future U.S. Secretary of the Interior Donald Hodel, *New York Times* senior editor Jack Rosenthal, space shuttle astronaut Gordon Fullerton, Stanford University Medical School administrator Howard Sussman, and New York Giants quarterback George Shaw.

Not surprisingly, Fred Packwood insisted that his son take one of Grant's toughest classes, freshman speech with Mrs. Opal Hamilton. Mrs. Hamilton recalled that "Bob was as smart as they come, but also shy and quiet." She did her best to draw him out through public speaking, but he was not interested in the treatment.

"I asked him to speak at our Veterans Day assembly his sophomore year. He turned me down, so I really gave him a lecture. 'Bob, you're selling yourself short. You'll probably go into law like your father—and you better get started with public speaking now.' He looked at me like I was nuts. But he went out and gave that speech in front of a thousand kids."

Most of Mrs. Hamilton's students loved participating in after-dinner speaking and humorous interpretation events. But while Bob appreciated a good joke, he lacked the social ease needed to tell one, unlike teammate Don Hodel. His quick mind thrived on debate, energized by the dance of intellect and ideas. At tournaments the debaters regularly switched between arguing the affirmative and negative side of issues such as Panama Canal policy. Bob excelled at arguing the affirmative, but he was peerless on the attack.

His debating successes raised his status at the large high school, and he began to reconfigure his image. He asked people to call him "Robert." He told his friends that he wanted to be either an engineer or a physicist. These fields required precision, organization, and logic, a perfect match for his intellect. His father approved of these career choices. Fred had personally tutored the boy in public affairs, but he discouraged politics as a vocation, having suffered too many setbacks in Salem. His introverted son needed little persuading. Robert immersed himself in advanced math and science coursework.

Meanwhile, he put his social life on hold. "I was a little afraid of women," he later said. As an upperclassman Bob spruced up his attire with sports coats and protected himself with an armor of pretention. "I initially identified with him because we both wore thick glasses, but he wasn't interested in me," said locker partner Roger Buchanan. "Bob would just plow right past me and throw his briefcase and books into my part of the locker. He seemed to think he was better than I was." When Buchanan ventured small talk about girls or sports, Packwood just scowled. "I began to dread having to deal with him," Buchanan said.

But Bob's academic pressures remained relentless. "If I could be half as smart as my dad," he once confided to Mrs. Hamilton, "I'd be happy." The disciplined youth graduated in June 1950 with near-perfect "A" grades and acceptance letters to Caltech, MIT, and the Carnegie Institute of Technology. He dreamed of becoming a mathematical engineer and decided on

Caltech in Pasadena, California. When Packwood left for college that September, it was his first trip to California and his first time on an airplane.

Located in the beautiful San Gabriel Mountains northeast of Los Angeles, the college seemed tiny to first-time visitors. But Caltech boasted a gigantic reputation.

Albert Einstein rejected the concept of a static cosmos and endorsed the expanding-universe theory while at Caltech. Since then, the Spanish mission–style campus had attracted nearly twenty Nobel Prize winners.

Shortly after the seventeen-year-old Packwood began attending classes, he faced the first crisis of his adult life. The absence of liberal arts courses and the brilliance of his fellow engineering students shocked him. In a few weeks he made clear his intent to drop out. The students at his residence assigned fellow Oregonian B.W. LeTourneau to dissuade him. "Bob was a very quiet boy but certain he wanted to transfer somewhere else to major in political science or pre-law," LeTourneau said.

Packwood wanted to make this decision himself, so he hid his desires from his quarrelsome parents. Fred and Mindy received the first word of trouble in October when Bob phoned from Portland International Airport. "I want your advice," Bob said, "but it won't change my mind—I'm transferring to Willamette University." He had, in fact, already withdrawn from Caltech and made plans to enroll at the college in Salem that same semester. Bob no longer desired a career as an engineer. He wanted to become a politically active lawyer like his father.

The new school seemed well suited for his political and social aspirations. Willamette's broad green lawns were literally across the street from the state capitol, the center of Oregon politics. The Republican-oriented, Methodist campus was just forty-five miles from home. And Fred was even closer: his capitol office stood three blocks away.

70 Willamette was an incubator of Republican talent. Among small Western schools only Santa Clara University exceeded it as a producer of American politicians.[4] But Willamette had its limitations. Salem offered less culturally than either Portland or Pasadena. And with an enrollment of just 800, the college was smaller, and in some ways narrower, than Grant High School, where Packwood had shared locker space, science labs, and lunchroom seats with a comparatively cosmopolitan student body.

"Willamette was a pretty uptight place," said history professor Ivan Lovell. The college expelled students for mere possession of beer—on or off campus. Residence halls had house mothers. Male and female students were not allowed to sit on the same blanket at beach parties.

Packwood pledged with Beta Theta Pi fraternity during his freshman year. Betas were known as the campus politicos, and alumni would include such future politicians as U.S. Senator Mark Hatfield, Congressman Denny Smith, State Treasurer Tony Meeker, and U.S. Senate candidate Harley Hoppe of Washington state. Bob became a house politician and eventually Beta president, but his peers admired him more than they desired to emulate him. His studious, fastidious habits set him apart from some of his rambunctious Beta friends. His bed was always made, and he tried to see to it that his roommates' beds were made, too. He declined to participate in pranks such as putting a cow in a dean's office or taking apart a car and reassembling it in a buddy's room. Instead he could always be found reading—even as he walked down the hallway.

During the Korean conflict, Bob's poor eyesight exempted him from military service. He still wore thick eyeglasses, which inhibited him socially. Beta Larry Standifer considered Packwood the ugliest guy in the fraternity. Bob never had a steady girlfriend, and most Saturday nights he ended up playing canasta with Harley Hoppe (who regularly hid Packwood's

---

4. Santa Clara University politicians, including President Bill Clinton's Chief of Staff Leon Panetta, Press Secretary DeeDee Meyers, Secretary of Agriculture Mike Espy, former Senator Paul Laxalt (R-Nevada), and former California Governor Edmund G. (Jerry) Brown.

glasses). "We probably set a world's record for asking girls out and hearing that they were washing their hair," Hoppe says.

One of the most popular girls on campus was Jane Notson Gregg, Bob's old elementary and high school schoolmate. "Bob was not very adept socially," she remembers, "and didn't really know how to ask a girl out." Gregg became engaged to a Beta who sometimes had Bob escort Jane to dances for him. Those were often bad experiences. "He also came on strongly with my friend Mary Campbell. She wasn't pleased with what happened," Gregg said.

But Packwood conducted himself decorously in the classroom. Professor Lovell, who taught constitutional history courses, was impressed with Packwood's agile mind. Another faculty member expressed unqualified praise. "His senior year oral thesis was among the four or five best that I heard in twenty years at the college," says history professor Robert Gregg.

Packwood's intellectual prowess drew considerable notice on campus. "I admired his quick mind and his ability," Jane Notson Gregg admits. "He was the sort of person who enjoyed playing devil's advocate."

The only classmate who rivaled Packwood intellectually was fraternity brother Jim Hitchman, who later became a Western Washington University history professor. "We had some real arguments, and [Bob] would just sort of total up the objective or tangible factors," said Hitchman. "He didn't give much weight to sentimental or ethical considerations. Those seemed to be lost on him."

But it was political science professor Mark Hatfield who became Packwood's greatest influence—and certainly his most interesting role model. The twenty-eight-year-old Willamette alumnus had just returned to the campus, following World War II duty and graduate school at Stanford.

"We called him 'Dean' Hatfield but regarded him as a cool, young hipster," said student Ruben Menashe. "Hatfield was good-looking, dashing, and well dressed. And Packwood was particularly admiring."

Hatfield had helped found the Beta fraternity in the 1940s, and he now served as an advisor. He often dined at the house,

72   regularly sitting next to Packwood. The charismatic bachelor professor also supervised the Young Republicans club, in which Packwood served as an officer.

The same fall that Packwood arrived on campus, Hatfield successfully ran for the Oregon legislature. Students flocked to help him in his election bid. Some classmates pitched in just for fun, but Packwood had a more practical goal: to learn about running a campaign.

The student who was once headed for life as an engineer now plunged headfirst into the hurly-burly of GOP politics. His Young Republicans chapter took conservative foreign policy positions such as opposing United Nations membership for Communist China, yet they were daringly liberal on social issues. Packwood attended a Young Republicans conference in October 1951 that supported federal civil rights legislation and opposed McCarthy-era "loyalty oaths."

In the spring of 1952 the Young Republicans gave a spirited reception to Senator Wayne Morse, probably the most liberal Republican in the country, who attacked the national GOP leadership for treating working people "like second-class citizens." Morse denounced Senator Joseph McCarthy (R-Wisconsin) as a danger to the party and the nation.

Emotions rode high. After twenty years of Roosevelt-Truman rule, Republicans smelled blood. They knew the country wanted a change, and the winner of the GOP nomination would quite likely become the next president of the United States. Young Republicans were too young to vote, so they poured their energies into staging a mock convention pitting conservative U.S. Senator Robert Taft of Ohio against retired General Dwight Eisenhower.

Most Betas idolized the stately, principled Taft, and Packwood became the brains of the Taft campaign. But as Taft began to falter in the real primaries and caucuses, Packwood switched sides—clinching the mock convention for Ike. "We were delighted that Bob came over," said Eisenhower partisan

Dolly Montag. "He was the best debater, and we didn't want to argue with him anymore."

———

Academically, Bob thrived at Willamette. His senior year test scores sparkled, and he won the top political science award. Leadership in the Young Republicans helped him cultivate friendships with future politicians such as Hatfield, Governor Tom McCall, Secretary of State Clay Myers, and House Speaker Larry Campbell. Instead of plugging into the Oregon political scene, he sought—and won—a coveted Root-Tilden scholarship to the prestigious New York University Law School. This was a prize scholarship—only two winners were selected from each federal court district. The full scholarships were designed to draw top talent from across the nation, and they became so successful that the *New York Times* regularly printed a list of the winners.

In the fall of 1954 Packwood traded Willamette's restrictive atmosphere of mandatory chapel and fraternity house mothers for the wide-open world of Greenwich Village. The new atmosphere swarmed with artists and intellectuals, the fabulously rich and the desperately poor. Packwood, fresh from the open spaces of Oregon and its predominantly white, Christian population, was impressed by the sheer numbers of people of all colors and religions that he saw on the streets of New York City.

And in this more varied cultural milieu, he began to make some interesting friends. Many NYU students were Jewish, some Holocaust survivors. Paul Berger, Packwood's Orthodox Jewish roommate, often asked Bob to run errands on the Jewish Sabbath and other holidays when Berger could not perform work. Berger shared his thoughts about Jewish culture and Old Testament scripture with his roommate; and during the 1956 Arab-Israeli War, Packwood became aware of the vulnerability of Berger and other Jewish students.

Packwood was one of about twenty Root-Tildens in the incoming class of three hundred law students. To groom them for success, NYU sponsored tours of top law firms and hosted

74 luncheons featuring such speakers as NAACP counsel Thurgood Marshall and Senator Jacob Javits (R-New York). NYU Law School alumni, such as Javits, Secretary of Education Lamar Alexander, New York City mayors Rudolph Giuliani and Ed Koch, and several senators and congressmen—often went on to success in state and national politics. Packwood now ventured into larger worlds than he had ever known.

At NYU, Packwood blossomed. Academically, he quickly climbed to the top of his class. He won a first-round national moot court competition. "He became one of the leaders. It was obvious he was going somewhere," said law professor Julian Marks. The teenage introvert who had been too timid to seek a class office at Grant or Willamette was elected NYU Law School student body president. In the past, such competitions had been low-key affairs, but Packwood changed that by printing sophisticated campaign brochures. He proudly sent copies to Fred and Mindy in Portland.

Encouraged by his academic successes, Packwood began to venture out socially as well. His baritone voice rang out at glee club performances, and he dated more women—including one he considered marrying.

The New York years shaped Packwood in many ways. The friends he made became important connections later in life. Berger eventually became a lawyer-lobbyist on issues including Israel; the roommates remained friends and would later be political allies. Packwood also befriended NYU stars such as future Metropolitan Life Insurance CEO John Creedon and Lester Pollack of Lazard Freres Bank. Both men greatly contributed to the success of Packwood's fund-raising campaigns.

NYU also influenced his political philosophy. Until moving to New York City, he had never been east of Boise, Idaho. The overcrowding of the Washington-to-Boston corridor shocked him, making him wonder about the tolls that spiraling population growth would take on the economy and the environment. This anxiety planted the seeds of his future decision to become the first American politician to advocate abortion as a population-control strategy.

A new Bob Packwood emerged from the NYU cocoon. He didn't intend to remain a lawyer for long, and he had a plan. His first step would be the Oregon legislature, then perhaps Portland's Congressional seat, and then the seat of a man he admired from his Willamette days, U.S. Senator Wayne Morse. His ambitions didn't go unnoticed. According to one classmate, mid-1950s student body president Howard Greenberger, "I thought Packwood had the makings to become president of the United States."

5

In the autumn of 1957 Bob Packwood began his legal career as a law clerk for Oregon Supreme Court Chief Justice Harold Warner in Salem. That year, which marked the birth of a career for Bob, turned out to be the end of a downhill spiral for Fred.

Rookie lobbyist Tom Doneca first met Fred Packwood in 1955, in the fourth-floor capitol office where Packwood wrote the daily bill calendar. As Doneca entered he saw the bald, bespectacled Packwood sitting behind a desk with three stacks of bills on it.

Packwood pointed to the tallest pile, which was two feet high, and explained, "These are our bills that have come through before and I don't even have to read. I already know what's in them."

He then pointed to the next stack and said that those bills were simply variations of old ideas. He did not need to spend much time on them.

And then Packwood pointed to the smallest pile of papers. "These are the only bills dealing with new subjects. They're the only ones I actually need to read," he said.

Fred Packwood, who authored most of Oregon's tax laws in his thirty-two years as a business lobbyist, may have been the most talented legislative analyst of his generation in Salem. "I learned more about legislating laws sitting at Fred's elbow than [I could have learned from] anyone else," says former partner John Lansing. Packwood could rip apart two-hundred-page bills and sew them back up seamlessly. If the powerful taxation committee ground to an impasse, Representative Giles French of Eastern Oregon would often adjourn, look wearily into the audience, and ask Fred to "take this damn thing and work it out for us." Packwood would invariably return several hours later with a compromise that most sides could stomach. Even his opponents knew that if Fred gave you his word, you could rely on it.

Packwood had become industry's point man for their lucrative taxation and workers' compensation bills, but his low salary belied his heavy connections. He never rose to the top rungs of capitol influence, and one didn't have to look very far to see why.

"Fred had zilch social skills," said Ed Armstrong, a top advisor to Republican governors Douglas McKay and Paul Patterson. "He was the kind of guy who'd irritate you by the way he said good morning." Indeed, Packwood sometimes seemed to delight in aggravating people. He regularly invited himself to Lansing's restaurant table to eat whatever was on his colleague's plate. People never knew whether to attribute Fred's behavior to his drinking, to absentmindedness, or to the fact that he just didn't seem to care.

"I respected Fred, but I really didn't like him," Lansing says. "He was a flat-out, abject drunk, and when he drank became as mean as a cobra."

Lansing and other Packwood colleagues were amazed at the way the veteran lobbyist "could put away bourbon at night and still make it to work at 7:30 A.M. the next morning. But you didn't want to be downwind from his breath," he adds.

In 1957 Packwood's two longtime employers, Columbia Empire Industries and Oregon Forest Industries Council, merged to create the new Associated Oregon Industries (AOI).

78   The timbermen had placed some provisions on that merger: they wanted Packwood out. The lobbyist had once given them trouble on a workers' compensation proposal, and they thought he was too independent and too drunk.

Tom Doneca, now an AOI lobbyist, recalls Packwood's ouster. "They fired Fred in 1957 without severance pay, without pension—without anything." Lobbyist Ken Rinke offered an insight into Fred's downfall. "He wasn't proud of some of the things he maneuvered through the legislature. I always suspected down deep Fred was kind of a closet liberal, but his employers definitely were not. For all his ability, I believe Fred thought he ended up prostituting himself."

"Bob never forgot the way the timber people treated his dad," says Doneca. The lumber barons didn't care much about the feelings of Packwood's twenty-five-year-old son, but the young man would settle that score in the future.

Fred was now a pariah at the capitol. But even pariahs have families to support and bills to pay, and at sixty-two he began a new career as an AFL-CIO consultant. With Fred's income plummeting, Mindy got a job to make ends meet.

"Those were tough times," Bob once recalled. Perhaps worse than the cut in salary was the loss of friendships, prestige, and a lifelong rhythm. Fred had more reasons than ever to stare into the bottom of a bourbon glass, and his drinking binges now became more difficult to conceal. Friends frequently carried him home from the Salem drunk tank, and he was often seen staggering down Stanton Street. Severe bladder-control problems plagued him, leaving him embarrassed and depressed at wetting his pants in public.

Bob never really got the recognition he sought from his complex and troubled father. In the mid-1950s, when colleagues asked how Bob was doing, Fred would usually grouse, "When's he ever going to get out of school?" But when pressed for details, he reported proudly on the law classes his son aced. Bob's mastery of NYU's tough tax-law courses particularly tickled Fred, but no one was really sure if Bob knew that his father was paying attention.

In October 1958 Bob landed a job with Koerner, Young, Mc-Colloch, and Dezendorf, a top Portland law firm. The firm wanted a talented attorney to represent employers in labor disputes, an ironic task considering that Bob's father now worked for the AFL-CIO.

Packwood was thinking hard about his political aspirations. Few people could have advised him better than Fred, but the boy who once raced to keep up with his dad was now a man who kept him at arm's length. Fred's public drinking around the capitol was not only an embarrassment, but a hindrance to his son's political dreams. "Bob distanced himself from his father," John Lansing said. "It was painful to watch."

At age twenty-six, Bob Packwood also hit his social stride. He had traded in his Coke-bottle eyeglasses for the then-exotic—and expensive—contact lenses just before Christmas 1957. The lenses were awkward, nearly the size of a quarter, and had to be removed with a handheld suction device, but they changed his life.

In 1958 Packwood and some bachelor friends began meeting at a downtown bar once a week after work. Several of the men had been classmates at Grant High School, and were destined for success.[5] Three of them would gain national renown: future U.S. Secretary of the Interior Donald Hodel, *New York Times* senior editor Jack Rosenthal, and Bob Packwood. Packwood christened the gathering the "528 Club," after a page of text he particularly admired in Irwin Shaw's best-seller *The Young Lions,* a World War II adventure tale of young men who killed Nazis by day and bedded women by night. In one of the book's Normandy battle scenes—on page 528—the American protagonist takes off his combat helmet and puts it over his groin to protect his organs "for women everywhere." The club's informal rule, which Packwood concocted, was that each man bring a different woman each time.

---

5. Steve Forrester. *Northwest Newsletter.* 1983.

Lobbyist Ken Rinke remembers being warned in the late 1950s that the ambitious young lawyer was an inveterate womanizer. One of the partners at Packwood's firm, Frank McColloch, visited Rinke in the capitol, and the discussion turned to the firm's new lawyer. "Bob's doing a good job," McColloch told Rinke, "but I just have one problem with him. Bob can't keep his eyes off the girls." The senior partner described how Packwood was always spinning around in his swivel chair, conspicuously ogling secretaries as they walked by. He asked Rinke to talk some sense into Packwood before it damaged his political career.

Rinke, then a railroad lobbyist, gave the young attorney some advice in the form of a story about a dog that gets its tail cut off by a locomotive in the switching yard. Angry, the dog turns around and snaps at the train—and gets beheaded by the caboose. The lesson, said Rinke, was, "Don't lose your head over a piece of tail."

But Bob had a larger goal than making partner at the law firm, and soon he began to survey the state's political landscape, which had been changing even before he left Willamette in 1954. That year, Republicans controlled every statewide and congressional elective office in Oregon and had recently dominated the Oregon House of Representatives by 51 to 9. The *New Republic* had described Oregon as the "Vermont of the West."

Then everything began to change. The Columbia River hydroelectric dams that had been constructed during the Roosevelt-Truman era had triggered a metamorphosis in Oregon and Washington when they allowed the region to have the cheapest electricity rates in the world. Industry poured in, transforming these states from hidebound agricultural provinces to robust industrial hubs. Scores of thousands of newcomers entered the region. Most were Democrats, and they revamped the Northwest with amazing speed.

Senators Henry Jackson and Warren Magnuson led Washington's shift into the Democratic column. In Oregon, West Portland Democrat Dick Neuberger won a U.S. Senate seat in 1954. Republican Senator Wayne Morse bolted dramatically to the Democratic party the next year. Democrats swept the gov-

ernorship, the state legislature, and three of the four congressional seats in 1956.

As Republicans lost power in the Pacific Northwest, the
party gained surprising strength in the East, where Packwood
was then immersed in studying law and politics. Just a few
years earlier, many thought the East Coast GOP was doomed
to second-party status as their Yankee-Protestant base shrank.
But the party responded with a new formula: conservatism on
tax issues, moderation toward labor unions, and unflinching
liberalism on civil rights.

By attracting blue-collar, Jewish, and black voters, New York
Republicans such as Governor Nelson Rockefeller, U.S. Senators Jacob Javits and Kenneth Keating, and Senator Prescott
Bush of nearby Greenwich, Connecticut, all won smashing victories in the mid-1950s. Young Packwood took notes.

In 1958 Packwood's old political science professor Mark
Hatfield was elected governor of Oregon in an upset over Democratic incumbent Bob Holmes. That victory was the first good
news for the Oregon GOP in several years, and the *Saturday
Evening Post* published a lengthy photo spread predicting national stature for the new Republican governor.

Hatfield's victory nurtured Packwood's own aspirations. If
Oregon's conservative Republican industrial, utility, and even
timber interests accepted a young moderate such as Hatfield,
they might someday promote Packwood, too.

Packwood proudly announced his political intentions to his
father, who was shocked by the scope of his son's ambitions. Fred
just smiled when he heard Bob's grand scenario for challeng-
ing Morse, a darling of American liberals who used his rapier
wit to attack President Eisenhower, Vice President Richard
Nixon, and Secretary of State John Foster Dulles. Fred discouraged Bob, warning that politics was "a man-killing profession."

But the son had been following the beat of his own drum-
mer since leaving Caltech. He had confidence in his own decisions, and he pursued his plan with vigor.

Packwood became a Republican precinct committeeman
in 1959, and one year later—with no serious opposition—was
named party chairman of populous Multnomah County. At

82 twenty-seven, Packwood knew how to make the best of the unpaid position. He described himself as "the youngest party
chairman of a major metropolitan area in the United States."

Packwood's most impressive achievement came in recog-
nizing a huge source of untapped energy and talent. At NYU, he
had come to appreciate the skills of female law students. He now
saw that similarly talented women—some with Phi Beta Kappa
keys—were cut out of meaningful roles in Republican politics.
Patriarchal tradition shunted them away from real power and
into the wasteland of "women's auxiliary" committees. As chairman Packwood dismantled the auxiliaries and merged women
into the party proper. In this one move he not only corrected a
sexist injustice, he served his own more pragmatic interests: by
opening up more roles to women, he made the party more pro-
ductive and thereby increased his own influence.

———

If he wanted to run against Wayne Morse someday, the
young chairman needed to watch a U.S. Senate campaign. The
opportunity came in 1960. Conservative Republican Elmo
Smith opposed Democrat Maurine Neuberger, who was running to fill the Senate seat of her husband, Dick Neuberger, who
had died of cancer that spring.

Packwood identified with the moderate Rockefeller wing of
the Republican party. Smith—a colorless, small-town Rotary
Club candidate whom Oregon voters increasingly rejected—
represented the antithesis of that. Smith was also expected to
lose. But Packwood welcomed the chance to volunteer and
learn the ropes.

The Smith campaign employed Packwood as a "bird dog"
to attend Neuberger's public appearances and needle her with
well-crafted questions. Neuberger survived those annoyances
and beat Smith that November, but Packwood was making his
mark as a rising political operative.

Local college professor Donald Balmer hosted a postelection party on the Oregon coast for Democratic and Republican
operatives to rehash the election. The group eventually ad-
journed to a cocktail lounge for stiff drinks and storytelling.

Well into the evening, one of the Democrats made an off-the-cuff remark about a particular campaign. While the rest of the Republicans nodded and reached for another glass, Packwood jumped on it. "No, no, no, that's not right," he insisted, and yanked out a three-ring binder stuffed with newspaper clippings. He pored over it, looking for the right piece of information to refute the Democrat's casual aside. Everyone else at the bar rolled their eyes in disbelief. "Bob didn't know when to turn it off," said fellow reveler Mike Katz, a Portland attorney.

Frank Roberts, who was then Multnomah County Democratic party chairman, affectionately called his Republican counterpart a fellow "political junkie." Packwood supported his habit in peculiar places. Once, at a Democratic committee meeting, Roberts counted more votes than Democrats in attendance. He later realized that Packwood had mischievously sneaked into the balcony to vote along with the Democrats in an effort to shape the opposition's policies.

Ironically, just as Packwood was garnering recognition, he faced his gravest threat from within the GOP itself. In the early 1960s a new ultraconservative organization was rapidly gaining momentum, especially on the West Coast. The John Birch Society took its name from an American pilot who had been captured and executed in 1945 by Chinese Communists. They regarded John Birch as the first casualty of the Cold War.

The John Birch Society grew by playing on people's fears of Communism and their apprehensions about Supreme Court Chief Justice Earl Warren's decisions against segregation and school prayer. Using the Communists' own techniques, the Birch Society infiltrated school boards and town hall meetings, and eventually seized control of Republican party organizations on the West Coast. They stymied Richard Nixon's 1962 California gubernatorial race and energized Barry Goldwater's presidential campaign two years later. Chairman Packwood now had a beast on his hands.

Birch Society members attempted to overthrow the Packwood-led moderates at the 1961 and 1962 Multnomah County conventions, and the young chairman found himself in a lose-lose situation. If the Birchers won, he lost his office. But if he

84 opposed them any longer, he risked making enemies for life. Fortunately, Packwood's own political script called for him to exit the stage. He had always considered the county chairmanship as a springboard to the Oregon legislature, and in the spring of 1962 he resigned in order to run for office.

———

Even as he campaigned for a seat in Salem, Packwood was focused on his ultimate goal: Wayne Morse's seat in the U. S. Senate. Toward this end, he became a student of elections. In June of 1961 the young attorney had written to ex–Vice President Richard Nixon requesting county-by-county breakdowns of Nixon's red-baiting defeat of U.S. Representative Jerry Voorhis fifteen years earlier. He began to create foreign policy credentials for himself by joining the board of directors of the World Affairs Council. He also began to make some Washington connections. He sought out newly elected Republican Senator John Tower of Texas, who had stunned national political observers by winning Vice President Lyndon Johnson's vacant Senate seat in 1961. Packwood persuaded the conservative Tower to speak in Portland, promising a capacity crowd and front-page headlines. Tower spoke, Packwood delivered, and a mutually beneficial friendship was cemented.

Packwood worked hard to ensure that no one else knocked off Morse before he got a shot at the seat in 1968. As former GOP State Treasurer Sig Unander geared up to challenge Morse in 1962, Packwood went to work. In September 1961, just a few days shy of his twenty-ninth birthday, Packwood traveled to a Western Republican National Committee meeting in Sun Valley, Idaho, where he undercut Unander's chances in a private meeting with GOP moneymen. The *Oregonian*'s front-page headline read: PACKWOOD DISCOUNTS UNANDER.

The patrician Unander personified the era of pre-television candidates, lacking both campaign sparkle and the common touch. Despite these weaknesses, and the GOP bad-mouthing by Packwood and others, Unander almost beat Morse.

A statewide poll showed Unander closing to within two points of Morse in October 1962, and he might have won if not for the Cuban Missile Crisis. On 14 October, American surveillance planes identified Soviet nuclear missile launching sites in Communist Cuba. President John F. Kennedy immediately dispatched Air Force jets to fly Morse and other Foreign Relations Committee members back to Washington to advise him during the country's closest brush with nuclear war. The reflected glory of Kennedy's missile crisis triumph enabled Morse to reverse Unander's momentum and win by an 8 percent margin.

Packwood had an epiphany watching that race. According to Bob Elliott (Packwood's successor as Multnomah County GOP chairman), "Bob just couldn't believe that a candidate as bad as Unander almost beat Morse." Packwood scrutinized the race and noticed—years before anyone else—the holes in Morse's senatorial robes. Republicans loathed his stand on most issues. But even many Democrats disliked Morse, a stern Congregationalist with a moralistic, pedantic style.

If Morse needed an event the magnitude of the Cuban Missile Crisis to stave off a weak opponent, how could he possibly prevail over a challenger who had great television savvy, a massive organization, and no embarrassing legislative baggage?

In the early 1960s, Republican campaign volunteers were predominantly business owners and retirees. But Packwood tapped into a huge reserve of energetic volunteers—members of the Junior Chamber of Commerce. Jaycees had always been a source of financial contributions, but Packwood harnessed their political potential.

He joined the Portland Jaycees and persuaded interested Republicans to join a spin-off group he named the "Trumpeters." These young attorneys and professionals became Packwood's campaign officer corps, dishing up impromptu political speeches at their weekly Toastmaster-style breakfasts. The energetic young leaders included future federal judges James Burns and Robert E. Jones, state Attorney General Lee Johnson, Jack Faust, Dave Barrows, and Tom Doneca. They were later joined by future Governor Tom McCall and Secretary of

State Clay Myers. As one newspaper reported at the time, "One Trumpeter is worth ten regular volunteers."

Their scientific campaign methods instantly made the plodding systems of other candidates obsolete. Packwood was also prescient enough to foresee—perhaps before anyone else in the country—a massive constituency that male politicians had long ignored: women. At Packwood's behest, the Trumpeters solicited their college-educated girlfriends and wives, and they worked the watercoolers and telephones to recruit female office workers. Women soon filled eleven out of fifteen positions on Packwood's 1962 legislative campaign committee.

In the year before Betty Friedan wrote *The Feminine Mystique,* such a high level of female participation was unheard of in U.S. politics. But Packwood's campaign experience validated his beliefs. He told friend Jack Faust that women's talents were the greatest wasted resource in the country.

Packwood also revamped door-to-door canvassing strategies. While most candidates just had volunteers drop literature behind the aluminum screen door, Packwood's "doorbell-ringers"—a battalion of college-educated women who did not hold jobs—"interviewed" voters about their preferences, attitudes, and likelihood of voting.

Candidates typically loved to display massive, ego-boosting highway billboards, but they were expensive. Packwood observed how one underfinanced congressional candidate, Edith Green, cleverly compensated by posting small signs in her supporters' front yards. For the price of one billboard, Packwood reasoned, a candidate could make one hundred smaller signs that would reach far more people. The lawn signs also suggested a grassroots dynamism. Packwood adopted Green's idea and popularized it throughout the state.

He began looking for locations for his lawn signs more than a year in advance of his legislative race. One day in 1961 he shared an elevator ride with a legal secretary from another firm in his downtown office building. Out of the blue, he asked, "What are you doing this weekend?" The secretary replied that she and her husband were moving to NE Fifty-eighth and Klickitat.

"That's in the legislative district I'm running in next year," he said, and asked permission to place a sign in her yard that following year.

The secretary, Julie Myers—the same Julie Myers who would later figure so prominently in the sexual misconduct scandal—thought that sounded crazy. But she politely gave her address, certain that he would never follow through on such an unusual request. But one year later, a Packwood volunteer appeared at the Myers's door with a sign for their lawn.

Packwood also adapted an idea that John Kennedy had popularized during his Massachusetts congressional and Senate campaigns, when his mother and sisters went into the poorer neighborhoods to host "teas." Packwood's women volunteers now began sponsoring similar "coffee klatsches" throughout Portland.

Not everyone was receptive to this campaign wizardry and salesmanship, and the most impervious were die-hard ideological foes such as the Birchers. The right-wingers disliked Packwood's Rockefeller-style ideas and support for public education, and they posed a real threat to him in the May 1962 GOP primary. So Packwood couched his position in terms no one on the far right could oppose. His statement in the voters pamphlet that Oregon election officials sent to all registered voters read: "Robert W. Packwood is for better education for our children to strengthen America against the Communist threat."

Packwood won the primary handily, and six months later he won the general election in a similarly lopsided race. But this time he didn't prevail because of state-of-the-art campaign science; he won the old-fashioned way—by dodging the issues. Packwood wrote just ninety-four words in the voter pamphlet, half the size of other candidates' statements. And to fill up all that extra space he ran an oversize photo of himself, studio lights glinting off his hair, which was styled à la Jack Kennedy. His brief statement cited his pioneer ancestry, law clerkships, and Republican party chores, but didn't mention a single issue. He won big.

In January 1963, at age thirty-one, Packwood became the youngest member of the Oregon legislature. With good reason, the business lobby excitedly anticipated that the son of master

88 lobbyist Fred Packwood would now advance their interests on the House Labor Committee. But the rookie refused to cooperate. He voted with business but at the same time publicly needled them for "hypocrisy" in wanting too many government handouts themselves.

Such impolitic statements made it harder for the House Republican leadership to trust him. But Packwood did not want to be a House insider. He eschewed the career track of aspiring to become Majority Leader and eventually Speaker of the House. The legislature was merely a means to an end.

"Bob deliberately avoided taking controversial stands on issues in order to help his chances to run for the U.S. Senate," said John Lansing, who was then an executive for Pacific Power & Light Utility Company. Fellow freshman Representative Richard Kennedy (D-Eugene) concurs with this view. "I think Bob believed that the more he spoke out, the more he'd offend interest groups he needed to run for the U.S. Senate."

While some Republicans resented Packwood's go-it-alone style, they knew he could butter their bread. Everyone had noticed the newcomer's brilliant campaign acumen, and several business groups hired him to recruit, coach, and coordinate GOP candidates for the 1964 general election.

Packwood attacked the project with a vengeance. He wrote a one-hundred-page campaign "cookbook" for first-time candidates, detailing every conceivable skill—from mastering a bone-crunching Dale Carnegie handshake to rehearsing for a live radio interview. He hit the road, traveling from Ashland, near the state's southern border, to Tillamook, on the Oregon coast, mining the ore of Jaycee, Republican party, and bar association contacts to find good candidates. Once they stepped into the arena, Packwood coached them on campaign expertise.

His strategy was a knockout. In 1964 the Oregon House was the only legislative chamber in the nation to switch to GOP control. Fifteen of his nineteen candidates won, despite Lyndon Johnson's landslide victory over Republican nominee Barry Goldwater that November.

Packwood, barely thirty years old, had become a major player in the state.

6

Bob Packwood's reputation "as a skirt-chaser began right off the bat," according to historian Cecil Edwards. Packwood relished the so-called cocktail lounge "Trapline," where capitol males sought diversion with female staff members, lobbyists, and waitresses. Briefly, the thirty-year-old legislator dated college intern Susan Swearingen, but that relationship ended after Packwood chased her around a table. Swearingen switched her attentions to another suitor, whom she eventually married: Les AuCoin, who would run an arduous race against Packwood a couple of decades later.

A Portland State University student recalled that "Bob saw himself as glamorous. He was young, single, kind of good-looking, and always cruising on women. Bob loved people thinking of him as a 'wolf.' That shtick seemed to be his life." She interned with Packwood's 1964 legislative campaign, and that fall she attended parties where Packwood leered at women, pinched them, and snapped their undergarments. "Most men weren't like that back then," she said.

By all accounts, Packwood kept his dance card full. "I don't mean to be sexist, but the sheer volume of beautiful women on his campaigns was amazing," says then–Portland State University professor Marko Haggard. "No one else had campaigns like that." The women, not surprisingly, attracted male volunteers. "I wanted to work on that campaign because he picked the best-looking women," lobbyist Ted Hughes said. The endless parade of women even caused Packwood's sister, Patricia, to wonder, "When's Bob ever going to settle down?"

In the 1960s the issue of wives had become more complex for young male politicians. Jackie Kennedy and Lady Bird Johnson had begun to change the public's expectations, and politicians saw that sophisticated wives who were interested in the community and the arts could be a real asset. The lesson was not lost on Packwood.

With the single-minded energy he put into political campaigning, he devoted himself to the task of finding the proper wife. According to one campaign aide, "Bob now wanted to marry a woman from a socially prominent family who could walk, talk, and help him politically." His friend Tom Hatfield (no relation to Mark Hatfield) remembers telling Packwood once that his wife wanted to fix Bob up with a date.

"What does her father do?" Packwood asked.

Hatfield replied that he didn't know. The topic was dropped, and Packwood never met the woman.

Packwood briefly pursued an elegant socialite from Northwest Portland's wealthy Ainsworth neighborhood. She was gracious, proper, and well connected, and Packwood was infatuated with her. Eventually, however, the woman broke off the relationship. She considered marrying Packwood the attorney but drew the line at becoming a politician's wife.

At this point an ex-girlfriend of Bob's reentered the picture: an athletic and intelligent young woman named Georgie Oberteuffer Crockatt. Georgine Ann Oberteuffer had grown up in Lake Oswego, an affluent Portland suburb, the only daughter of a family that sincerely valued the idea of public service. One ancestor had helped found Gallaudet University for the deaf. Her father, George "Obie" Oberteuffer, was a Pacific Northwest legend in scouting: he cofounded the National Camp Fire Girls in the 1930s and worked as executive director of the Portland Boy Scout Council during his daughter's childhood.

Her family's social prominence may have helped Georgie become a junior princess in Portland's Rose Festival. The grand floral parade annually attracted nearly one hundred thousand spectators, and the crown was cherished by many of the city's little girls.

She attended Portland's Lincoln High School, which served the city's elegant and sometimes snobbish West Hills and was a step higher on the social ladder than Grant High School. The year she graduated, the yearbook ran a photo of her mother that was larger than the one of herself. The caption read, in part: "Mrs. G. H. Oberteuffer, well-known Portland club woman, is the current president of the Lincoln P.T. A. . . . ."

Georgie, however, avoided the social spotlight. Whereas an exasperated teacher once complained that Georgie's older brother, Bill, "acted like a Reed College kid," referring to Portland's nonconformist university, Georgie became the good daughter. The soft-spoken introvert participated in all the right Lincoln activities but much preferred swimming and horseback riding in the countryside. Her scoutmaster father taught her to ride a horse when she just three years old, and she cherished the childhood memory of riding with him on the Skyline Trail in the Cascade Mountains.

Following Oberteuffer tradition, Georgie attended the University of Oregon and pledged Kappa Alpha Theta—Georgie and a dozen other pledges were daughters of Theta mothers—and her family was very pleased with her choice. Her parents often visited her at college, and one sorority sister admired how "Georgie came from a very secure home."

She joined service clubs, worked on the *Oregon Daily Emerald* school newspaper, and became Theta president. Although her friends were Thetas, her acquaintances included rebel Gretchen Grondahl Edgren, who would later become a *Playboy* magazine editor, and Antoinette Kuzmanich, who would marry rising politician Mark Hatfield.

Oberteuffer graduated from the University of Oregon with a degree in psychology and a minor in special education. She also left with a fiancé—David Crockatt, the son of a Salem merchant family. One sorority sister had previously dated Crockatt and described him as "extroverted and very sweet." Portland's

92   society pages reported on Georgie and David's 1952 wedding, which was held at the First Presbyterian Church in downtown Portland. Georgie's parents hosted the wedding reception at their Nine Acres estate outside Lake Oswego.

Crockatt had entered the military before the wedding, and the couple spent the next two years living at army bases across the country. When his hitch was up they returned to Salem, where David became an executive at Meier & Frank, a department store. But despite the fact that he came from a good family, had a decent job, and enjoyed the outdoors as Georgie did, the relationship faltered. Georgie filed for divorce in 1958; Crockatt went into the clothing business.

After the marriage dissolved, Georgie decided to move to England and reassess her life. Just before she left, in 1959, she was casually introduced to Bob Packwood, but nothing came of that meeting. For the next two years she lived in London, where she worked as a secretary for the U.S. Third Air Force overseeing the needs of servicemen and their families.

Georgie arrived back in Portland on election night 1960. Unlike Bob, who was intensely scrutinizing the Kennedy-Nixon returns, the jet-lagged expatriate barely knew the election was under way. She soon took a new job as executive secretary at the National Primate Research Center near Portland and spent her spare time teaching horseback riding to adults and children.

Early in 1962, at age thirty-one, she again met Bob Packwood, and they began dating seriously. At first glance, they were an odd couple. Georgie had never been in the smoke-filled room of political campaigning, and Packwood knew nothing about Pendleton saddles. Georgie was two years older than Bob, and at five-foot-nine she was the same height with heels. Sensitive and intelligent, she was miles away from the kind of woman that Packwood regularly escorted to "528 Club" cocktail parties.

Georgie was relaxed and open with her feelings, whereas Bob's intensity permeated everything he did. In fact, he was quite different from the men she was accustomed to seeing in her own polite social group. "He was the first man I'd ever met who didn't know how to flirt and didn't even try," she said.

The relationship ground to a halt when Packwood asked her to work on his upcoming rookie legislative race.

"What do I have to do?" asked Georgie.

When he launched into the litany of telephone canvassing and envelope stuffing tasks, she replied, "No, I don't think I want to do that."

She did not see him again for six months.

But something drew Georgie back to him. In 1962 the chances that a divorced woman in her thirties would find another husband were not good, and Georgie was intrigued by the scope of Bob's ambitions. She changed her mind and joined his campaign, soon becoming a member of his steering committee. By the time his 1964 campaign began, she was in charge of his mammoth door-to-door canvassing operation, a program so effective that it left potential rivals in the dust. Packwood became such a shoo-in that he was free to travel throughout Oregon to coach at his GOP campaign schools, sometimes with Georgie at his side.

Georgie admired Bob's energy and intellect, and she was captivated by the aura of a young man on the rise. Nonetheless, she had other serious suitors, and Bob was jealous. Georgie later explained to a reporter how she "got" Bob: "First become a first-rate secretary and make yourself indispensable to somebody who is going places . . . just enough so he can't quite get along without you." He finally proposed in the summer of 1964 after she threatened to accept a job offer in Europe unless they got married.

They delayed the wedding until after the November 1964 election, and were married on Thanksgiving Eve at his parents' home on Stanton Street. Judge Robert E. Jones, one of Packwood's Trumpeters, performed the ceremony, and Bob's sister, Patricia Packwood Richardson, served as a witness.

The marriage helped Packwood's career by quieting, although not quite dispelling, the rumors of his philandering. But the trouble continued. Those who liked Georgie disliked Bob, according to Harold Hughes, then the Oregonian's political

94   writer. "People predicted from the very start that the marriage wouldn't last," Hughes said. Former sorority sister Geraldine Pearson observed both of Georgie's husbands. "I thought Davy Crockatt was a better catch than Bob," she says. "He was gentle, smooth, and good-looking, while Bob was a little too ambitious and rough for our group." The young legislator annoyed Pearson by trying too aggressively to convince her to enter Republican politics. "I felt sorry for Georgie when they became engaged," says another woman who worked on Packwood's campaigns. "It was obvious what Bob was like."

The start of that troubled relationship came just as another ended. Shortly after Bob and Georgie were married, Fred Packwood died at age sixty-nine. After Fred was fired, he had virtually dropped out of sight. Colleagues in Salem remember seeing him only once, in 1963, when he and Mindy returned to Salem to see their son, the freshman Oregon legislator. The House Speaker learned in advance that the Packwoods were coming, and handed Bob the gavel to preside over the chamber that day. When Fred and Mindy arrived, they walked onto the House floor and embraced their son, as legislators stopped and applauded.

"The affection between them was special to see," recalled Fred's former partner John Lansing, "because it was so rare."

Few winters in Republican party history have been as grim as the one following Barry Goldwater's failed presidential bid in 1964. Many Republicans feared that if Lyndon Johnson translated his wide margin of victory into an equally triumphant presidency, the GOP would permanently become the minority party.

Packwood, now thirty-three, was still aiming his sights at Wayne Morse's Senate seat and was working hard at building an organization. Intuitively, he knew that his success in 1968 would depend on distancing himself from the party's conservative Goldwater wing, no matter how much that angered Republican insiders.

State GOP chairman Elmo Smith, a Goldwater conservative, now viewed his former campaign volunteer as suspiciously liberal. Packwood, no longer able to count on his help, engineered an end-run around Smith to mobilize moderate Republicans. He organized a statewide conference based on the model of a group of Washington liberal Democrats, who incubated ideas and passion through an annual conference at Lake Keeleseh, in the mountains east of Seattle. He decided to hold his conference at the Dorchester Hotel, located on the Oregon coast near Lincoln City, and sent invitations to the hundreds of Jaycee and party activists he met as he crisscrossed the state in 1964; he particularly cultivated those newly elected Republican legislators he had helped win.

Georgie had now become Bob's full-time political partner, and the couple barely had time to say "I do" before they began hatching plans for the conference. Together, the newlyweds saw to every detail. "Dorchester," Georgie said, "became our first baby."

Packwood made clear his intent to break with the Goldwater conservatives in his conference invitation to hundreds of progressive Republicans. The letter to future liberal GOP Governor Tom McCall read, "On April 9–11, there is going to be a Republican political retreat. . . . Far right-wingers will be deliberately excluded."

The first conference attracted more than three hundred participants and more press—both good and bad—than Packwood had anticipated. Party regulars were not amused. Smith mortified Packwood by asking party officials to "censure" the event. Governor Mark Hatfield, Packwood's college hero, was now suspicious of the rising young star. Tom McCall wrote that Hatfield's people regarded the Dorchester gathering as "a Trotskyite cell."

Most of the Dorchester delegates were Jaycees, Trumpeters, and young professionals who thought campaign work was exciting and glamorous. However, some established Republicans, even liberals such as Representative Connie McCready of Northeast Portland, were less intrigued.

96   She found Packwood's single-mindedness to be self-serving and frequently insensitive. Packwood once came to her Irvington home to speak to some volunteers McCready had recruited, including Jalmar Johnson, a retired *Oregonian* editor, and his wife. Packwood continually emphasized the importance of attracting and retaining young people in politics. That was well and fine, McCready said, but he repeated the mantra of "young people, young people, and young people" until finally the Johnsons, both about seventy, mortified their host by saying, "Well, I guess that excludes us," and bowed out.

The young attorney also agitated McCready in the same way that Fred Packwood had needled people. "Sometimes I'd be having a private lunch with a lobbyist when suddenly Bob invites himself down, orders something on the lobbyist's tab, eats that, and then walks off," McCready said.

Packwood may have viewed McCready, a future Portland mayor, as a potential rival. She clearly had little use for him and joined colleagues in mocking what she called Packwood's girlish hips and feminine walk. The *Oregonian*'s Harold Hughes remembered the allegedly swaying hips but suspected some of the ridicule betrayed a grudging respect for Packwood. "A lot of legislators knew that Bob's campaign skills were taking him places."

In fact, the word had spread nationwide that Packwood was becoming known as one of the savviest young Republican strategists. Researchers at the national party headquarters began to examine his campaign innovations, which now included the Dorchester conference, candidate training schools, and sophisticated door-to-door canvassing.

Meanwhile, new opportunities opened up for Packwood as a legislator. The GOP takeover in 1964 put him in the majority party for the first time, and in 1965 he became chairman of the House Local Government and Elections Committee. Georgie joined him as a legislative secretary. At first the committee was a de facto Dorchester booking agency; but once Bob got down to legislative business, he tenaciously focused on what would be the defining issue of his career in Salem: creating single-member districts.

Packwood believed that Oregon's system of electing legislators from "at-large" districts prevented Republicans from winning more seats in populous Democratic-dominated Multnomah County. If he could divide the 500,000-person county into more than a dozen individual House districts, the Republicans would reap a partisan windfall, picking up several seats.

"Maneuvering to create single-member districts was Bob's whole agenda during his last years in Salem," said his nemesis Frank Roberts, a veteran of Packwood's local government committee. Eventually, after the 1970 reapportionment, the state adopted the model. But as dedicated as he was to that issue, Packwood kept his priorities straight. "Frank," he told Roberts on a spring day that year, "I'll get to Washington, D.C., before you will."

As the 1967 session concluded, Packwood was in position to enter the Senate race. He enjoyed excellent relations with big business, which regarded him as one of their own, and he had the potential to woo liberal voters, who were kept ignorant of his more conservative views. These views included support for a sales tax, opposition to labor unions for schoolteachers, and writing workers' compensation laws that favored insurance companies over injured blue-collar workers.

Organizationally, Packwood had an energetic and effective statewide volunteer network. He just needed to touch base with his personal contacts nationwide. He began by calling his NYU Law School friends, who were now entering their peak earning years. Howard Greenberger remembers listening to Packwood detail his strategy for unseating Morse.

Puzzled, Greenberger said, "But I thought you *liked* Morse."

"I do," Packwood explained, "but he's getting old, and somebody can take him out."

By now he had practically dropped any pretense of practicing law. Legal peers had long predicted that Packwood and lawyering would not mix. After joining Koerner, Young, McColloch, and Dezendorf, Packwood switched to the Spears, Lubersky law firm and then to Mize, Kriesien, Fewless, and

98 Douglass before joining friend Garry McMurray in 1966. That arrangement provided Packwood with a desk and a telephone and, most importantly, time for campaigning.

Spears, Lubersky attorney Lew Scott worked with Packwood on several labor cases and noticed his colleague's obsession with politics.

"He had a greater interest in politics than in practicing law. I once gave him a modest case and later dropped by the courtroom and listened in the back as he tried to get something admitted as evidence. Bob didn't know how to do it. He kept asking the wrong questions until I finally I walked up to the counsel table to help him get it done.

"That really demonstrated to me his lack of preparation for even a simple case. He might have been a great attorney, but you could never tell because he never put the time in," Scott says.

Packwood did invest extraordinary energy into his political career. According to Scott, he would "spend company time writing [campaign] letters and was able to get people, usually young ladies, to work on his legislative campaigns." Packwood also proved adept at befriending wealthy people, including Bob and Nannie Warren. Nannie's father was Ernest Swigert, an industrialist and former John Birch Society national board member.

In the early summer, Packwood made his move. "I thought Morse might be vulnerable, but everything had to go right— including things I could not control," Packwood told a reporter. These variables ranged from being denied the nomination by another Republican to public opinion on the war shifting Morse's way. And there was always the danger that stories of Packwood's behavior with women might be leaked to the press.

He launched an exploratory committee in July 1967. A poll showed he only had 10 percent name familiarity, but money could fix that problem. And national Republican leaders suspected Morse was vulnerable. They passed over Packwood to promote Governor Tom McCall as their top general election candidate. Senate minority leader Everett Dirksen of Illinois lobbied McCall at the Republican Governors Conference in December 1967. "In his whiskey-baritone voice," McCall wrote, "he said I would, in running [against Morse], be making a contribution to the state, the nation, and the Republican party." Senator George Murphy (R-California) showed McCall a poll that predicted he could defeat Morse in the general election.

Back in Oregon, Packwood watched helplessly. The popular McCall dwarfed Packwood in stature and financial resources, and he appealed to the same moderate wing of the GOP. Packwood knew he wouldn't stand a chance against McCall. But, as it turned out, he didn't have to try: McCall decided to serve out his term as governor, and declined Dirksen's overture in January 1968. The hour had grown late for another major Republican to enter the race, and Packwood emerged as the lone serious candidate.

Packwood's Dorchester experiment had succeeded beyond his wildest dreams. Through his vision and hard work, Dorchester had bloomed into one of the most prestigious annual GOP gatherings on the West Coast. Presidential aspirant Nelson Rockefeller attended in February 1968; future candidates Ronald Reagan and George Bush followed in the ensuing years. The 1968 conference attracted one thousand party activists, Jaycees, and new recruits who comprised a private Packwood army.

Others saw danger signs. As journalist Floyd McKay wrote in the *Nation:*

> Dorchester seemed more a Packwood personality cult than an issue-driven movement. The format was elastic, too elastic. Would anyone remember, a year later, what resolutions had been passed?. . . It mattered little if Dorchester urged withdrawal from Vietnam, or the negative income tax or whatever. It mattered little if Packwood later took opposing views in his Senatorial campaign.

And the womanizing rumors persisted. One veteran Portland television reporter who covered the early Dorchester conferences recalled, "Some mornings of the conference Bob came in bleary-eyed, and reporters suspected he had been sleeping with some Republican babe. Packwood was playing close to the edge for someone recruiting women for key roles in his campaign."

100   In stark contrast to Morse, who rivaled Sam Ervin and J. William Fulbright as one of the Senate's leading constitutional lawyers, Packwood seemed to have tepid interest in advancing moderate Republican issues—or any issues. Morse's convictions were as blunt as Packwood's were elusive. Nothing was firmer than Morse's almost obsessive opposition to United States involvement in the war in Vietnam.

Twenty years later, Pulitzer Prize–winning historian Barbara Tuchman's *The March of Folly* cited the war in Indochina and England's needless loss of the American colonies as examples of how governments can tragically pursue policies against their own interests. Tuchman called Morse prophetic for sounding an early alarm against the perils of President Lyndon Johnson's decision to escalate the conflict into a war.

But Morse had fulminated on too many issues to be fully effective. He had called Harry Truman a liar, bedeviled Dwight Eisenhower, and patronized John Kennedy. And mavericks risk defeat if they fail to create new friends at the same rate that they make enemies. Such was Morse's fate. Republicans had hated him for years as an article of faith, but now his own party began to turn against him.

On 4 August 1964, an attack by North Vietnamese patrol boats on U.S. Navy destroyers in the Gulf of Tonkin created a protracted crisis destined to determine Morse's Senate future. That evening, a Pentagon intelligence officer telephoned the senator with the information that President Johnson had ordered the destroyers into North Vietnamese waters in order to deliberately provoke a reaction and widen the war.

Johnson subsequently asked Congress to pass the Gulf of Tonkin Resolution authorizing bombing attacks against North Vietnam. The Senate endorsed that resolution 98 to 2, over Morse's vocal opposition. The proposal was tantamount to a limited declaration of war, and Johnson used the Tonkin Resolution as authority to send more than 500,000 American soldiers to Vietnam.

Morse threatened to crush Johnson's credibility by calling for a Senate Foreign Relations Committee investigation of the Tonkin Gulf issue. Johnson supporters defeated Morse's attempt, but the senator persisted. The White House retaliated by ordering FBI surveillance on Morse and his national supporters. Over the next two years President Johnson's personal vendetta against Morse became blatantly apparent.

In July 1966 Johnson secretly ordered the FBI to extend surveillance on Morse and ninety-three of his key national supporters. Four days later the FBI reported uncovering "embarrassing" facts on seventeen Morse followers.* On 10 February 1967, the FBI sent a memo to the White House discussing possible "Communist and subversive" influences on Morse and another antiwar senator, Mark Hatfield. Hatfield had narrowly defeated pro-LBJ Democrat Bob Duncan to win the state's other Senate seat in November 1966. Morse had crossed party lines to endorse Hatfield, which infuriated the White House. This act advanced Morse's anti-Vietnam agenda, but irrevocably fouled the political waters he had to swim in. LBJ Democrats now burned for revenge, as did Duncan, who announced in December 1967 his intent to challenge Morse in the May 1968 Democratic primary. Duncan led the incumbent by a two-to-one margin in an early poll; Morse faced the race of his life.

Feelings about U.S. involvement in Vietnam now defined every individual in the Senate race except Packwood. He had certainly been exposed to all sides of the issue. He served on the World Affairs Council board, which regularly debated war policy. A key contributor had served on the John Birch Society national board, which advocated pursuing the war until North Vietnam surrendered. And Packwood's sister, Patricia, belonged to an antiwar group, which advocated exactly the opposite.

Some politicians, including conservative California Governor Ronald Reagan and liberal Senator Eugene McCarthy (D-Minnesota) remained true to their beliefs and impervious to shifts in public opinion. But nonideological candidates had great incentive to dodge this volatile issue, and this was particularly true of Packwood. The hawks loathed Morse, and even

---

* The complete records of Johnson's domestic spying against Morse remain classified at the Lyndon Johnson Presidential Library in Austin, Texas, until 2025. There is no evidence that Packwood or Morse's Democratic rival, Bob Duncan, had any knowledge of the FBI's activities.

102 some doves were not enamored with his often self-righteous style. If marginal doves perceived Packwood as too pro-war, they'd stick with Morse, warts and all. But if hawkish voters saw Packwood drifting to the center, they had nowhere else to go. For Packwood, the solution was simple: obfuscate the issue.

Packwood staked out unique center ground: the U.S. government should give South Vietnamese leaders several billion dollars to forcibly buy out rural landowners and deed over the land to peasants, thereby increasing their incentive to fight the Communists. As voters tried to pin down his position on Vietnam, he easily sidestepped the issue by responding that America needed to try land reform *before* debating the issue of military involvement.

Conservative South Vietnamese President Nguyen Van Thieu viewed such socialistic land reform schemes about as kindly as North Vietnam's Ho Chi Minh viewed laissez-faire capitalism. Packwood's vague proposal had no mechanism, no time line, and no cost controls, and no one in Congress or in academia took it seriously. But it worked for the voters, and Packwood spread the land reform line with a well-heeled campaign largely financed by manufacturing and banking interests.

Packwood's cynical dodge rivaled GOP presidential nominee Richard Nixon's promise of a "secret plan" to end the war. David Halberstam's characterization of Nixon's attitude in *The Best and The Brightest* is equally applicable to Packwood. For both men,

> the issue was not the compelling tragedy it was for so many other Americans, something that you had to come to terms with on its merits. Something which the failure had to be traced and explained to a troubled and divided country. Rather, it was an issue, like others, something to maneuver on, to watch Johnson, Humphrey and Wallace on. . . .

Or, in Packwood's case, to watch Morse on. The Democratic senator struggled to defeat Duncan by 1 percent in the May 1968 primary, while Packwood won the GOP nomination virtually uncontested. And the explosive events of 1968 presented

Morse with even more obstacles. Antiwar demonstrations were beginning to become violent, which created voter backlash. The assassination of Martin Luther King, Jr., triggered race riots in major cities. A *Newsweek* poll showed 43 percent of Duncan's supporters intended to vote against Morse in November.

Democrats everywhere were on the run, besieged by a growing number of Americans who blamed Johnson's "Great Society" and the marked "permissiveness" of the second half of the decade for the rise of black militancy, the worsening situation in Vietnam, and the general social disorder personified by hippies, drugs, and demonstrations. In California, Governor Ronald Reagan pulled out all the stops to support Republican Max Rafferty's unsuccessful race against Democrat Alan Cranston. In Kansas, Republican candidate Bob Dole rode the antiliberal wave to an easy Senate victory. Republican challenger Richard Schweiker flayed dovish Senator Joseph Clark in Pennsylvania. The New York Conservative party exploited white middle-class anger at liberal Jacob Javits by fielding James Buckley in the general election. Florida, Missouri, Indiana, and Oregon all became battlegrounds for the Richard Nixon–led GOP ticket.

Young Bob Packwood had the opportunity of a lifetime.

Nixon now led the Democratic nominee, Vice President Hubert Humphrey, by nearly 2 to 1 in Oregon. Packwood rode Nixon's coattails in his Senate campaign, even improvising on some of Nixon's material. Nixon had condemned as "revolutionaries" a group of antiwar students at Columbia University who had taken over the university president's office. Packwood reworked that theme for the home state crowd, with the subtle implication that Morse, a Columbia alumnus, was sympathetic to those tactics.

Packwood also applied variations of the red-baiting tactics that Nixon had used against his opponents in the past. When reporters asked Packwood where he stood on Vietnam, he sometimes answered, "Well, I'm not going to give propaganda for Hanoi," implying that Morse was a Communist dupe. His approach worked. A statewide poll in the *Oregonian* showed

104   Packwood overtaking Morse. It later turned out that the poll was inaccurate, the challenger admitted, but it boosted him nonetheless.

In Oregon, Humphrey had chided Nixon for refusing to debate him, which undercut Morse's efforts to avoid debating Packwood. Morse reluctantly agreed to a televised debate with Packwood before the Portland City Club on 25 October.

The debate further heightened national interest. The *New York Times* decided to endorse Morse, an unusual response to an out-of-state race. The national press, including the *Christian Science Monitor, Newsweek,* and *Time,* flew in to cover the debate. With all this attention, City Club organizers were forced to move the event to the cavernous eight-hundred-seat Masonic Temple in downtown Portland.

The two rivals entered the auditorium together to take their seats on an elevated stage. Morse spoke first. With his charcoal-colored glasses, wavy white hair, bushy eyebrows, and silvery mustache, the sixty-eight-year-old senator looked stately, distinguished, and old. Packwood's appearance contrasted vividly. His unlined face, tan skin, and blue eyes radiated vitality, not only to the audience at the auditorium but to voters who were watching the debate on color television.

This was the audience that particularly interested Packwood, and he had been thoroughly coached on his speech by Portland television personality Ben Padrow. While Morse delivered a lengthy stem-winder, Packwood spoke in the crisp, aggressive sixty-second bites that, new research showed, would keep television viewers interested.

In the *New York Times,* Lawrence Davis reported that the business audience gave its biggest applause to Packwood's response to a question about the right to dissent:

> If we're talking about people carrying signs—walking barefooted, bead-wearing guys, they're not my cup of tea.
>
> If they want to go up to the hills and raise turnips or get permits and parade around like the rest of us have a right to do, that's their business.
>
> But when they cross that line and say this society is so rotten it has got to be destroyed to save it, then I say, stop.

When I see that crazy kid at Columbia University sitting in the president's chair with his feet on the desk and smoking a cigar, I get mad. And I'd put that kook in jail. . . .

Packwood's supporters cheered as he accused Morse of favoring "the unilateral and unconditional" surrender of South Vietnam. The response was not unplanned. Packwood's campaign manager, Jim Elias, had strategically placed Trumpeters in the audience who repeatedly rose to ask Morse well-researched, well-crafted, and hostile questions. "We set Morse up," one Trumpeter admitted.

Morse answered everything, but the questions kept him on the defensive and may have pushed him past the point of no return. Ten days later Packwood won the election, beating Morse by a slim margin of three-tenths of 1 percent. Incredibly, he had reached the goal he had been aiming at since college. As he later told a reporter, "I'm as happy, as excited as anybody could ask to be. It's what I've wanted to be all my life. Very few people are lucky enough to achieve, at a relatively young age . . . what they really wanted to do all their lives." At the age of thirty-six, Bob Packwood replaced Ted Kennedy as the youngest member of the U.S. Senate.

Part III

7

In December of 1968 Bob and Georgie arrived in Washington, D.C., never having had a moment to spare after the election. In mid-November, just as the Packwoods began a long-planned Hawaiian vacation, Morse demanded a recount and Bob had to return to Oregon, accusing Morse of seeking to "steal the election." Morse refused to concede until 30 December, which left Packwood scrambling to assemble a Senate staff.

On 3 January 1969, the day he would be sworn in by outgoing Vice President Hubert Humphrey, Packwood was still interviewing potential employees. Georgie drove Bob to work that day, steering the car to a halt outside the Capitol's members' entrance. The couple barely had a chance to say good-bye before a veteran senator approached the vehicle. He greeted her husband, and the two men bounded up the granite steps, disappearing through the august high-framed door.

"I felt I had just lost my husband," Georgie remembered. Alone in a strange new city, she realized she did not even know how to return to their newly rented home in suburban Virginia.

During the flight from Portland, Georgie had turned to her husband and said, "Bob, all during the time in Salem and in the

Senate campaign, I knew my role was to help you. But now that we've won the election and we're going to Washington, I don't know what my role will be."

Bob nodded at her affectionately and told her to just keep being herself. But after all these years as his wife, she wasn't sure what that was. Georgie had loved political work, and she had been good at it. In many ways Georgie was better suited than Bob to the more personal aspects of campaigning. While Bob performed masterfully in pressure-packed debates, he often recoiled at the simple one-on-one interactions Georgie took pleasure in. She remembers a day during the 1968 Senate race when they had some unscheduled time in the small Columbia River town of St. Helens:

> There was nothing doing in this town, and we had to kill a couple hours, so whoever did the schedule filled in "Just walk up and down Main Street shaking hands," right? Wrong. Bob was scared to death. I mean, he just froze. He said, "I can't just walk up to somebody on the street and stick out my hand and say, 'Hi, I'm Bob Packwood, running for the Senate.'" And I said, "Okay, I'll do it." And I'd just walk up to somebody and say, "Hi, I'm Georgie Packwood. My husband is running against Wayne Morse." And then I would take these people and introduce them to Bob. Then he could shake their hands.

Life inside the Beltway was quiet and suburban. Without campaigning to keep her busy, she had more time to reflect on their marriage, which had been troubled almost from the start. Noting their first anniversary on her personal calendar in November 1965, she had written, "Bob got drunk and wants a divorce. Well, we almost made it through one whole year."

Eventually, Georgie came to expect three or four particularly unpleasant drinking binges every year, when her husband would get drunk, pick a fight with her, and repeat what came to be his standard cry: "I want a divorce! We should have never married! I want to be a bachelor!" She told writer Peter Boyer that they never discussed those incidents. The next day Bob would be up and out of the house early, as usual, and would return home after work as if nothing had happened. Despite these scenes, Georgie was committed to making the marriage work.

Both Packwoods wanted children, but Georgie's two pregnancies had ended in stillbirths. The tragedy of their second stillborn child in 1967 seemed to tighten their bond. "After Bob was told that our child was dead," Georgie said, "he arranged for me to be in a private ward so I wouldn't be around babies who had lived." Tearfully, Bob suggested they adopt a baby.

She called that moment one of the most precious of their lives and said it gave her "something positive to think about." That same year, they adopted a son and named him after Bob's great-grandfather, gold rush politician William Henderson Packwood. In 1971 they would adopt a baby girl, whom Georgie named Shyla, after a favorite horse.

In Washington, Georgie immersed herself in Bob's life, accompanying him to receptions and parties. Society writers observed the couple, and Georgie got good notices in the press. "Georgie Packwood is just like her home state of Oregon . . . open, refreshing," wrote *Women's Wear Daily*. "The Packwoods are new, young, attractive . . . and everyone wants to get a look. So they're out four and five nights a week. . . . Georgie's five-foot-nine, size ten, and a sports woman. She's been a swimmer and expert rider all her life, and her taste runs to the more tailored . . . woolens, leather, paisley and pants, but she also loves hostess gowns for at-home. And she adores her husband."

Women's Wear Daily also took a brief dip into the waters of the Packwoods' relationship. What first attracted her, said Georgie, was "his brightness, sense of humor and complete dedication to the idea of the moment. He has such purpose in life. He's his own man." But another quote hinted at trouble. "The biggest problem is [that] I'm further away from what Bob is doing than I've been in eight years."

———

Bob, however, was reveling in his new role as Senator and was getting ready to carve out his own territory. Packwood had

112 spent his career in the Oregon legislature intentionally avoiding controversial issues, and many Senate watchers had low expectations for him. But he astonished them with his talent and energy. The intensity he had focused for so many years on winning the Senate seat was now aimed at achieving something in that office.

He sought assignments on the Interior and Agriculture committees—where issues concerning Oregon's forests are debated—but fellow Oregon Senator Mark Hatfield had already nailed down those seats, along with a coveted Appropriations Committee pork barrel position. Packwood had not forgotten—and would never forget—that Hatfield had secretly crossed party lines to help Wayne Morse in 1968. Now, as he began to climb the Senate ladder, all he could see was Hatfield above him.

"Bob really chafed at how many voters perceived that Hatfield's serving on Appropriations made him 'Oregon's Senator,'" said writer Bill Keller, formerly of the *Oregonian* and later of the *New York Times*. "I believe Packwood even tried to get on Appropriations himself, but Senate leaders said 'No way will we let two guys from the [same] state get on it.'"

To Packwood's chagrin, Senate elders marooned him on the lower-ranking Banking and Housing and Labor and Public Works committees. The newcomer tried to reshuffle his hand with a clever but ultimately ill-advised scheme called the "Packwood Communications Plan." Under that plan, his Senate race contributors and lobbyists could annually donate $100 for a $40,000 supplemental fund to cover additional staff and travel expenses so Packwood could tend to Oregon's constituents and political affairs.

He cleared the idea with the Senate Ethics Committee, but the public saw the plan as a slush fund that gave lobbyists more access to Packwood than regular citizens could get. Packwood dropped the idea quickly. He would not trip over a financial embarrassment again for another twenty years.

Now Packwood was forced to take a backseat to Hatfield, and he resented the power that Hatfield's committees gave him with Oregon voters. Personally, the two men were at each other's throats. "Watching the Senate floor is like watching a laboratory of mice," said Keller. "The senators forget about the visitor galleries. They put their arms around each other, tell jokes, sometimes obscene ones. You never saw Packwood and Hatfield doing anything with each other." Hatfield told Senator Jacob Javits that he would no longer attend the Javits-led liberal Senate Republican "Wednesday Club" meetings if it meant sitting next to Packwood. Members could invite either him or Packwood, Hatfield said, but not the two together. He even told a colleague that "Packwood was an unscrupulous son of a bitch."[6]

Their relations deteriorated further when Packwood traveled to Tom McCall's home to personally lobby the governor to challenge Hatfield in the May 1972 GOP Senate primary. If the governor defeated Hatfield, Packwood would become senior senator. When McCall turned him down, a disappointed Packwood said, "If you wait until 1974 to eventually run against *me*, you'd still be junior senator to Mark Hatfield and, let me tell you, that's no fun."

But Packwood, ever the outsider, soon distinguished himself from others in his freshman class. In his inaugural speech, he stunned colleagues by pointedly criticizing the Senate's seniority system. "Even the law of the jungle operates on the principle of survival of the fittest. But Congress only operates on the principle of survival—period. . . . Long service does not necessarily produce expertise. Natural ability, devoted interests, and detailed study do," he declared. According to Keller, a veteran political reporter, "That was a helluva speech, courageous, dynamic, a lollapalooza."

Packwood proposed bills calling for committee chairs to be elected rather than automatically promoted according to longevity. It was nothing new for a freshman senator to loathe the seniority system, but to openly show contempt, as Packwood did, was unheard of. He knew what the rules were, and he refused to abide by them.

6. K. Ross Baker. *Friend and Foe in the U.S. Senate* (Rutgers University, 1981).

In the early 1970s Oregon's demographics began to change radically. The 1950s had seen an influx of blue-collar Democrats hoping to make a living from Oregon's evergreen forests. Now, however, the newcomers tended to be middle-class California and East Coast residents fleeing urban areas for the open and underpopulated Northwest. They advocated looking at forests rather than logging them, and many Oregonians, particularly in the Portland suburbs, began to feel that way, too. Packwood saw early on that he needed to distance himself from his Republican timber constituency to appeal to these new voters, and he did it with relish: he had never forgotten the shabby way that the timber lobbyists had terminated his father's career.

He now delighted environmentalists by sparing the French Pete Valley forest east of Eugene from logging, helping to inspire a crusade that eventually made logging old-growth forests an international issue. In 1973 he again defied the timber lobby by creating the Hells Canyon National Recreation Area to protect the 6,000-foot-deep gorge along the Snake River that divides the remotest regions of Oregon and Idaho (his great-grandfather had run ferries there one hundred years earlier). Saving the magnificent gorge, the deepest in North America, became one of the major U.S. conservation victories of the 1970s and 1980s.

Packwood raised eyebrows even higher with his next cause: population control. Bob Packwood first met Stanford University biologist Paul Ehrlich over dinner at the scientist's home in California. Ehrlich's best-seller *The Population Bomb,* which alleged in relentless detail how unchecked population growth would endanger the economy and peace of the planet, would help to create a mass movement and give Ehrlich a permanent following among many ecology scientists.

In the late 1960s, the Stanford professor was seeking out American and European politicians to champion his Zero Population Growth movement. He had hopes for Senator Joseph Clark (D-Pennsylvania), but Clark lost his 1968 Senate reelection race. Ehrlich also targeted Texas Congressman George Bush. The proabortion Republican chaired a liberal House GOP task force on population growth and invited Ehrlich to testify in June 1969.

The Ehrlich/Bush relationship would be a fruitful one. That June, Bush announced his intention to support a "strong national family planning effort," and he persuaded the Nixon administration to hook up with him. Nixon's urban affairs advisor, Daniel P. Moynihan, voiced the president's support in a letter to Bush on 16 September 1969. The Texas congressman immediately led passage of the Tydings-Scheuer-Bush legislation, which increased congressional spending for family planning clinics from $29.2 million in 1967 to nearly $1 billion in 1971. That success would firmly establish federal involvement in family planning for a decade, until the election of Ronald Reagan—and, ironically, George Bush—would bring it to an abrupt halt.

Family planning was a euphemism for legalized abortion, and the term was fraught with danger in some quarters. The ambitious Bush, who had moved to Houston from his home in Connecticut, had decided to oppose Democrat Lloyd Bentsen for a U.S. Senate seat in Texas. He knew he would have enough electoral trouble in the heavily fundamentalist Christian state without further associating himself with Ehrlich's Zero Population Growth agenda.

Ehrlich began to search for another champion. He decided to approach the rookie lawmaker from Oregon, who seemed to have some interest in overpopulation. The scientist couldn't believe his fortune. Bush's commitment to legalizing abortion paled in comparison to Packwood's fervor. The senator has cited at least four influences behind his pioneering abortion views: the overcrowded cities he saw during his NYU Law School days shocked him into seeking viable means of population control; the suffering he and his wife had endured with two stillborn babies proved to him the need for people to be able to terminate problem pregnancies; the support he had received from women over the years had exposed him to the intellectual arguments for abortion, including women's rights; and through studying English common law he began to see reproductive freedom as a basic civil liberty.

116   Packwood quickly put his name on the line. In February 1970 he introduced—with no cosponsors—legislation to allow abortions within the District of Columbia. Sixty days later he would ask liberal senators George McGovern and Walter Mondale to join him in advocating legalized abortion for the entire country, but they timidly declined.

Undaunted, he proceeded to sponsor—again alone—the first nationwide abortion bill, and followed up with legislation that would restrict income tax exemptions to two children. "This legislation encourages families, but it encourages smaller families, and with smaller families we have a chance to save our environment," he intoned. In addition to his own bills, Packwood cosponsored another for a federal family planning center to conduct research on contraception and distribute information about birth control.

His opposition to unbridled population growth defied traditional main street business boosterism and spat in the eye of the country's prevailing religious beliefs. Few American politicians since the 1950s had smashed more taboos than Bob Packwood. No senator had gone farther out on a limb for a social issue. His actions did not go unnoticed.

Evangelical Protestant and Catholic leaders excoriated Packwood. One of the country's leading Roman Catholic Archbishops, Robert Dwyer, characterized the senator's agenda as "an Orwellian nightmare." Other conservatives condemned Packwood as "Senator ZPG," "Senator Abortion," and "Senator Death." And that was just the beginning.

Packwood also had a different intellectual starting point than many politicians. The absence of religious connections is common on the secular West Coast, but is rare throughout the rest of the country.

He never had to reconcile the abortion issue with his religious philosophy because, for better or worse, he didn't have one. When friend Jack Faust told a roast audience how "Bob's religion is part Unitarian, part Huguenot, and—depending if it's an election year—part Jewish," Packwood guffawed louder than anyone. He did give religion some thought, however. As he once told a reporter, "This world and universe did not happen scientifically. God has some purpose in this creation, but

The senator's father, Fred Packwood, near the Oregon State Capitol, where he spent three decades as a business lobbyist.

Gladys Taft Packwood at one of her son's early Dorchester political conferences, which helped springboard his career into the U.S. Senate.

The senator, then-wife Georgie, and baby Bill in a happy moment shortly after arriving in Washington, D.C., in 1969.

The Class of 1957 honor student at New York University Law School, where his provocative views on population control and Israel took root.

Gladys Packwood Collection

Packwood and Mary Jane Dellenback, wife of U.S. Representative John Dellenback (R-Oregon), meet Oregon high school students in early 1970. The author is to the senator's far right.

Collection of the author

An introverted Packwood with peers at Willamette University, the Methodist college in Salem from which he graduated in 1954. The future senator is wearing glasses and Hawaiian shirt.

The Willamette Young Republican advisor, Packwood's favorite professor, and later rival U.S. Senator Mark Hatfield (R-Oregon).

Willamette University

Willamette University

In 1969, Packwood with Gayle Rothrock, an aide for Senator Len Jordan (R-Idaho) who would later accuse Packwood of sexual misconduct.

Gayle Rothrock Collection

Oregon Magazine

Packwood cultivated a close political alliance with feminist leader Gloria Steinem during his 1980 reelection that paid dividends for a decade. Steinem initially supported him after the November 1992 misconduct revelations but later sided with the women. Georgie stands between the two.

Then Finance Committee Chairman Packwood, Senate Democratic Leader Robert Byrd (D-West Virginia), ranking Finance Democrat Russell Long (D-Louisiana), and Majority Leader Bob Dole (R-Kansas) enjoy a collegial moment before tax reform debate.

Longtime Chief of Staff Elaine Franklin and the senator strategize. Former aides claim that in 1992 Franklin orchestrated a coverup of the sexual miscon-duct charges.

Associated Press

Associated Press

Associated Press

Packwood had championed employer-mandated health coverage for two decades, only to completely reverse his views when First Lady Hillary Clinton came calling in 1994.

People Weekly © 1992 Diane Walker

Former Packwood aide Paige Wagers, a Virginia resident who accused Packwood of two incidents of sexual misconduct.

Robbie McClaran/New York Times

Three of the senator's accusers, former volunteer campaign worker Gena Hutton, former aide Julie Myers Williamson, and Gillian Butler.

Ross Hamilton/The Oregonian

Demonstrations broke out in several cities as Packwood met constituents for the first time after The Post *revelations. A melee surrounds Packwood and Franklin during a January 1993 visit to Eugene.*

San Francisco Chronicle

Rejecting Packwood's privacy arguments, as did San Francisco Chronicle's *Tom Meyer, the Senate voted 94 to 6 ordering Packwood to turn over the diaries.*

Packwood gained allies against ethics charges, including Majority Leader Bob Dole (R-Kansas), by faithfully following Dole's opposition to health care, deficit reduction issues, and lobby reform throughout 1993 and 1994.

Associated Press

Associated Press

Gloria Allred of the women's legal defense organization of Los Angeles and Julie Myers Williamson of Portland leading efforts against the senator.

I'm not sure I understand exactly what that purpose is, and [I] doubt that anyone else does."

Packwood expounded on this when Senate prayer breakfast members unwittingly invited him to share some personal reflections. He shocked the button-down group by condemning the hypocrisy of legislators who pray in the morning and backstab in the afternoon.

Years later, when the Bible group finally invited him back, Packwood prepared to give a fiery proabortion speech, but his staff discreetly intervened. The senator ended up with a quotation-stuffed talk extolling the views of Hume, Hegel, and Toynbee: that democracies with religious freedom survive, and dictatorships with rigid religious controls do not—just as, by implication, any prayer breakfast senators who ascribed their own opinions to God's will, would not.

———————

"Population stabilization is the foremost challenge facing the nation and the world," Packwood warned fellow senators as he introduced the 1970 National Abortion Act. "If we can restrain population growth through voluntary means, we have a chance to save our environment; if we do not, we are lost.

"One has only to look at the heavily populated Northeastern section of the United States to see how inhumane man can be to the environment. Man has literally raped and ravished the landscape from Washington to Philadelphia to New York to Boston."

When Packwood threw the abortion issue before an astounded Congress, the pace of work at his Capitol Hill office immediately intensified. Lawrence Spivak, producer of television's *Meet the Press*, invited the senator to be on the show. On 17 May 1970, Americans received their first long look at an abortion advocate. The panel—NBC news correspondent Nancy Dickerson; *Newsweek*'s chief Capitol reporter, Samuel Shaffer; and Spivak—interrogated Packwood.

Dickerson: In Red China [abortion] was a national policy and was abandoned after there were profound adverse psychological effects. Have you given a lot of thought to this?

118 *Packwood:* I have. And I have seen good studies out of Japan, where they have had legalized abortion for twenty-one years. The psychological effects are almost nil. The population stabilization they have achieved is quite well known, and the amount of ill-treated . . . illegitimate children is almost insignificant.

With that answer, the panel shifted gear. Their questions became softer, more supportive, and even obsequious.

Shaffer: One aspect of this abortion legislation [of yours] we haven't covered. It is a cliché in politics that a politician doesn't vote against motherhood. That is what you are doing. Do you think you have a future in politics if you do?

Packwood: Mr. Shaffer, I hope so. I like the Senate and I would like to stay here, but if, because of my abortion legislation, I am defeated, I will go back to practicing law in Portland, which isn't the worst of the lives I could lead.

Dickerson: Senator, do you think if we have two-children families we will be breeding a different kind of people than we have had before, that have been nurtured on those old-fashioned virtues of the big, loving American family?

Packwood: The big, loving American family, Mrs. Dickerson, is gone, and it went with the day when we quit being an agricultural country and moved to an urban nation.

The newcomer's performance placed him on the national political radar screen. *Newsweek* columnist Kenneth Crawford gave Packwood a positive review. "Packwood is preempting a cause bound to be high on the agenda of the 1970s, thus stealing a march on his elders who have been hesitant about grasping this nettle."

Packwood had made the overpopulation case for abortion. He crafted arguments showing how restrictive abortion laws violated an individual's constitutional right to privacy. "No state has the right to tell a woman she cannot have an abortion any more than it has the right to tell her she must have one," he said in an August 1970 newsletter to national supporters and con-

stituents. "The decision to terminate a pregnancy must properly be left to the woman and her private conscience."

Senator Ted Kennedy, at that time an opponent of abortion, refused to give the Packwood bill a hearing. But even Kennedy could not shut out debate. "Packwood's bill became symbolic for those in the abortion movement," said veteran Planned Parenthood lobbyist Jeanne Rosoff. Indeed, the senator set the pace on the issue. The states of New York and Hawaii legalized abortion that year, and as Packwood pushed open the gates, California, Texas, Washington, New Jersey, and his home state of Oregon followed suit.

Congress failed to pass his reforms, but Packwood refiled the National Abortion Act in May 1971. Representative Paul McCloskey (R-California) joined the fight, and Packwood's rhetoric became more hopeful. "In contrast to last year, when Congress avoided abortion legislation like the plague, Packwood is optimistic his legislation will receive public hearings this year and that Congress may have to commit itself on the issue," he told a reporter.

Abortion legalization in New York and Hawaii convinced liberal Democrats that they could follow Packwood's lead and survive. Even Ted Kennedy promised to hold congressional hearings. But most senators dodged the issue by insisting that abortion was a "local" issue that Congress should not touch. Packwood fought back by reintroducing his abortion bill in the nation's capital. Because Congress directly administers the local District of Columbia government, senators could no longer use the local control excuse to avoid taking a position. "Well," Packwood told reporters, "I've localized it for them now."

The senator, perhaps naively, believed that President Nixon might support him—after all, the president had strongly endorsed Bush's family planning bill. But an examination of the Nixon Presidential Library records reveals that Nixon's decisions were based more on pragmatism than on personal conviction. In a private memo to presidential assistant Patrick Buchanan on 5 January 1971, White House counsel John W. Dean III informed Buchanan that the latest Harris Poll showed a majority of voters against abortion. "It appears from a review

120 of this poll that the feeling of Americans in the Midwest and South [Nixon's constituency] makes it a political plus for the president to take a position opposing legalization of abortions." The White House aides persuaded Nixon to volunteer his "personal opposition" to abortion on the eve of Packwood's reintroduction of the National Abortion Act in May 1971.

Packwood told reporters that Nixon's opposition "struck a telling blow . . . he's certainly entitled to his personal opinions, but he didn't have to let the whole world know how he feels." Packwood defiantly predicted that he would pass an abortion bill in five years—"with or without the president's support." As he planned for committee hearings on the District bill, he told reporters that its chances were "much better than those for the national act."

The White House planned for that, too. In a private memo dated 22 July 1971, John Dean decided to withhold Nixon administration support from Packwood.

Packwood's prediction that abortion rights would become federal law within five years was pessimistic—the Supreme Court proved him right sooner than that. On 22 January 1973, the court's decision on *Roe* v. *Wade* turned Packwood into a prophet and abortion into the law of the land. But it would have to withstand some powerful blows.

When Packwood first introduced legislation for abortion reform in 1970, the Right to Life group did not have a single office in Washington, D.C. Now the shock of the *Roe* decision gave the antiabortionists new energy. They labeled 22 January "Black Monday" and mounted local, state, and congressional offensives.

The biggest target of all was Bob Packwood, and that complicated matters as his 1974 reelection bid approached. In 1968 his liberal views had been a secret to social conservatives who had passionately supported him over Wayne Morse. Now that this support was gone for good, he needed to attract new voters. And he found them in the tens of thousands of pro-choice women who now saw Packwood as their leader.

Packwood, once again, was in on the ground floor of a new movement. He broadened his agenda beyond abortion to become a national leader on all women's issues: the Equal Rights Amendment, discrimination in the workplace, day care, and parental leave. It would be twenty years before his supporters realized that his pro-choice views had arisen from fears of overpopulation rather than from a core belief in a woman's right to have control over her own body—and that his private behavior toward women was something less than honorable.

8

U.S. Senator Howard Baker of Tennessee had known for a while that his father-in-law, Senate Republican leader Everett McKinley Dirksen, could die at any time. So when the gravel-voiced senator died on Sunday, 7 September 1969, it came as no surprise. On Monday morning, as the *Oregonian*'s A. Robert Smith made his daily Senate rounds, he found Baker and his friend Bob Packwood talking intently in Packwood's office. "Old Ev Dirksen's body hadn't even grown stiff—and Packwood and Baker were already inside scheming to get Baker elected as Senate Republican leader," said Smith.

No senator seeking to overturn the country's 200-year-old tradition of restricting abortion could be meek in pursuing that agenda. Packwood needed powerful allies and Howard Baker became the first one. He selected fellow rookie Packwood to manage his campaign. The two men, among the youngest in the Senate, had served together on the Senate Labor and Public Works Committee.

Baker wasn't the only one running after the Republican prize; moderate Hugh Scott of Pennsylvania was right there with him. The race would become a generational fight between Scott, sixty-eight, and Baker, forty-three. Scott was popular with

Northerners and party traditionalists, but he was on less firm ground with the newcomers. Many new senators, including Bob Dole, stood to gain more from fellow freshman Baker than the veteran Scott, who had already established his friendships.

As Baker and Packwood worked on this front, they also appealed to Southern conservatives, including Strom Thurmond of South Carolina and John Tower of Texas, who regarded Scott as too liberal on civil rights. Packwood had gotten to know Tower when he hosted the Texan's 1961 visit to Oregon, and found that he was an easy sell.

Although Scott eventually defeated Baker in a close vote, Baker and Packwood gained momentum from the race. They had gambled and had nearly toppled the old guard. In doing so, they had become rising Senate stars in impressive time. Baker immediately began to position himself for the future, aiming first at minority leader and ultimately at the presidency. Packwood harbored similar long-term ambitions, but he knew that he first needed to advance his abortion and environmental causes.

The defining issue of the era—the war in Vietnam—was not a priority for Packwood. He had never pursued legislation to enact one of the key platform proposals of his campaign, South Vietnamese land reform. That scheme had already served its purpose—getting Packwood elected to the Senate.

By early 1970 the war had cost more than a quarter of a million lives, and the American public was deeply divided on what should be done. Packwood, however, managed to straddle the fence, never taking a firm stand. In a December 1969 newsletter, he told constituents: "After talking with the president, I am even more convinced that he's going to have our ground combat forces out of Vietnam by the end of 1970." But when asked about that statement, Packwood waffled. "I've been fairly supportive of the president, but—I don't remember saying that, but if I did—I was wrong. I think I supported one of the Mansfield amendments, but beyond that, I think I've been fairly constant in my support."

The Senate and the nation hotly debated the Hatfield-McGovern amendment, which called for the gradual withdrawal of all American troops. Although Packwood joined conservative

124   and Southern senators to oppose the amendments, he also supported the liberal Cooper-Church amendment to restrict the president from using any U.S. forces in Cambodia.

His independent voting record soon earned Packwood a reputation as a maverick. Politicians who play their own hand, like Jerry Brown of California and Barry Goldwater of Arizona, are a rare breed in the East but hardy perennials in the West. The frontier, settled by people who wanted to break free of tradition, never had the East Coast–style patronage systems that created omnipotent political parties that politicians depended on for cash, volunteers, and allies.

Oregon, on the Western edge of the nation, created a system that fumigated every crevice and cranny of conventional party politics. In 1902 the state gave voters the sweeping ability to use initiatives and referenda. Woodrow Wilson, then president of Princeton University, praised the "Oregon System" as a national model. The reforms and lack of patronage made political parties largely irrelevant, giving lawmakers great freedom over their own actions. Oregon voters expected their lawmakers to act independently of the president and prevailing opinion, and now they were beginning to see that Packwood was following this tradition.

The senator had voted with the Nixon administration two-thirds of the time but seldom on the high-stakes issues that Nixon most wanted, including the B-1 bomber, supersonic transport (SST), and the Trident submarine. Packwood actually contributed to two of Nixon's most embarrassing defeats: the Senate's rejections of the president's conservative nominees to the U.S. Supreme Court, Clement Haynsworth and G. Harrold Carswell.

Nixon had appointed Haynsworth, a South Carolina federal judge, at the behest of the powerful Senator Strom Thurmond (R-South Carolina), who had supported Nixon for the 1968 Republican presidential nomination. As Haynsworth faltered, Nixon was on the verge of becoming the first president since Herbert Hoover to have a Supreme Court nominee rejected. He needed every Republican vote, including Packwood's, to turn it around.

Nixon dispatched then–Solicitor General William Rehnquist to lobby Packwood, but Rehnquist reported that he didn't make much headway because Packwood said lawyers in Oregon were against Haynsworth. "But Packwood said he would be quiet," according to a confidential memo written by White House aide Bryce Harlow.[7]

Nixon summoned Packwood to the White House for what the senator thought would be a meeting with Nixon and several Republican solons. Instead, the president had arranged a private forty-five-minute session. Nixon began by explaining to Packwood how much the nomination meant to the administration, and to him personally. When Packwood expressed his strong reservations about Haynsworth's civil rights record, the president said that he understood. Signaling that the meeting was over, Nixon placed his hand on the freshman senator's shoulders and said that, just this once—as a personal favor—he needed this vote.

The White House waited for the senator's answer, but Packwood did not budge. Nixon never forgave Packwood for that.

Harlow reported that after Packwood turned down the president's request, he boldly asked for Nixon's help in derailing Wayne Morse, who was thinking of running for the U.S. House of Representatives seat that year as a springboard to challenge Packwood for reelection in 1974. To assuage Nixon, Packwood promised to help Haynsworth in other ways. The senator agreed not to influence other Republicans against Haynsworth, reported author Richard Harris in the book *Decision,* and he also helped the Haynsworth camp on procedural votes. Minutes before the Haynsworth nomination vote, Packwood was summoned off the floor to take a phone call from a Nixon aide. The aide breathlessly told him that the result was going to be very close, and asked Packwood to hold back his vote on the first roll call to make the margin look even narrower. That might persuade other senators that a pro-Haynsworth bandwagon had begun.

Packwood held back; but to his bitter embarrassment, the bandwagon turned out to be rolling in the other direction. The final 55-to-45 vote against Haynsworth made Packwood look not only like an opportunist, but one who couldn't count.

7. Nixon presidential archives, White House central files.

The senator was furious at Nixon. In early 1970, when the president appointed another conservative nominee, G. Harrold Carswell, Packwood responded in kind. He deceived the administration into believing that he supported Carswell, but later became one of the few Republicans to reject that nominee, pointedly contributing to another humiliating Nixon defeat.

The president's troubles had just begun. That May the U.S. invasion of Cambodia would set off protests culminating in the deadly fusillade that killed four students at Kent State University in Ohio. Nixon, watching his support slip away, decided to close ranks. According to presidential records, the White House began to monitor political opponents, including Packwood. In a memo dated 16 March 1970, Nixon Chief of Staff H. R. Haldeman reported to the president that Packwood had organized a conference of 250 young GOP moderates who were critical of Nixon. Haldeman wrote that "one speaker suggested that we 'devote our energies to denying [Nixon] renomination in 1972.'"

As Nixon began his reelection campaign, Haldeman stayed on the trail of the troublesome senator. One of the linchpins of the president's reelection strategy was to wrest labor support away from Democrats. The Teamsters loathed likely Democratic nominee George McGovern's liberal views on Vietnam and social issues, but they couldn't stomach endorsing Nixon either—unless the president dropped the antistrike legislation he had put before Congress.

Nixon had invested two years on this issue, even recruiting Packwood, the former Portland management attorney, to push the antilabor bill. But on 21 July, desperate for labor support, the president yanked his own bill. That same day, Haldeman wrote a confidential summary about the reaction of the news media:

> NBC's [Paul] Duke said for more than 2 years RN has asked for the law and Packwood, *"prodded by the Admin" has worked long and hard for it* and now, *when he seemed about to succeed for his good friend RN* (shot of RN-Packwood), the WH has backed down in an action followed shortly by Teamsters support.
>
> On NBC film *Packwood said he had 47 backers to 45 opponents. . .*

He [Packwood] said he'd not work so long and hard again on a bill which gained him animosity of labor only to have rug pulled out from under him. . . .

"Nixon Veers" was title of ABC's report w/ [reporter Tom] Jarriel saying it was regarded as one of RN's most important bills and supporters thought it 1 of most significant labor bills ever. . . . Packwood who had steered bill w/in few voters of passage, "suspects an election-year sell-out," said Jarriel.

Packwood was angry. Nixon's betrayal emboldened the senator to challenge something that the president cherished even more than a labor endorsement: a harmonious Republican National Convention that would peacefully celebrate the president's renomination for four days on national television.

Almost all the delegates to the Republican National Convention were white and male, partly because of tradition and partly because of a rigged delegate selection process that favored rural, conservative states. Nixon's people wanted to keep it that way, but Packwood exhorted Republicans to "open up" the convention with McGovern-style reforms that would attract more women and minority delegates. Packwood and his allies, Illinois Senator Charles Percy and Representative Tom Railsback, also of Illinois, proposed redrawing the rules to help Northern liberal, industrial states rather than conservative Southern and Midwestern states.

The Nixon forces beat back the Railsback/Packwood reforms by a vote of 910 to 434, and the August convention triumphantly renominated Nixon. Free of embarrassing convention setbacks, the Nixon-Agnew ticket sailed unscathed to an eventual landslide victory over McGovern in November.

But hard times lay ahead for Nixon. Soon after *Washington Post* reporters Bob Woodward and Carl Bernstein broke the news of White House involvement in the 17 June burglary of the Democratic National Headquarters in the Watergate apartment complex in Washington, D.C., all hell broke loose.

The White House hoped the convictions of the seven burglars in January 1973 might put the issue to rest, but *Post*

128   disclosures implicating former Attorney General John Mitchell created a major scandal for Nixon and potentially hurt all Republicans seeking reelection the following year. To placate the American public, who were by turns confused and enraged, the Senate created a Watergate investigation committee led by the Democratic Senator Sam Ervin of North Carolina, and Packwood's ally Howard Baker.

Packwood had his own troubles. As he had feared, Wayne Morse was now preparing to run against him in 1974. The mood of the country was such that any ethical scandal that took Nixon down would also threaten Packwood's reelection. In addition, he seemed to be genuinely outraged at the behavior of Mitchell, G. Gordon Liddy, and the others, and he certainly had no goodwill left toward Nixon. It was the country's ironic fortune that Watergate broke when it did. Packwood had plenty of reasons to lead Republican opposition to Nixon, and he crafted his attacks for maximum political advantage.

The Democrats needed his help. Alone, they could not have forced Nixon out of office. Packwood's early dissent lent credibility to their charges. As the senator kept the heat on, he made it harder for conservative Republicans to ignore evidence. His actions helped create the unity that would heal the nation after Nixon's resignation.

That January, Packwood described the scandal as "a dagger to the heart of the Republican Party" and called on the president to tell the truth. Historian and Nixon biographer Steven E. Ambrose later identified that as the first crack in Nixon's united Republican front. Virtually every other GOP lawmaker had leapt to Nixon's defense, as had much of the nation. Despite Watergate, the president's Gallup Poll approval ratings remained at a respectable 50 percent.

But that soon changed, and Packwood was leading the charge. On 13 March, Haldeman assistant Bruce Kehrli dispatched a news summary labeled "Watergate" to domestic policy advisor John Ehrlichman, congressional relations advisor William Timmons, and Haldeman. The document signaled to the White House inner guard another dangerous breach in party ranks.

The nation lacks the kind of spirit which JFK gave it— and, says Packwood, "it's not going to come from this Admin.". . . In *Oregonian* interview titled "Packwood not convinced WH 'clean' on Watergate; Feels party hurt badly, and RN won't listen," the Sen. also says there's no justification for alleged Admin "paranoid fear" of media.

He charges WH feels [Capitol] Hill is "irrelevant" and doesn't even care about views of Senate GOP, even when presented by [minority leader Hugh] Scott.

Packwood says Watergate "has cast a permanent pall over Republicanism" and he feels RN should have ordered a complete investigation of it when it occurred and "gotten rid of everybody involved" no matter how high up they were.

As Sam Ervin later wrote, "Republicans in high places expressed their misgivings publicly. Senator Robert W. Packwood described Watergate as the most odious issue since Teapot Dome." The Watergate Committee subpoenaed Mitchell, Haldeman, Ehrlichman, and John Dean for nationally televised hearings. Nixon feared that Dean would finger the White House in supporting the burglary cover-up. On 30 April, to appease critics, the president fired Ehrlichman and Haldeman.

Packwood now declared that the scandal was "reaching disastrous proportions."

The Watergate hearings began on 1 May in the historic chandeliered and marbled Russell Senate Office caucus room. They became the most watched televised political drama in American history, dominating the evening news and daytime ratings for eight weeks, making household names of such low-level Nixon operatives as Magruder and Liddy, and adding the terms "stonewall," "Deep Throat," and "twisting in the wind" to the American lexicon.

Nixon's approval ratings dropped like a rock down a rain chute, plummeting from 68 percent in January of 1973 to 40 percent by the summer. Watergate had long since eclipsed Teapot Dome, the Warren Harding administration land swindle of 1923, which had long served as the standard for U.S. political corruption.

Muckraking columnist Jack Anderson gave Packwood reason to believe he would survive Watergate with his reputation intact. On 9 July Anderson reported that Haldeman had drawn up a secret blacklist of Republican senators whom Nixon disliked. "We called it the shit list," said one White House source. The blacklist included Packwood, Lowell Weicker, Jacob Javits, Charles Percy, and Clifford Case. As punishment for their disloyalty, Haldeman cut off patronage, campaign assistance, invitations, and even routine White House tours for these men.

On 21 July the Watergate Committee was galvanized by the information that the president had tape-recorded all White House office conversations. Ervin and special prosecutor Archibald Cox immediately filed a subpoena for Nixon to turn over the tapes. On Friday, 19 October, Cox refused Nixon's order to stop. Late in the evening of Saturday, 20 October, Nixon ordered Attorney General Elliott Richardson to fire Cox, but Richardson resigned rather than do so. Nixon then fired Deputy Attorney General William Ruckelshaus for refusing to carry out the same order. Finally, Nixon appointed Solicitor General Robert H. Bork as acting Attorney General.

Packwood joined others in condemning Nixon for what was inevitably called the "Saturday Night Massacre," declaring that "the office of president does not carry with it the license to destroy justice in America." Voices on Capitol Hill began to whisper a word not heard in 105 years, since the days of President Andrew Johnson: impeachment. Dozens of Democrats readied resolutions to do exactly that.

Under the Constitution, the House of Representatives votes on articles of impeachment against a president, who then must stand trial before the Senate. It takes a two-thirds majority of the Senate to impeach—and Nixon knew that without Republican support, the Democrats couldn't swing enough votes.

On 15 November a desperate Nixon invited a select group of GOP senators—including the renegade Packwood—to a private White House meeting to seek their support. Press Secretary Ronald Ziegler ushered the ten senators into the White House solarium, which had recently been renamed the California Room. As cocktails were served, the president—wearing a sports coat and slacks—joked nervously about being too "sportily dressed" for his audience.

Finally, Nixon made a few opening remarks and then called on one senator after another to speak. Several senators, including Strom Thurmond of South Carolina, William Scott of Virginia, and Peter Dominick of Colorado, were lockstep Nixon men. Others, such as William Schweiker of Pennsylvania and Robert Stafford of Vermont, lacked either the seniority or the self-confidence necessary to challenge a president.

Then it was Packwood's turn. He told Nixon he had a statement and that he would prefer to make it without interruption. The room grew hushed, and he sensed the others thinking, "Oh God, what's he going he say?"

"All of us, Mr. President, whether we're in politics or not, have weaknesses," Packwood began. And then, in words that would one day come back to haunt him, he told Richard Nixon that some politicians have a weakness with alcohol.

> For others, it's gambling. For others, it's women. None of these weaknesses applies to you. Your weakness is credibility. This has always been your short suit with the news media and general public. The problem with the public is that they no longer believe you. They no longer trust the integrity of the administration. . . .
>
> Most members of Congress, furthermore, believed that you broke your word by firing Archibald Cox. Congress has come to expect that many people who testify before it lie. It's an entirely different matter, however, when one person gives his word to another. That is a bond which those of us in politics revere highly. Those who breach that bond suffer an incalculable loss of credibility.

The senator then seized on a remark Nixon had made minutes earlier: that he would most certainly not resign, because he had not even been convicted of any crime. "That struck a nerve with me," Packwood recalled. "It hit me that that was the crux of the whole Watergate thing."

He told Nixon, "For too long, this administration has given the public the impression that its standard of conduct was not

132 that it must be above suspicion but that it must merely be above criminal guilt. Mr. President, that is not an adequate standard of conduct for those who have been accorded the privilege of governing this country."

As an example, Packwood cited the indictments of former Commerce Secretary Maurice Stans and Attorney General John Mitchell. "If they are cleared," Packwood predicted, "there will be great trumpeting from this administration that the court system has vindicated them and revived their credibility and inferentially yours.

"If Stans and Mitchell are acquitted, it simply means that evidence beyond a reasonable doubt was not presented to convince jurors of their criminal guilt. It does not mean they were innocent of wrongdoing."

After hitting the president with this stick, Packwood dangled a carrot. He made two suggestions:

One, disclose everything—the confidential notes, the tapes—everything bearing on the scandal. There can't be a missing tape accidentally disposed of by a janitor. There can't be a memo uncovered by an inquiring reporter.

Two, hold an open-ended, no-time-limit news conference with only six or seven reporters [the senator specifically plugged his friend Dan Rather of CBS]. I recommend this first because you are good at adversarial proceedings, and second because the public must be convinced that you have opened yourself up to your harshest critics.

Throughout the long statement, the president looked toward the young senator, but not at him. When Packwood finished, Nixon said coolly, "Thank you," and moved on to the next senator.[8]

That meeting propelled Packwood to a place alongside Watergate Committee member Lowell Weicker as the leading Republican scandal critics. R.W. Apple of the *New York Times* wrote how Nixon aides acknowledged that the forty-one-year-

---

8. J. Anthony Lukas. *Nightmare: The Underside of the Nixon Years* (Viking, 1976).

old senator gave the president the most stinging critique of the two hundred Capitol Hill Republicans.

Packwood continued to hammer the president. Speaking on the CBS radio program "Capitol Cloakroom" on 21 November, he concluded that "Nixon had hurt the office of the presidency more than any occupant since Warren Harding." The senator exceeded even most Democrats in mobilizing public opinion against Nixon. A majority of Democrats believed in Nixon's culpability in the cover-up, but impeachment calls remained risky. What if the tapes exonerated the president?

———

As 1974 began, no Republican senator endorsed impeachment proceedings as a means of determining the president's innocence or guilt. No Republican senator or congressmember even suggested that Nixon resign. Only four of the fifty-eight Democratic senators—George McGovern, Daniel Inouye of Hawaii, Phillip Hart of Michigan, and John Tunney of California—had endorsed impeachment or resignation.

On 19 February federal prosecutors began criminal trials against John Mitchell and Maurice Stans for obstruction of justice, perjury, and conspiracy. The two men became the first cabinet members in fifty years to face criminal charges.

Now, there was more at stake than Richard Nixon's career. It was clear that all Republicans seeking election in 1974—including Bob Packwood—would pay the price.

The trail of felonies leading into the Oval Office outraged Oregon voters more than most Americans. Voter revulsion against Republicans could end Packwood's career after only one term. Packwood had done his best to insulate himself from the Watergate fallout; he could only hope that the voters had taken note.

The following week a federal grand jury source called Packwood with a dramatic disclosure. The source revealed that jurors would indict the president's inner sanctum, Haldeman and Ehrlichman, on Friday, 1 March. They would also file more charges against Mitchell, and charge former Nixon aides

134   Charles W. Colson, Robert C. Mardian, Gordon Strachan, and Kenneth W. Parkinson with criminal counts.

Gambling that his friend's information was correct, Packwood took a big step. On Wednesday, 27 February, he called *Los Angeles Times* bureau chief Jack Nelson to say he would become the first Senate Republican to support impeaching Richard Nixon.

Packwood confidently told Nelson, "There are already sufficient reasons to go ahead and impeach the president and try the case on its merits in the Senate.

"I think most senators would prefer not to face up to impeachment, but it doesn't bother me. I would just look at the facts. It's frustrating to me to see politicians spend so much time asking people to elect them as their representatives, and then doing everything they can to avoid their responsibilities."

Nelson then asked, "But how will your calling for impeachment affect your reelection chances?"

"Certainly, impeachment is an election issue," Packwood answered. "And I get teed off with the attitude that the way to get reelected is to avoid controversial issues, whether it's abortion or marijuana or war or impeachment." [Though Packwood had done exactly that on Vietnam.]

Nelson began writing up the exclusive for the *Los Angeles Times–Washington Post* news service.

Minutes later, the telephone rang again. It was Packwood, apparently having second thoughts.

"Jack," he asked sheepishly, "how were you going to quote me about impeachment?"

Nelson read the quote back to him.

After several seconds of silence, Packwood said, "I will stand behind what you wrote." After more silence, Packwood tried another tack—to make Nelson feel guilty for holding him to his words.

"I don't want to crawfish. But I know what will happen; the Oregon newspapers will have headlines saying, 'Packwood Calls For Impeachment.' And I shouldn't tell the House how to vote. So you can use the story the way I told you, if you want to, but if I am called by the Oregon papers, I will say that was what

I told you, but what I had meant to say was that the House should vote on impeachment."

Packwood now backpedaled from nearly everything he had originally told Nelson. He was not "breaking" with Nixon. In fact, he had a "reasonably good relationship" with the White House and was "delighted" to be steering Nixon's health-care bills in the Senate.

"I'm for impeachment in the defense of the president as much as anything else," he said, not explaining what "anything else" might be. "He can't continue to hang this way, and the Senate should try him and if it exonerates him, fine, and if it convicts him, fine. But let's get on with it."

The Oregon reporters whom Packwood feared might hold him to his words greeted him at Portland International Airport the next day, Thursday, 28 February.

But this time he was better prepared. He staked out a position—and stuck to it—for the remainder of his reelection campaign. He endorsed an impeachment trial as if he was doing the president a favor. "There is no way [President Nixon] can be exonerated save impeachment," he said.

Packwood declared—somewhat hypocritically, given his attempts to change his statement to Nelson—that "there's a tendency in Congress not to vote on controversial issues."

Twenty-four hours later the senator opened the Dorchester Conference at the beach resort town of Seaside, Oregon. It had been ten years since he had created the conclave as a springboard for his U.S. Senate dreams, but none of the preceding conferences had the national impact that this one would.

Packwood's anonymous source had given him the jump on the national media all week. As promised, the grand jury indicted Mitchell, Ehrlichman, Haldeman, and others on Friday, 1 March. And as reporters looked to the nation's hinterlands for reaction stories, they followed Packwood to Seaside.

The *Congressional Quarterly* reported that Packwood and Dorchester keynote speaker, former New York Governor Nelson Rockefeller, endorsed an impeachment trial as "the proper course" to determine the president's responsibility in the Watergate cover-up. Remarkably, the Dorchester delegates voted

136 286 to 119 to support impeaching their party's president. Packwood's good friend and alter ego, attorney Jack Faust, helped lead the floor fight for impeachment.

As anticipated, old nemesis Wayne Morse now joined the Senate race against him. The widespread unpopularity of the Republican administration and the war in Vietnam had vindicated the Democrat with many Oregon voters. "Bob became very agitated when Morse entered the race," a campaign aide said. The public was unaware that the seventy-three-year-old Morse was fighting serious health problems. The Packwood campaign hoped the press might pick up this information, but Morse easily won the Democratic nomination, setting the stage for a general election rematch with Packwood.

In late April the U.S. Supreme Court ordered the White House to release the tapes of Watergate-related conversations. The dialogue between President Nixon and counsel John Dean incriminated some Republicans but liberated others:

Dean: So there are dangers, Mr. President. I would be less than candid if I didn't tell you there are. There is a reason for not everyone going up and not testifying.

Nixon: I see. Oh, no, no, no. I didn't mean to have everyone go up and testify.

Dean: Well, I mean they are just starting to let it hang out, and say here's our story . . .

Nixon: I mean putting out the story to the people, here is the true story of Watergate.

Dean: They would never believe it. The two things they are working on is Watergate . . .

Nixon: Who is they?

Dean: The press, the intellectuals, the . . .

Nixon: [interrupting] The Packwoods.

The tapes boosted Packwood's reelection bid against Morse by giving Oregon voters irrefutable evidence of his independence from the unpopular Nixon administration.

Packwood claimed to have read the entire 1,250 pages of transcripts that week. "It was like reading Machiavelli," he said. "In all the years I've been in politics, I've never seen such an amoral attitude. You look in vain for a scintilla of evidence of ethical considerations."

Nixon resigned on 9 August to avoid certain Senate conviction on impeachment charges. But even resignation could not relieve Packwood's reelection fears. When newly sworn-in President Gerald Ford pardoned Nixon for all possible criminal charges, voter furor was refueled. GOP senators seeking reelection, among them Packwood, Dole, and Schweicker, denounced their new president's action.

The protracted scandal had traumatized the electorate, and Republicans suffered for it: the percentage of voters registering with the GOP plummeted to 20 percent. The party faced its greatest electoral disaster since the Stock Market Crash of 1929 rocked Herbert Hoover's administration.

Packwood, however, got a macabre break. Morse died in July, and the Democrats scrambled to replace him with state Senator Betty Roberts—the ex-wife of Packwood's enemy Frank Roberts—who had lost that year's gubernatorial primary. She had a depleted treasury but an energetic organization of liberals and feminists and good name recognition. At fifty-one, her relative youth made her in some ways as good a candidate as Morse.

"We had to run against two opponents, Betty Roberts and Richard Nixon," a Packwood campaign aide said. "Watergate made it harder than hell to get volunteers. Every day people called saying, 'Take my name off your list. I don't want anything to do with a Republican.'"

While Roberts pelted him with charges of Republican corruption, Packwood fought back with all the innovative ammunition he could muster—and that was formidable. He utilized the new videotape technology, recording Roberts's campaign appearances to probe for weaknesses and get instant material for television and radio commercials. As in 1968, he planted staff members at his opponent's speeches to ask pointed questions. Packwood saw nothing unethical or objectionable

138 about this, feeling that it was necessary to "learn Roberts's position on various issues, including gun control." Packwood believed that her supporters had also planted questioners in his audiences.

Roberts, a strongly pro-abortion candidate, threatened to steal some of Packwood's clout with liberal women voters. The Republican, however, was prepared for that. No American politician had ever had the foresight or resources to appeal to feminists on a national scale. Ever the campaign innovator, Packwood developed a sophisticated direct mail campaign to reach a national feminist audience. But he also danced close to danger.

This senator who lectured Nixon about "weaknesses" such as "women" and "lack of credibility" recklessly displayed his own foibles. Packwood frequently visited the Hells Canyon Recreation Area near the Idaho border and, along with fish-and-game ranger Bill Brown, usually ended up at the Black Anville tavern in La Grande. "Packwood always seemed to have five or six real good-looking women on his staff," and they joined him for beer drinking and partying at the Black Anville. The women vied for Packwood's attention, and "he'd figure out which one it was for that night," Brown said.

The volume of extramarital sex created great anxiety among the women who were running his 1974 reelection campaign. "You couldn't let him out of your sight," said one campaign scheduler. "There was a code. 'Don't let him spend the night in Salem because of "Susan." Don't let him spend the night in Medford because of another woman,' and down the line," the aide said.

But Packwood skated by those cracks in the ice, and in November he defeated Roberts by 55 percent to 45 percent of the vote. The triumph was particularly sweet because Watergate had sent other GOP candidates across the country crashing down.

The 1974 Watergate election wiped out a generation of Republican talent. The GOP lost forty-three seats in the House, four in the Senate, and four governorships. The election weakened the party but strengthened Packwood. The retirement and defeat of older GOP senators cleared his path to power. Pack-

wood hoped for Senate leadership within a few years—and
maybe more than that.

Important people had noticed Packwood's leadership on women's issues and Watergate. *Newsweek*'s Samuel Shaffer described the senator as "one of the brightest young men the Republicans have elected to the Senate in decades." Columnist George Will even suggested Packwood as a future Republican presidential nominee. The senator warmed to that suggestion.

9

After Fred Packwood died in 1965, Mindy moved from the family's spacious Northeast Portland home to a small apartment downtown. She directed her considerable energies to her volunteer job at a YWCA consignment store. According to shop manager Corrine Jennings, she served as treasurer for eighteen years without making a bookkeeping mistake.

Her husband's death brought respite from marital wars, but not from loneliness. Bob's spectacular successes had only slightly improved their relationship. After all, he was his father's son, and Mindy had made no secret of her disdain for Fred. She seemed ambivalent over Bob's election to the Senate. She cried joyful tears as she watched him being sworn in, but his move to Washington, D.C., made him even less a part of her life, and she spoke very critically about him to strangers. She once snapped back to a reporter, "I don't know anything about Bob Packwood—except he was a bratty boy."

Bob Witeck served longer with Packwood than almost anyone else, working with him from 1976 to 1982, and 1986 to 1989. "I knew him for a lot of years and we'd have drinks together. He'd sometimes talk about his father and how much he admired his dad's intellect. He never talked about his still-living parent, his mother, and that relationship—or nonrelationship. He never talked about his sister," Witeck says.

Mindy felt closer to her daughter, Patricia, the family nonconformist. In the late 1950s Pat married Campbell Richardson, one of Bob's law school classmates and an attorney for Davies, Strayer, Biggs, Stoel—among the Northwest's largest law firms. The couple's social life centered around the firm, especially the monthly bridge club dinners, where Pat met the wives of other attorneys, including Barbara (Mrs. Donald) Hodel and Linda McAlister Peters.

Peters was intrigued with this fast-talking, energetic young woman. She had never met anyone as interesting and daring as Pat Richardson. "Pat had chosen to *not* play the society role the law firm expected of the wives," Peters said.

While her brother immersed himself in mainstream Republican and Jaycee affairs, sister Pat threw herself into the wave of social change that swept through the sixties. She declined to join Junior League and other like-minded women's organizations. Instead, she was attracted to the nontraditional message of the West Hills Unitarian Church social committee. Pat listened raptly to the stories told by a church member who had just returned from registering black voters in the South after the Freedom Rider bombings. "She developed an enormous, throbbing social conscience," said Peters.

Richardson didn't keep her opinions to herself. She explained her position to the resistant lawyers and their wives at the bridge club. Peters, at least, was grateful. "It was because of Pat that I stopped having automatic Republican responses to every subject." The society page of the *Oregon Journal* observed that while her mother, Mindy, loved the piano, "Patricia prefers her life as a social activist, intent on civil rights, better schools, and fair housing."

Pat joined an anti–Vietnam War group at a time when that was a rather daring move, and she persistently lobbied her brother on that issue. Although one of Bob's campaign aides dismissed her as a "March hare," she acted on her convictions. Pat shocked her friends by transferring her daughter from their affluent Raleigh Hills school to a largely black grade school in

142   Northeast Portland. "I was blown out of the water. I couldn't imagine anyone doing that," Peters recalled.

Her lifestyle slowly became as provocative as her politics. In the late 1960s Bob preferred the music of Frank Sinatra. Pat, just five years younger, listened to the Jefferson Airplane.

Pat and Linda Peters eventually became closer than most sisters, discussing nearly everything in their lives. But during those intimate and wide-ranging conversations, Pat never divulged anything about her childhood or parents. Peters didn't press. "I knew that wasn't safe for me to ask about."

A central theme of their talks was Pat's "sense of not belonging and feeling different from other people." Peters thought her friend's feelings were shaped by the disruptive effects of her dysfunctional family. She could never find her place in the parental warfare, and she lived in constant fear of her father's alcohol-induced outbursts. "I think her social conscience came from those experiences," Peters said. "She had a strong desire to set things right [in her life and society]."

Unfortunately, Pat's desire to "set things right" eventually led to her death. Around 1970 she became immersed in raising money for several black organizations that had sprung up in Portland's inner city. At this time she became lovers with Donald Louis Merchant, an ex-convict, believes then–Assistant District Attorney Robert S. Gardner. Merchant had found his way to Portland after serving time at federal prisons in Terminal Island, California, and Sandstone, Minnesota, for unlawful possession of narcotics. Gardner believes that Merchant purportedly took money from Richardson to establish a camp for underprivileged black boys in Alaska.

Whatever the circumstances, late on the night of 15 October 1971, a white 1968 Jaguar driven by Merchant, with Pat in the passenger seat, slammed broadside into a large fir tree on Skyline Boulevard near the Sunset Highway in the West Hills, pinning the couple beneath the wreckage. By the time police arrived, Pat Richardson, thirty-four, was dead. Merchant, thirty-five, was taken to St. Vincent's Hospital in critical condition.

The family held Pat's funeral four days later at First Unitarian Church. "It was horrible," said Mary Lou Oberson, an old Packwood family neighbor. "It was terribly sad to see Pat's two little children there, with no mother."

Packwood, pained and red-eyed, bravely greeted guests. Oberson thought he was holding it together, "but his mind was somewhere else." His thoughts may well have been on the circumstances surrounding his sister's death, which gave him the first political crisis of his career. The public perception of his socially prominent sister flaunting a love affair with a black ex-convict and dying in a mysterious accident would not help Packwood win law-and-order votes.

Meanwhile, Gardner and fellow prosecutor Michael Bailey were investigating whether Merchant, as the driver, might have committed negligent homicide. The night of the accident the two prosecutors went to the hospital to get a statement from Merchant, but doctors said he was in no shape to talk. Packwood showed up later that evening, and doctors allowed him to see Merchant. Bailey stood near the door as Packwood entered the patient's room. He couldn't hear the conversation, but he could see Packwood lean over the bed to speak.

Bailey promptly called District Attorney Desmond Connall, who told him to subpoena Packwood. That seemed bold to Bailey, a twenty-five-year-old rookie prosecutor. He called a shift supervisor at the D.A.'s office who told him, "Oh, Des gets a little worked up sometimes. Let's not subpoena anyone tonight."

The next morning Gardner and Bailey went to talk with Campbell Richardson about his wife's accident. The house was barren. Bailey had to sit on a camping cooler in the vacant living room, and he saw blank spots on the wall where paintings used to hang. He was pretty sure Merchant had used an Alaskan boys home spiel to obtain a considerable sum of money from the Richardsons, and in fact, Campbell Richardson told the attorneys that his wife had given Merchant a lot of money, Bailey says.

While they were talking to Richardson, Bailey remembered that Packwood walked in. The senator told the two men that he'd never seen Merchant in his life. Bailey believed that was a lie because he had seen Packwood visit Merchant at the hospital just hours earlier. He did not let on that he had seen the senator there.

144   On 29 October, the district attorney's office filed negligent homicide charges against Merchant that carried a maximum sentence of five years and a $2,500 fine.

But before the case ever came to trial, Multnomah county circuit court judge Robert E. Jones instructed another assistant district attorney, Helen Kahlil, to get the Merchant file from Bailey's office and report to his chamber. Kahlil later told Bailey that Jones pushed through an agreement where prosecutors dropped the negligent homocide felony charge and accepted Merchant's guilty plea to the lesser misdemeanor charge of reckless driving. As a result, instead of facing a possible five-year sentence in the state prison, Merchant received a six-week sentence in the Multnomah county jail, five years probation, and a fine.

Bailey believes that Jones showed poor judgment in reducing the charge. The reduced sentence understandably delighted Merchant's attorney Stephen Walker. Walker, later a county circuit judge, acknowledged that "Bailey was right in saying that it was a light sentence" and especially for an ex-convict.

Packwood and Jones remained friends—Jones had officiated at Packwood's marriage to Georgie—and the senator later nominated Jones for a U. S. District Court judgeship in 1990. The senator and Jones declined to be interviewed. Gardner eventually became a county circuit judge. Bailey later entered private practice, where, two decades later, he voluntarily resigned from the bar pending some client complaints.

———

"Losing a child is the worst thing that can happen to you," Mindy said after her daughter's death. To fight her loneliness, she decorated her apartment with artistic, stylized photos of Pat and framed several photo collages of the entire family, including a separate shot of Bob and Georgie. She suffered a second loss when infirmities forced her to stop playing the piano. "I used to rely on piano playing to make friends," Mindy said. She treasured those memories by filling her apartment with busts of Bach and Beethoven, music boxes, and framed copies of her favorite sheet music.

Although Mindy kept friends posted about Bob's accomplishments in Washington, relations between them remained cool. "When he'd come to town, he'd take her to dinner—but he didn't spend as much time as we thought he should," Corrine Jennings said. One of her closest friends, Viola Oberson mused, "Maybe Gladys [Mindy] didn't know how to express love, and Bob didn't know how to accept it."

Georgie tried hard to penetrate Bob's defenses, working to become essential to his life. Before the world had ever heard of activist political wives like Rosalyn Carter, Tipper Gore, or Hillary Clinton, Georgie sought to play a major role in her husband's legislative agenda. She influenced his decision to expand his issues to include national leadership on such issues as the Equal Rights Amendment, gender discrimination in employment, and day care. She also served on the Women's Campaign Fund, a political action committee that assists women in both major parties.

But Georgie had powerfully mixed emotions about Bob's career rise. "She was a partner in his early career, make no mistake about that," says a female aide, "but that required she look away from the philandering. . . . I think Georgie thought that, 'as bad as this is, it's still a marriage, and a marriage to a U.S. senator at that.'"

That struggle was not easy. Georgie threw herself into campaigns to be closer to Bob, but her efforts sometimes drove the campaign staff to exhaustion. One staffer said, "I'll never forget one meeting when Georgie instructed me to 'create the kind of campaign where when Bob is driving a convertible in a parade, people run out to touch him the same way they did for Bobby Kennedy.'"

The couple did enjoy some happy moments. They loved hearing their son, Bill, perform at high school concerts, and Packwood's eyes grew moist at the sound of his son's voice. But father and son never had an easy relationship. Bill worked one summer as a Capitol tour guide, but that was as close to politics as he wished to get. When his father once pressed him about a political career, Bill reportedly replied that he would not want to be away from his family that much. He studied science at Penn State University and now lives in Michigan. "It became clear," one Packwood aide said, "that the senator and the son did not have a lot to do with each other."

Bill and his sister followed a more conservative path than their risk-taking father. Bill recoiled at the fast-paced designer drug culture of his affluent Bethesda public high school. He suggested that his parents send sister Shyla, three years his junior, to a private school, which they ultimately did.

Shyla shares her mother's love of nature. She enjoyed summers horseback riding at her uncle's ranch in the Blue Mountains near Elgin, Oregon, much as Georgie treasured riding and hiking with her father four decades earlier. Shyla chose to shun the East Coast and attend Southern Oregon State College in Ashland, an outdoor mecca in the Siskiyou Mountains near the California border.

But despite her enjoyment of her children, Georgie lived with an undercurrent of pain concerning her husband, which only grew deeper. Packwood aide Mike Salsgiver remembers a day when Georgie made an unexpected visit to Packwood's office and asked him about her husband's schedule. Before he could answer, Georgie snapped, "I am so tired of being passed around. I can't believe the life we have. We have absolutely nothing to show for it." Salsgiver was startled. Her cry of pain was so deep that he reshaped his views of both her and the senator.

Georgie heard rumors of Bob's womanizing but tried to discount them. On the few occasions that she confronted him, he denied that he was unfaithful. In retrospect, she realizes that she probably didn't really want to confirm the rumors. "I was concerned that perhaps he was doing some womanizing," she told a reporter. "I thought, 'Well, I can weather that.' It hurts so deeply, but he keeps coming back to me."

Alcohol further clouded their marriage. Georgie was very concerned about Bob's binge-drinking, and as early as his 1974 reelection campaign she pleaded with him to do something, even asking Jack Faust to persuade Packwood to get help.

Packwood normally drank heavily, but Georgie absolutely dreaded campaign years. Then Bob would go through periods of manic fund-raising and personal paranoia, during which his alcohol consumption would spike. His voice grew louder and, in the privacy of their home, he cruelly berated her. "I'm an enabler," she has said, referring to the times she covered up for her husband's behavior. "It's natural to do for people you love, but then when you're in public life, you want to protect him doubly. . . . It goes on and on. I used to marvel at it when I went to the Senate wives' lunch the First Lady gives every year at the White House. There'd be a roomful of capable, bright, loving, devoted women—a whole get-together of enablers."

———

The senator, who as a youth wanted to be an engineer, continued to think like an engineer. He was always seeking certainty and control through almost limitless research, much like another engineer turned politician, Jimmy Carter. The need to control everything, however, was both a strength and a weakness.

Attorney Peter Friedman served as Commerce Committee counsel working for Packwood and other senators. "I could brief most senators in twenty-five minutes about an upcoming issue, but Packwood was a son of a bitch. It'd take me one-half day to answer everything he wanted to know."

On the right issue, that made Packwood a legislative powerhouse. "I remember aides for Senator Inouye and other senators calling to challenge Packwood about a bill, and if I answered, 'Well, let's just debate that on the floor,' a lot of senators would back off because they wouldn't do the work to master the issue like they knew Packwood would."

Unfortunately, Packwood sometimes misapplied his prodigious talent for research. "Packwood had a psychological need to convince people that he was right," Friedman says. "It isn't just enough to pass the bill. Sometimes I could place a bill on the unanimous consent calendar where bills sail through, but Packwood said no. He'd say, 'Let's argue it on the Senate floor.'"

Julie Myers Williamson remembers one night when she and another aide, Roy Sampsel, sat down with Packwood at a

Portland restaurant. The three had been dashing from one appearance to another since about 7 A.M. and now they were finally able to take a break. But before a waitress could lay down a menu, the senator began analyzing every speech, meeting, and telephone call of the day.

Williamson interrupted, "Can't we talk about something besides politics?"

Packwood replied quizzically, "What else is there to talk about?"

Anyone who requires more than six or seven hours of sleep a night, or does not thrive in an ultraregimented office environment, should not work for Bob Packwood. He is typically at his desk by 6:30 A.M., two hours before many aides arrive. He has written a thirty-six-page memo instructing his staff on writing memos. A student of time management, Packwood uses a reading light on his dashboard and a stopwatch to time commuting routes. He orders beers two at a time so he never has to wait for a refill.

Close friend Dan Rather, the CBS anchor, who shares some of Packwood's intensity, nevertheless found it overwhelming after visiting the Senate office. "I'm not sure I could work for him. He drove himself and everyone around him unmercifully." Former aide Bob Van Brocklin, who ran on the same University of Oregon track team as Olympian Steve Prefontaine, said that his teammate's workouts consisted of running at a brutal pace until he threw up. "[Working for] Packwood reminded me of that," said Van Brocklin.

This lawmaker placed women in positions of importance in his campaigns as early as 1962; since coming to the Senate women have comprised the majority of his staff and a woman has almost always been his chief of staff.

Packwood's motives may not have been totally altruistic, however. Williamson remembers Packwood cynically saying that he liked hiring divorced women, or women with bad marriages, because they did not have relationshps that competed with working for him.

The type of women Packwood hired sometimes raised concern. A. Robert Smith covered Packwood more closely during the senator's first ten years than any other journalist. "You can tell a lot about a senator by the kind of people they hire," Smith said, "and Packwood's staff wasn't very reassuring in that regard. I had the impression that he mainly hired cute little girls."

Packwood also had a reputation for high staff turnover, translating into poor service for his constituents and missed legislative opportunities. Williamson, Paige Wagers, and other aides fled after Packwood allegedly harassed them. Such turnover threatened to jeopardize all that he had worked for, especially the feminist agenda.

But despite those problems, Packwood had long received more national press than most senators. He usually devoted three staff assistants to his media desk, whereas most senators used one or two. And he cultivated friendships with media stars. The Packwoods befriended Dan Rather, and columnist George Will became a regular at office parties. The senator hired William Safire's son as an intern, cementing their relationship.

Packwood traditionally returned journalists' phone calls before almost any others. "He is the only politician I know who'll call you with news tips," said Associated Press reporter Scott Sonner. "Press secretaries do that all the time, but Packwood's the only politician I've ever known who does." And this senator can fill reporters' television tape cans and notebooks faster than anyone. "He is articulate, funny, and charming—just an excellent interview," said ABC-TV Capitol correspondent Brit Hume.

But Hume saw signs of trouble. "At times Packwood struck me as bored. He suffers from the malaise of many bright people who don't see many things in black and white. Senate procedures are also very tedious, and I'm not sure that's always been his thing."

———

In the mid-1970s Packwood, who had long worn contact lenses, began having to squint to recognize people. His vision soon became so cloudy he could not identify some senators at all. Doctors gave him the grim diagnosis: rapidly developing cataracts that might blind him.

150   He could no longer drive from his home in suburban Bethesda to the Capitol—in fact, he couldn't drive anywhere. Georgie told their kids not to leave toys around because daddy might trip over them. Packwood could only read by turning his eyes to the side and looking through the edge where the cataract was thinnest. Staff members tried writing memos in huge type.

Portland's *Oregonian* dominates Oregon news coverage, and anything the paper reports is usually picked up by the rest of the Northwest's media. Packwood understood that but found the newspaper's new Capitol correspondent Bill Keller annoyingly undeferential. So Packwood planted the story of his failing eyesight in the less-respected *Oregon Journal* to underplay the news. Packwood's office invited *Journal* reporter Joe Berger to the senator's home, where sitting by the backyard pool, he mundanely explained the seemingly routine corrective surgery. He showed Berger some unusable surgical photos, and they soon moved on to other subjects. The story ran in the *Journal*, but it received little play elsewhere.

The *Washington Post* gave Packwood's health problems more coverage than his home state did. The *Post* reported that Dr. Charles Kelman, a New York City physician, successfully removed the senator's cataracts during the Senate's 1976 August recess, using a technique he had pioneered. Packwood told the *Post*, "I thought if worse comes to worse, I could handle this job blind. I thought what the components of the job are—being able to listen, pick up facts, and dictate. Other people can read to me. As for campaigning, I thought I'd do it the same as now. Go to a Rotary or high school." But it never came to that. Packwood survived the threat, and Oregon voters were hardly aware that there had been a crisis.

———

After rolling out his taboo-breaking abortion legislation, Packwood gathered no moss. In the fall of 1971, he began a campaign to inform his colleagues, sometimes in startling terms, of the effects of unchecked population growth. On the first of each month, he delivered a brief message into the Congressional Record similar to this entry dated 1 November 1971:

I wish to report that according to current Census Bureau approximations the total population of the United States as of today is 208,259,635. This represents an increase of 170,369 since Oct. 1, or roughly the size of Kansas City, Kansas. It also represents an addition of 2,128,810 since Nov. 1 of last year, an increase which is approximately three times the size of San Francisco.

In the two years following the *Roe* v. *Wade* victory, the right-to-life movement fought against federal abortion funding for low-income women. Packwood beat them in 1974 and 1975 but could not stem the tide in 1976. That year, a defeated Packwood vowed, "I do not think that, somehow, someway, God has spoken on one side of the issue. . . . I want you in the U.S. Senate tonight at six o'clock to write and freeze in your Constitution a final and definitive view of abortion that shall not be changed forevermore."

In 1977 Packwood offered an amendment to delete an anti-abortion provision from an appropriations bill. "If we do not fund abortions, these 250,000 to 300,000 women who now receive abortions, paid for by federal or state monies, are either going to have babies they do not want or are going to go to backroom abortionists," he said.

The debate erupted into a shouting match between Packwood and Senator Jake Garn (R-Utah), an abortion foe. "I pray to God that the Senate is not that haughty and not that disdainful," Packwood said. Jesse Helms countered that "the bottom line" on abortion is that it constitutes "the deliberate termination of an innocent human life."

Packwood led pro-choice brigades in every abortion battle over the next decade. He stood alone in opposing abortion critic Joseph Califano as Secretary of Health, Education, and Welfare. He pilloried the Carter administration for backsliding on abortion issues.

Never totally content with being just a senator, he now focused on his national ambitions and became a man who transcended single issues. His agenda expanded to encompass a full range of women's issues, including leadership on the Equal Rights Amendment, pregnancy leave, and day care. ERA

152 replaced ZPG as the defining acronym in his lexicon. Very quietly, Packwood distanced himself from population-control champion Paul Ehrlich. With greater fanfare, he advertised his friendship with feminist Gloria Steinem.

Packwood and Steinem had shared dinners together in New York City. "Don't say [dinners] alone," Steinem once begged a reporter. They made an unlikely couple. "You know, Gloria is a socialist," Packwood said. "She regards many of my economic views as absolutely wacky, but on women's issues she regards me as almost a hundred percenter. She appreciates the fact that women predominate in the upper echelons of this office, and are paid accordingly. She appreciates the fact that this was true long before it became an issue," he told reporter Tom Bates.

Steinem helped Packwood exploit his right-to-life foes, even when the threats were not viable. The senator claimed that anti-abortionists had raised a tremendous amount of money to use against him in the 1980 general election. In fact, they were nearly bankrupt and not about to contribute to his equally pro-choice Democratic opponent. Nevertheless, Packwood asked Steinem to sign a fund-raising letter claiming that right-to-life wolves jeopardized his future. The appeal raised an estimated $750,000 from concerned feminists nationwide.

After his 1974 reelection, he had lobbied hard for a seat on the Senate Finance Committee. He got it, in part, because of the seniority system he had tried to dismantle six years earlier. The panel oversaw family planning policy, which he continued to strongly support, but now he emphasized the aspect of women's rights rather than population control.

The Finance Committee also sets tax policy for every business and wage-earner in the country, an interest that was right up Packwood's alley, as well as that of his late father. The elder Packwood, after all, had been Oregon's nonpareil tax lobbyist for three decades, and he taught his son well. Bob taught himself that the committee was a splendid place from which to look for money from loophole-seeking corporations.

This special-interest cash would become the gunpowder for Packwood's national agenda. Finance had not previously been a workbench for advocating moderate Republican values, but Packwood—now much more issue-oriented than he was earlier in his career—made it into one. He crafted a plan to enable the GOP to better compete with Democrats for the votes of women, minorities, and the poor. His staff spent six months working out details of the proposal.

Packwood declared his position in 1977 before a friendly audience at the annual Dorchester Conference. Republicans were out of power in the White House, Congress, and most statehouses, and they needed new ideas. He opened with a rhetorical question: How could Republicans compete with Democrats for those voters who liked social services? The answer, the senator said, lay in the tax code. He advocated delivering services through tax credits and deductions rather than the costly bureaucracy-littered programs favored by liberal Democrats.

Unlike the progressive model of Rockefeller and Javits, which involved big government, Packwood used the tools of a conservative—personal and business tax incentives—to seek a liberal's goals of employer-mandated health care, pensions, energy conservation, day care, and pregnancy leave. Packwood's ideas appealed to moderate Democrats, but conservative Republicans saw the devil's handiwork. They feared that loopholes reducing Treasury revenues might increase tax pressure on businesses to make up the difference.

Conservatives excoriated Packwood's hybrid platform. "A prescription for a corporate state," sniffed Nobel Prize–winning economist Milton Friedman. The American Conservative Union's *Battleground* magazine satirized the senator with a front-page article entitled, "Packwood's Plan Mussolinism Warmed Over," accompanied by a cartoon of a GOP elephant dressed as Il Duce snapping a Fascist salute.

His environmental and social stances became similarly unique. The moderate label no longer neatly fit him. Packwood was seldom middle of the road about anything. "Moderate" simply meant the mean of his extremes. Even as church leaders loathed Packwood's relentless abortion advocacy, he continued to battle for hefty tuition credits for church schools. Environmentalists applauded his advocacy of solar energy, returnable

154 bottles, and bike paths, while oil executives considered him a champion for corporate tax breaks. "The environmental issues he supported tended to be ones where he didn't have to oppose a big business lobby," Keller says.

Packwood successfully placed his tax program onto the congressional agenda. But he needed more clout to advance the plan, along with his women's agenda and his ultimate dream of running for president. He got what he needed in 1977, when Senate Republicans chose him to run their campaign arm, the National Republican Senatorial Committee (NRSC).

The NRSC operated out of a converted men's room and had virtually no staff, but Packwood turned everything around. Using direct mail techniques, he increased the number of individual GOP contributors from 40,000 to 100,000 in two years. He also wanted to turn low contributors into high rollers. The problem was that donors could give $20,000 to the NRSC, but only $1,000 to individual candidates. Some fat cats gave no more than $1,000 to the NRSC because they had no influence over how the money was spent. Packwood solved that problem by letting big donors serve on "trust committees" to determine which Senate races received the most money. That encouraged them to give the maximum of $20,000 because they could aim more money toward their favorite candidates.

Another venue for gaining political clout was the Finance Committee chamber. While writing loopholes for day care centers to please feminists, Packwood penned even more for corporate special interests in the fields of banking, cable television, insurance, oil, and timber. These grateful contributors helped fatten the Packwood-run NRSC coffers from a paltry $2 million in 1975–76, to nearly $40 million by 1982.

Even better, the Democrats couldn't accuse Packwood of making *too* much money. The direct mail success increased the middle-class donor base, thereby lowering the GOP's average donation to about $20, and partially inoculating the party from charges of being in the grip of special interests.

The historic GOP campaign spending edge over Democrats widened, and in 1978 Republicans gained three Senate seats. Packwood dramatically increased GOP power in the Senate before the world had become aware of Jesse Helms's Congressional Club or Reverend Jerry Falwell's Moral Majority. Democratic pollster Patrick Caddell pinpointed those successes as the start of the Ronald Reagan–era surge.

NRSC chairmen served two-year terms, but Packwood remained the power behind the throne even after he stepped down in January 1979. He installed his own aides to continue running the committee, including executive director Bob Moore.

The NRSC aided the election victories of some conservatives, including such abortion foes as Helms, Roger Jepsen of Iowa, Bill Armstrong of Colorado, and Alfonse D'Amato of New York, but Packwood did not mind that irony. What mattered was that they were Republicans. They valued Packwood as the party's premier moneyman, and several moderate Republicans saw him as a role model. According to Packwood aide Bob Witeck, pro-choice GOP senators John Heinz of Pennsylvania and Larry Pressler of South Dakota plumbed Packwood's feminist fund-raising apparatus for ideas. A few years later D'Amato, representing a state with two million Jewish citizens, recognized Packwood's expertise in soliciting contributions from Jewish voters in Oregon, a state that had barely 10,000 Jews.

As Packwood's reelection approached, U.S. Secretary of Transportation Neil Goldschmidt and U.S. Representative Les AuCoin analyzed their chances of defeating him. Any Democratic opponent would need to squeeze every drop from traditionally liberal Jewish and women's groups to challenge the well-monied Packwood. Goldschmidt loomed as the toughest foe. The youthful, charismatic former mayor of Portland, who is Jewish, had a high-performance organization and the best fund-raising potential of any Democrat.

Packwood began hiring campaign staff in mid-1979. "We wanted to organize early to scare Goldschmidt out of the race," said campaign aide Gary Eisler. Packwood had been pro-Israel since his election to the Senate, but he seemed to intensify his pro-Israeli rhetoric as Goldschmidt's popularity rose.

As President Carter tried to maintain the Camp David peace treaties, Packwood teetered on the edge of demagoguery. At an

156 American-Israeli Public Affairs Committee event, he declared, "Not one inch of soil will the United States require Israel to give up without irrevocable treaties with her neighbors. . . . Not one inch will Israel have to give up for flimsy guarantees from the United Nations."

The waves from the Packwood splash reached Jerusalem. The *Jerusalem Post* reported that Packwood had accused "Carter and Assistant Secretary of State Harold Saunders, by name, of undermining Israel's negotiating position during the forthcoming West Bank and Gaza Strip autonomy negotiations" in a speech to a pro-Israeli political action committee in Washington.

"Carter was not present during the dinner at the Capitol's Hilton, but his chief political aide, Hamilton Jordan, and Saunders were there, sitting passively on the dais as Packwood lashed out against the administration's criticism of Israel's settlements on the West Bank."

Ironically, Packwood's hard-charging chief of staff, Mimi Weyforth, was capable of some startlingly insensitive remarks about Jews masquerading as rough humor. One day, as the office prepared for Goldschmidt's challenge, a campaign aide asked Weyforth to fill him in on the origins of Packwood's strong pro-Israeli views.

"Well," Weyforth answered, "don't you know the senator went to NYJew Law School?"

Shocked, the aide responded, "But Mimi, I'm Jewish."

Weyforth retorted with a strange pun: "You mean I hired Jew—and I didn't even know it?"

As their conversation came to an abrupt halt, she told her subordinate in an attempt at humor, "Weyforth is a German name, and don't you ever forget that."

Although the aide felt that Weyforth's attempts at humor were "cruel and uncalled for," he did not complain to Packwood; he sensed that the senator and his chief of staff were personally close, and he did not want to jeopardize his job. The aide did not accuse Packwood of any anti-Semitic remarks.

In January 1980 the *Oregonian* reported that the Packwood reelection organization was in full gear, and ran a photo of

Packwood proudly standing in front of one hundred of his campaign leaders. A few days later, Goldschmidt decided not to enter the race. "We believe that photo had something to do with that," Eisler said.

Two hundred delegates rose to applaud as the keynote speaker for the 1978 Oregon Women's Political Caucus convention buoyantly strode to the podium. Politicians dream of days like this, and Packwood basked in their adulation. As the premier male feminist in American politics, the senator's most supportive and, at times, even worshipful audiences were feminist conclaves. Packwood's grip on this liberal constituency had frustrated Goldschmidt and other Democratic rivals; but the women's movement was changing, and Packwood was about to trip.

As he began taking audience questions, a young woman asked: "Do you support antidiscrimination legislation for gay people?"

Surprised, he responded, "No, I think homosexuals are disgusting."

After a moment of awkward silence, the crowd burst into catcalls. "Several people just walked out," said Anne Greenfield, a National Women's Political Caucus board member.

Packwood might have gotten by with such a remark five years earlier, but by 1978 gay rights had become a central plank of the women's rights movement. If Packwood opposed gay rights, feminists would not endorse him no matter how exemplary his women's rights record.

Seeking to heal the breach, Greenfield arranged a summit between the senator and feminist leaders at the private home of a Packwood supporter active in abortion rights. The agenda included abortion, ERA, and an ominous new issue—gay and lesbian rights.

To make the senator comfortable, Greenfield invited several pro-Packwood Republican women and kept radical feminists away. But anxiety pervaded, and everyone tiptoed around the taboo subject. "It was tense," Greenfield said. Finally one woman raised the question everyone wanted to discuss. "Why do you oppose gay and lesbian rights?" she asked Packwood. The senator surprised them. "I don't oppose that. I'm reevaluating how I feel. Just be patient with me."

Greenfield saw hope in that answer. "He didn't expressly say no, as every other politician in the country had. I'd hoped we'd turned the corner." The state women's group mailed questionnaires to candidates in the May 1980 primary election asking about their views on a number of issues, including gay rights. Packwood responded by agreeing to cosponsor a federal gay rights law as soon as he dispatched three New Right opponents in the 1980 GOP primary. He won that election easily and subsequently joined Senator Lowell Weicker of Connecticut in sponsoring pioneer national gay rights legislation.

Packwood's positions on Israel and gay rights had outmaneuvered his rivals. Major Democrats declined to run, leaving the nomination to promising, but little-known state Senator Ted Kulongoski.

But nagging clouds obscured the blue reelection skies. Packwood's private behavior threatened to ruin everything. Brit Hume had first noticed Packwood's womanizing in the early 1970s. "My main impression [of him then] was he had quite a reputation as a ladies' man," he said.

The term *ladies' man*, however, connotes mutual consent, and some of the women Packwood approached saw that this was not his primary concern. One woman, Capitol elevator operator Kerry Whitney, found herself alone with the senator in the elevator in the summer of 1977. As soon as the twenty-seven-year-old woman closed the elevator doors, Packwood "cocked his head to the side and said 'Kiss' and immediately grabbed me by the shoulders, pushed me against the wall of the elevator, and started kissing me on the lips. He stopped as he felt the elevator coming to a halt."

Shocked, she wondered, "Where did that come from?" Packwood forcibly kissed her at least ten times during the eight months she worked as a Senate elevator operator.

One day Packwood asked if he could drop over to her apartment. Whitney, feeling intimidated, agreed. When he arrived that night he introduced himself to her roommate and asked for a drink. After Whitney got him a beer, he started kissing her. "Wait a minute," she said. "What do you want from me?"

"Two things," replied the senator. "First thing is, I want to make love to you. Second thing is, you have a job where you hear things, and I want to hear what you hear."

Whitney countered, "Well, you're married, aren't you?"

"Yes," he said, "and I love my wife very much."

As Whitney later told a reporter from the *Dallas Morning News,* "I just didn't have the backbone to say, 'Get the hell out of my house, you creep.' I was trying to be nice and hospitable. So I said, 'Let's go sit in the backyard, so we can talk.'"

He told her of his upcoming Senate reelection, "suggesting I might want to work on it," she said. The prospect didn't entice her. When he asked to spend the night, she told him no and led him to the door. Outside, he began banging on her door. Later, he telephoned her.

"I was afraid," said Whitney, who now runs a small fabric-design business. "No way would I let him in. I thought, 'This guy is weird. This guy is sick.'"

Packwood's advisors feared that he would cross the line and ignite a genuine scandal. They especially worried about the young women who were volunteering for Packwood's campaign in droves because of his pro-choice views. As his campaign prepared literature proclaiming him a "family man," Eugene-area chairperson Gena Hutton complained about Packwood's sexual conduct to Craig Smith, an NRSC veteran who was now chairing Packwood's 1980 reelection. Smith told her that Packwood had made similar advances to other women, and that staff members had tried many times to talk with the senator about changing his behavior.

A campaign organizer who traveled with the senator was told by a top aide to refuse Packwood's requests to help him pick up women. "I was warned that I might be recruited by him to pimp for him, especially in my position of recruiting volunteers," he told writer Trip Gabriel. "I can recall being taken aside and told: 'This kind of stuff happens. Don't let it happen.'"

But the senator's private behavior remained secret. Packwood spent $3 million to Kulongoski's $300,000, and confidently stumped alongside his old Zero Population Growth ally,

160 vice presidential candidate George Bush. Packwood defeated
Kulongoski by eight percentage points in November. And there
was more good news. The NRSC helped Republicans take control of the Senate for the first time in three decades, elevating
Packwood to powerful committee chairmanships and national
center stage.

More important for the Republicans, however, was the news
that Jimmy Carter and the Democrats were out of the White
House. Ronald Reagan, retired movie star, former Governor of
California, and formidable ideological conservative, had been
elected to the presidency on a wave of voter approval.

10

As soon as he took the oath of office, President Ronald Reagan went to work implementing the most far-reaching social agenda of this century: seeking to overturn abortion laws, halt busing as a means of integrating schools, and restore prayer in school. He began with a bang, convincing Congress to reduce spending programs and cut tax rates for the wealthy. His momentum seemed unstoppable—no new president had been this effective since Franklin D. Roosevelt's first one hundred days.

By the spring of 1981, the nation's conservatives were delirious with joy. But liberals, who saw the gains of the last two decades slipping away, were scared. Every evening at 6:30 P.M., as the "CBS Evening News" ended, the telephone consoles lit up at Planned Parenthood headquarters in Washington, D.C. The callers—mainly single and working mothers—were frightened by the nightly reports of newly elected President Ronald Reagan's pledge to outlaw abortion. They asked:

"Can this really happen?"

"Will I have to move to get an abortion?"

"No," Planned Parenthood lobbyist Bill Hamilton promised them, the Democrats could stop Reagan. But although Hamilton mouthed those reassurances over the phone, he worried how long the pro-choice lobby could withstand the assault. **161**

Reagan's surrogate in the Senate, Jesse Helms of North Carolina, began the social reform war with legislation to nullify the 1973 Supreme Court's *Roe* v. *Wade* decision, which had legalized abortion. Helms proposed granting constitutional rights to unborn human beings, which would make terminating a pregnancy the same as murder. He went further, seeking to strip the courts of their power to overrule antiabortion laws.

By March 1982, the bill had slowly proceeded through when Helms got Majority Leader Howard Baker's permission to pop the measure directly onto the Senate floor as an amendment. Helms, along with GOP Senators Dan Quayle of Indiana and Alfonse D'Amato of New York, had gathered more than fifty committed votes to ensure passage; their allies in the House of Representatives were similarly gaining momentum. Liberals had to do something: if they lost on abortion now, conservative school prayer and busing victories were almost certain to follow.

Planned Parenthood entered a coalition with the National Abortion Rights Action League (NARAL), National Organization of Women (NOW), the American Civil Liberties Union (ACLU), and Common Cause, to fight the White House and Helms. The coalition issued a nationwide call for people to join in the battle. At home in Oregon, twenty-nine-year-old activist Mary Heffernan heard the call. She was no stranger to the issue, having worked with Senator Packwood on abortion issues in Oregon. Heffernan had later donated money to Packwood's 1980 campaign and coordinated his campaign volunteers. He had even written her parents in Maine, lauding their daughter's hard work and talent. Now she responded to the need for pro-choice activists in the most positive way she could: by moving across the country to become a lobbyist for the beleaguered NARAL.

Coalition members knew that Helms stood to win a straight up-or-down vote. They decided to adopt a last-ditch tactic that the North Carolina senator had used himself in opposing civil rights for blacks: the filibuster. That strategy was fraught with danger. Heffernan and her colleagues knew Reagan would attack them as hypocrites for exploiting the maneuver, but they had no choice.

Now they needed a senator to lead the filibuster—a tall order in 1982. The power and energy of the New Right had intimidated even the staunchest liberal Democrats. One by one, they were turned down by Ted Kennedy, Bill Bradley, Joe Biden, Gary Hart, Daniel Moynihan, Alan Cranston, and Howard Metzenbaum. That left Heffernan and her allies with one final hope—liberal Republican leader Bob Packwood, the nation's premier abortion advocate.

Packwood had led many national abortion fights, but never against a popular president from his own party and for such high stakes. Now feminists were asking him to put his White House patronage—and quite possibly his future within the Republican party—on the line.

In perhaps the most courageous act of his career, Packwood accepted command of the filibuster army. Yet as Helms marched inexorably toward his goal in the early summer of 1982, Packwood grew somber at strategy meetings. The alliance, waiting for the right moment to launch a filibuster, picked the days after the August 1982 recess in the wan hope that as the general election approached, more senators would vote their way.

They unleashed the filibuster on 15 August. Filibusters, which generally consist of speaking interminably in order to hold the floor to delay or kill legislation, can become a mockery. In the 1930s, for example, Democratic Senator Huey Long of Louisiana conducted a filibuster by reading gumbo recipes into the Congressional Record. But Packwood took the high road and began the abortion filibuster eruditely, quoting his predecessor Wayne Morse on constitutional law, and pacing the Senate aisles while reading aloud from a 320-page tome entitled *Abortion In America—The Origins and Evolution of National Policy*. By the end of the first day he had progressed to the year 1840 in that book.

Suddenly, the abortion foes sensed the momentum turning. They needed sixty votes to silence Packwood. Helms appealed directly to Reagan to intensify White House lobbying efforts, and the president turned the pressure on. He even called some

164 wavering senators from Air Force One, telling them, "It is time to stand and be counted on this issue."

The NARAL office resembled a battle station where weary supporters regrouped for encouragement and intelligence reports before returning to the fray. Lobbyists and volunteers worked day and night, gathering information and actively seeking Senate votes. Heffernan and other lobbyists routinely went back and forth from the coalition offices to Packwood's office, discussing strategy.

One day, Heffernan arrived at Packwood's opulent Russell Senate Building suite and stepped inside his high-ceilinged interior office. Facing Packwood across his massive desk, she laid out her concerns: amendments to draft and votes to count. As she spoke, Packwood suddenly rose from his seat, walked around the corner of his desk, grabbed her shoulder, and kissed her on the lips. He held the kiss for several seconds, pushing his tongue into her mouth. Heffernan, almost as tall as Packwood at five-foot-nine, broke away from his grasp. She recoiled, glaring at him, trying to send him an unmistakable visual message: *This isn't going anywhere.*

She left the building in shocked silence, feeling that Packwood had betrayed their professional relationship. Packwood's act forced Heffernan to make a soul-searching decision: should she defend her feelings or her cause? She chose to continue working with Packwood as a lobbyist, explaining, "Abortion rights were on the line."

A lobbyist's lifeblood is access to senators. Anything that diminishes that access, including unwanted sexual advances, harms the movement that the lobbyist represents. Although Heffernan continued to work with Packwood, she saw him less frequently and made sure they were never alone. Eventually, she turned down a coveted Packwood staff job that she would have otherwise accepted.

———

In September, conservatives failed to get the sixty Senate votes they needed to break the filibuster. Packwood had stopped the New Right, and they would never regain their momentum.

Helms's efforts to imperil abortion rights were dead, and the
Packwood-led liberals also threw knockout punches to Reagan's pro-school prayer and anti-school busing measures. For
Reagan, the days of a subservient Congress were over. He
would not win another major domestic achievement until his
second term.

Packwood was now the most powerful feminist advocate in
America. Women's groups showered him with contributions
and boosted his dreams of running for president in 1988 and
1992. Although some knew firsthand about his womanizing,
their fear of politicians like Reagan, Helms, and Quayle exceeded their loathing of Packwood's private behavior.

Packwood began to plan a run for the presidency. As a
liberal Republican seeking his party's nomination against
a popular conservative incumbent, he would have to take
risks. Fortunately, the president gave him several targets. The
economy had slid into the doldrums, and unemployment
reached post-Depression highs. Two hallmarks of Reagan's
popular appeal—perceived decency and idealism—were damaged by budget director David Stockman's article in the
Atlantic Monthly, alleging that Reagan's team was greedy, de-
ceitful, and incompetent.

Reagan's policies had alienated blacks, Jews, and blue-collar
workers. Farmers were forced to accept near-Depression prices
for their produce. Even some business leaders were ridiculing
supply-side economics. Polls showed Reagan's approval rating
dropping to the lowest levels of the Nixon and Carter eras.

Packwood also saw that the nation's demographics were
changing—the country no longer fit the 1950s *Reader's Digest*
mold that Reagan epitomized. More and more women were becoming heads of households, and Hispanics and blacks already
outnumbered Caucasians in California, Texas, Florida, and
other states.

Seeing Reagan's weaknesses, however, made his situation
complex. Although it gave him plenty of places to attack, Reagan's vulnerability increased the risks for *all* Republicans
seeking public office. After the 1980 election, Packwood had
reclaimed the NRSC chairmanship, and he now feared that

166 Republicans would squander their hard-fought Senate majority in the 1982 general election. For Packwood, who had probably saved his career and that of many other Republicans by repudiating Nixon during Watergate, the choice was clear: to succeed, GOP candidates would need to break with the president.

In March 1982 the senator sought out Donald Rothberg, the chief national political writer for the Associated Press, and declared war on Reagan:

> [The president] has an idealized concept of America, and maybe Americans wish we were that, maybe Americans wish we all looked alike, and went to the same middle-of-the-road Protestant church, and we'd be better off. I don't think we'd be better off. . . .
>
> You cannot write working women off, the blacks off, and the Hispanics off, and the Jews off, and assume you're going to build a party on the white, Anglo-Saxon males over 40. There aren't enough of us left. . . .

Packwood was not finished. He recounted White House meetings with Reagan and majority leader Robert Dole, in which the president's anecdotal replies to complex problems seemed "on a totally different track." To make his point, Packwood described Reagan's response to news of the impending $120 billion deficit.

> And the president says, "You know, a person yesterday, a young man, went into a grocery store and he had an orange in one hand and bottle of vodka in the other, and he paid for the orange with food stamps, and he took the change and paid for the vodka. That's what's wrong.

After listening to Reagan's simplistic meanderings, Packwood said that he and other Senate leaders would "just shake our heads."

Packwood's public ridicule made the president furious, and he told the wayward senator off personally in a telephone call from Air Force One. In retaliation, the White House blocked Packwood recommendations for federal appointments and fired former Packwood aide Pamela Aycock as a Commerce Department congressional liaison. Reagan aides forced Packwood to tear up a $1 million NRSC fund-raising mail piece because the president objected to having his picture alongside Packwood's in the literature. The White House also encouraged beer baron Adolph Coors's efforts to boycott the NRSC as long as Packwood was at the helm.

But Packwood's high-risk tactics ultimately worked. By taking the brunt of Reagan's anger he enabled other moderates to distance themselves from Reagan with relative immunity. That November the GOP lost twenty-six seats in the House, twice as many as the post–World War II average, but Packwood's Senate Republicans made history by halting Democratic gains. They prevailed largely because several candidates—including Minnesota's David Durenberger, Vermont's Robert Stafford, and Connecticut's Lowell Weicker—made clear their independence from Reagan.

Some Washington pundits could now foresee a scenario in which the economy sank so low that it dragged the Reagan administration down with it. Who then could be a more compelling moderate Republican presidential candidate than the ultimate anti-Reagan Republican, Bob Packwood?

The president continued to retaliate. In December, Senate Republicans stopped Packwood's bid for an unprecedented second consecutive NRSC chairmanship term. Reagan loyalist Richard Lugar of Indiana defeated Packwood by a 29-to-25 vote.

Packwood had also surfaced as a major obstacle to Reagan's Middle East policy, just as he had been to Jimmy Carter's. In 1981 he had galvanized opposition to the White House proposal to sell AWACS radar aircraft to Saudi Arabia. As that debate began, the president personally lobbied Packwood at the White House. But the senator emerged from that meeting to blast the proposed $8.5 billion arms sale:

> Before we sell any more arms to the Saudis, including AWACS, they owe us and the world—if they are serious about peace—some evidence that they are willing at least to bargain with Israel. . . . All they have done is go around with a wrecking ball, breaking relations with Egypt, trying to stop traffic through the Suez Canal, leading the Arab boycott of Egypt, and financing the PLO.

168   The AWACS fight created a major threat to presidential prestige, and the White House went full throttle to edge out a 52-to-48 Senate victory. But in defeat Packwood became a hero to the pro-Israeli lobby, and he used that support to win campaign contributions from the Jewish community and its supporters. In the next major Middle East arms sale debate, in 1984, Packwood organized Senate opposition so well that Reagan withdrew a proposed sale of anti-aircraft missiles to Jordan. Reagan aides were frantic. They tried to embarrass Packwood by spreading rumors that he had emphasized the issue in order to attract Jewish campaign contributions for his 1986 Senate race. Packwood had indeed honed his speeches well to pro-Israeli PACs; former campaign aide Gary Eisler admired Packwood's uncanny ability to "talk the talk" in appealing to Jewish groups.

In comments to the American Israel Public Affairs Committee, Packwood explained that he had never known any Jews as he was growing up, but all that changed when he went to law school in New York City.

I love the people who say, "Some of my best friends are Jews." At NYU you had no choice. Or you had no friends: one of the two. When Yom Kippur came and I went to school, I thought I was there on Sunday; the school was 75 percent deserted, and I thought perhaps I had lost track of a day some place along the way.

I was there during the 1956 War. . . . And I gained a knowledge and appreciation and, yes, a love of the Jewish tradition, and lore, life and history, respect for civil liberties, and everything Americans think came only with the Magna Carta and the Anglo-Saxon world.

We really are unaware of how much we owe the "Judeo" part of our Judeo-Christian heritage.

Packwood always began raising money several years in advance of each Senate election. He asked his old NYU roommate Paul Berger, who was now with the Arnold and Porter law firm, to sign a direct mail piece identifying himself as "the guy who introduced Senator Bob Packwood to the Jews."

"When others caved in to political pressure, Bob Packwood led the fight against the AWACS sale to Saudi Arabia," Berger's letter read. The letter also contained an Israeli shekel coin pasted to a note from Packwood, in which the senator explained that he carried one in his pocket to remind him of Israel. Packwood urged readers to "please carry the attached shekel with you. And then every time you pull out a handful of change to make a phone call or feed a parking meter, you'll remember that Israel's future and growth depend on each of us doing our part."

Inevitably, Packwood's strong pro-Israeli stand came to the attention of hate groups. At one point, in December 1984, he received death threats from the Aryan Nation, a white supremacist group affiliated with The Order, whose members had connections with the group convicted of the murder of Alan Berg, a Jewish radio talk-show host in Denver. The FBI had to dispatch agents to protect Packwood's family for several weeks.

Packwood's presidential ambitions were no secret. Throughout the 1980s the senator displayed a color photo on his outer office wall that showed him enjoying an intimate conversation with Ronald Reagan in the wingback chairs of the Oval Office. The president had inscribed on the photo, "Dear Bob: I hope this is a picture of the future as well as the present. Best Regards, Ron."[9]

After defeating Reagan's domestic agenda in 1982 and 1983, Packwood's confidence soared. The timing was good. He could run for president in 1984 or 1988 without having to sacrifice his Senate seat; 1988 looked particularly appealing because Reagan would step down that year and Vice President George Bush was vulnerable.

This brazenly liberal Republican probably knew he could never capture the nomination, but people run for reasons other than winning. Packwood could out-debate any Republican candidate on the horizon, and he relished recognition of that fact. He also knew that his well-financed campaign could succeed in crowded primaries in liberal New York, Pennsylvania, and Illinois, where his pro-choice and pro-Israeli views had carved out a delegate constituency. Packwood might win enough overall

---

9. Steve Forrester. 20 October 1981, *Northwest Newsletter.*

170   delegates to influence the Republican convention, the nomination, and the future of the country.

In mid-1983 Packwood traveled to New Hampshire and Iowa to meet newspaper editors and feminist and Jewish groups. That autumn, he summoned key supporters to a resort on Maryland's Eastern shore to further discuss a presidential race. His wife, Georgie, accompanied him to that meeting. She had once been excited about working with Bob on causes that were important to her, including women's rights, but when Packwood aides asked for her thoughts about the race, she could scarcely disguise her displeasure, saying, "I guess I can get used to the idea."

Georgie had begun to spend many depressive hours in bed, thinking about the depths into which their marriage had fallen. At one Washington dinner party, Bob had gotten drunk and belittled her, embarrassing both herself and the other guests. The Packwoods left abruptly, and as soon as they got in the car Bob passed out cold. As Georgie drove home, he came to and began bemoaning his alcoholic father's failures.

When they returned home to Bethesda from the meeting on the Eastern shore, Georgie firmly told Bob that a presidential campaign was out of the question unless he quit drinking. Several weeks later he angrily shelved plans to challenge Reagan, and began referring to Georgie as his "albatross."

Georgie regularly confronted him about his binge drinking: "I would say to him, 'Tell me why it is that you drink.' And he'd say, 'Because I feel so socially insecure.'" In fact, Packwood could put away an enormous amount of alcohol with little obvious effect.

According to the *New Yorker*,[10]

> Witnesses to his binges are awed by the memory of them—Packwood ordering two drinks at a time at a bar, or going through several pitchers of beer as if it were water. "I drink immense quantities of liquid, it doesn't matter what it is," Packwood said. "I will, on occasion, drink a gallon of milk

---

10. Peter J. Boyer. 4 April 1994, *New Yorker*.

at dinner, or two or three pitchers of water. And when I drank alcohol I would go through beer and wine the same way." He was seldom a sloppy drunk, his companions remember, and he almost never paid the price of a hangover. "It's not my fault," he said. "Chemistry."

Packwood's drinking puzzled Georgie because he almost never drank at home. She belatedly realized that drinking had become his "way of life at the office."

The moratorium on presidential campaigning changed none of his habits. While on a road trip, Packwood and aide Mike Salsgiver once spent the night in the Columbia River town of The Dalles, and Packwood invited Salsgiver to dinner at the motel cocktail lounge. Salsgiver had served on a sensitive military assignment in Turkey near the Soviet Union border, and Packwood pumped him for details over dinner and drinks.

At about 10:30 P.M., Packwood had satisfied his curiosity about Turkey. He abruptly told Salsgiver, "Okay, you can take off now."

As Salsgiver left the cocktail lounge, he walked right into Elaine Franklin, then one of Packwood's senior aides.

Franklin: Where is the senator?

Salsgiver: In the cocktail lounge.

Franklin: Where?!

Salsgiver: In the, uh, bar.

Franklin: [erupting in anger] Don't you ever leave him there alone with his worst impulses.

Salsgiver: Elaine, he told me to leave.

Franklin: You need to have balls in this job—and stay with him. [Pause] Well, you've done enough damage for the night.

Former Packwood aide Ann Elias originally recruited Franklin to volunteer on the senator's 1980 campaign. Packwood soon hired her as a staff assistant, and by summer she was managing the Portland office. She steadily rose up the hierarchy. Georgie was not alone in noticing that Franklin managed to spend time alone with Bob in a hot tub, wearing a skimpy bikini on a swing through Oregon. Franklin denied any sexual relationship. "The senator is fond of hot tubs, and he does a lot of his thinking in them," Franklin explained to writer Tom Bates. "On many occasions he'd suggest that someone get their bathing suit on and meet him in the hot tub, me included."

Packwood's leadership on women's rights and the Middle East had made him well known to the media and political activists. His next issue, tax reform, brought him to the attention of nearly everyone else.

Just weeks after dispatching Walter Mondale in the 1984 presidential election, Ronald Reagan rocked Wall Street with rumors of a surprisingly progressive tax reform that would alter the rules by which Americans spent, saved, and borrowed.

At half-past ten on 27 November 1983, a cluster of U.S. Treasury Department brass walked up the blue carpet of the opulent cabinet press room. Bullnecked Treasury Secretary Donald Regan led the way to the dais. Beaming proudly into the bright television lights, the secretary stroked his crimson and silver tie, pinched his reading glasses, and grandly read the summary of the "President's Tax Proposals for Simplicity, Growth, and Fairness"—the Reagan tax reform.

Forty-eight hours later, reporters spilled out of Senator Robert Packwood's office into the 250-foot-long sunlit colonnade of the Russell Senate Office Building. He had just succeeded Robert Dole as chairman of the tax-writing Finance Committee. Almost in unison, the reporters asked what the senator thought of Reagan's proposed tax revolution. Packwood had already singled out a *Washington Post* reporter to quip coyly, "I sorta like the tax code the way it is."

Sixteen blocks away, Donald Regan and White House aides were infuriated by Packwood's flippant answer. Packwood was the man that Ronald Reagan least wanted chairing the Senate Finance Committee, with its life-and-death power over tax reform. No one had forgotten how Packwood had ridiculed Reagan for allegedly snubbing women, blacks, and Jews, and discussing vodka-drinking welfare recipients.

Perhaps most important, the president could not overlook Packwood's unreliability as an ally in this issue. "Packwood has built a career by filling the tax code with the kind of special credits and incentives that Reagan's tax revision is designed to pare away," wrote the *Wall Street Journal*.

Packwood had the smoothest pipeline into corporate and women's campaign contributions of any American politician. He did not need the White House's fund-raising assistance, and he was not obliged to tow the Reagan line. This senator had won feminists' acclaim by advocating tax benefits for day care and pregnancy leave, but he had written even more loopholes for corporate special interests.

Enacting tax reform that stripped away loopholes has never been easy, and its successes have been aberrations. In 1969 Congress cracked down on abuses by foundations and initiated a minimum tax for the wealthy—but only after the outgoing Lyndon Johnson administration Treasury Department caused a national uproar by revealing that hundreds of millionaires didn't pay any income taxes.[11] In 1975 Congress repealed the oil depletion allowance for major oil companies—but only after long gas lines and soaring prices forced the issue.

Reagan had raged against the tax system his entire political career, and he tied high taxes to Jimmy Carter's tail in the 1980 presidential election. But when he became president himself, Reagan showed no interest in reforming tax rates, only in slashing. And that decision unwittingly sparked reform. When he sent his three-year, 30 percent rate cut to Congress in 1981, the bill included so many business giveaways that his own budget director, David Stockman, publicly complained how "the hogs were really feeding." But Reagan predicted a budget surplus by 1984.

Instead, the country was hit with record deficits and recession, and the momentum for tax reform built. Two Democratic senators, New Jersey's Bill Bradley and Missouri's

---

11. Jeffrey Birnbaum and Alan Murray. *Showdown at Gucci Gulch: Lawmakers, Lobbyists and the Unlikely Triumph of Tax Reform* (Random House, 1987).

174   Richard Gephardt, teamed up to write a bill trimming loopholes
and tax rates. The president kept silent, but was quietly changing his stand on the issue. After finishing off Walter Mondale's
call for a tax increase in the 1984 campaign, Reagan stunned
special-interest lobbyists with his postelection proposal.

The Reagan plan redrew the rules for how Americans spend,
save, and invest. It replaced the fourteen individual income-tax
brackets with just three: a 15 percent rate on income up to
$29,500; a 25 percent rate on income up to $38,000; and a 35
percent rate on all income above that. Reagan had already
chopped the top rate down from 70 percent.

His proposal for replacing the $100 billion that would be
lost from the reduced rates astounded people: the White House
penciled hundreds of Treasury-draining loopholes for the
waste bin, including state and local tax deductions, tax-free
employee fringe benefits, and write-offs for second homes and
business lunches.

Reagan also saw great political opportunity in historic tax
reform, which he believed could pull conservative Democrats
into the GOP. That was the kind of partisan talk that Packwood
listened to. Tax reform could be the jewel in the Republican
crown for the 1980s and 1990s. Few politicians ever get a chance
to shape such a landmark issue.

But Packwood bewildered lobbyists who thought they knew
him. The "I sorta like the tax code the way it is" statement now
haunted him, and the *Post* quoted a White House official as saying that, "If anybody can screw up tax reform, it will probably
be [Packwood]."

Packwood told the White House that taxing fringe benefits
was unacceptable. He forced James A. Baker III, who had replaced Regan as Treasury Secretary, to withdraw the entire tax
bill in March for "revisions." In May, the White House released
a new plan designed to placate the Senate Finance Committee
chair. It included fringe benefit taxes only on the first $10 in
health insurance premiums for individuals and the first $25 for
families—precisely the figures that Packwood had told Reagan
he would accept.

After Packwood endorsed tax reform that May, some thought he might do a good job selling the package to Middle America because he was middle-income himself. Although more than half of his Finance Committee members were multimillion-aires—including Bradley (D-New Jersey), Lloyd Bentsen (D-Texas), Ralston-Purina heir John Danforth (R-Missouri), and Heinz heir John Heinz (R-Pennsylvania)—no one had ever accused Packwood of personally profiting from the tax code.

But this fourth-generation Oregonian, despite his continuing reelection, had never been overwhelmingly popular in his home state. He had won reelection by a surprisingly close margin in the 1980 Republican landslide. Packwood realized that Oregonians' perception of tax reform would have a big impact on his chances of being reelected in 1986.

A state Department of Revenue study in late June showed that Reagan's proposal would cripple the state's timber economy and raise the taxes of many Oregon families. "This isn't tax reform," Packwood said of the Reagan proposal. "It's a deliberate act of sabotaging an entire industry and thereby the state of Oregon. If I cannot remove the timber provision from the legislation, I will do everything possible to kill the entire bill," he declared defiantly. "And I've made that *very* clear to the Treasury Secretary [James Baker]," he told a conference of Oregon Rotarians.

It seemed as though the senator had drawn his line in the dust, but a phone call from Baker had a strange effect. Whatever he said in that call caused Packwood to recant a second time. Twenty-four hours later he released a brief statement saying that while he opposed more timber industry taxes, he would not "oppose the bill" on that basis alone.

The senator now suffered the worst media drubbing of his career. "Packwood Eats His Words," declared the *Oregonian*. "Packwood has made it clear where he stands on tax reform: all over the place."

When reporters asked Senator Bill Bradley where Packwood stood, Bradley could only mutter, "I don't know. I figure at this

176 stage, uh, he, I don't know where, I mean, I don't know, I mean you know, you just take him at what he says." Packwood had now changed his position four times since saying he liked the tax code "the way it is."

Fortunately, the House of Representatives soon began to deliberate on tax reform, distracting critical attention from Packwood. The media was more interested in scrutinizing House Ways and Means Chairman Dan Rostenkowski. The Chicago Democrat closed so many business loopholes that Republicans abandoned the bill.

Reagan intervened to try to save the bill in the final hours before the 1985 Christmas recess. In mid-December, as visitors reveled at Packwood's holiday office party, the senator's eyes were glued to the C-SPAN broadcast of the House tax reform debate. "We held our breath to the last minute," a Packwood aide said, "hoping something would go wrong." But tax reform passed, and that presented Packwood with a critical choice: support a reform that home-state voters mistrusted, or oppose reform and be labeled a special-interest pawn.

Political events in Oregon, meanwhile, looked like they might relieve some of the pressure. One prospective foe, Democratic Representative Ron Wyden, declined to enter the Senate contest. But an earnest Baptist minister, Reverend Joe Lutz, challenged Packwood for the GOP Senate nomination. Conservative Republicans had long disliked Packwood, but they had never had a charismatic candidate to challenge him. Lutz might be that person.

———

Packwood's behavior was becoming riskier. Columnist Jack Anderson assigned his reporters to conduct several interviews exploring whether the senator had acted inappropriately with taxpayer-financed female employees, but none of the women would speak for the record. Former Anderson staffer Mark Zusman had not been connected with that project, but he launched his own investigation after becoming editor of *Willamette Week*.

As the tax reform battle geared up, Zusman assigned Washington, D.C., reporter Theresa Riordan to check out stories on

Packwood and female aides. Riordan identified a former aide who had quit her job with Packwood because he had made sexual overtures toward her, but the woman declined to go on the record.

The *Willamette Week*'s digging provoked sharp denials from Packwood's inner circle. Etta Fielek called allegations of sexual misconduct a "bum rap" that came from the fact that Packwood worked so closely with women. The senator constantly championed women's issues, she told Riordan, something unusual in the "old boy" mentality.

The senator's closest advisor, Jack Faust, tried to dismiss the stories as "just gossip." As an example, Faust described how he once received a telephone call from a big Packwood supporter. "She said she had it firsthand that last night Bob was at the Prima Dona [restaurant] around 9 P.M. with a little black-haired girl, both drunk and making out like crazy." A few hours later, another person called Faust to complain about the incident. Faust explained that the story was untrue. He had been with Packwood at the restaurant that night, and the "black-haired girl" was Faust's wife. They had all been dining together, and nothing was going on, but in twelve hours it had grown into a tale about Bob Packwood making out with a little black-haired girl. "I'm sure there must be hundreds of little black-haired girl stories running around," he said.

But despite Faust's assurances, the old media attitude that anything about a politician's private life was off-limits was slowly changing. NBC News reporter Roger Mudd had fired a warning shot at Packwood when he interviewed the senator on the television news magazine program *1986*. He read the senator a list of adjectives people used to describe him, including "ladies' man." Packwood replied, "Different people see different things."

On 19 March 1986, fifteen months after Reagan had presented his tax proposal, the Senate Finance Committee began its deliberations amid the pewter chandeliers and tobacco-brown walls of room 219 in the Everett Dirksen Building. Packwood

178 opened with a victory. Committee members restored the timber, oil, and gas loopholes that Rostenkowski had taken away.

Other senators now followed Packwood's lead in proposing giveaways for their home-state lobbies. Packwood's pleas for restraint went unheeded; he was in no position to condemn anyone. Eventually the Senate voted for $10 billion in tax relief for computers and telephone equipment, gave new benefits to farmers, and created loopholes affecting hundreds of industries, from oil refineries to casket-making. Packwood tried to compensate for that lost revenue by proposing $62 billion in excise taxes on beer, wine, and cigarettes. Speaker of the House Tip O'Neill shouted him down.

As Packwood strived to hold them back, the Finance Committee clamored for still more loopholes. New giveaways gashed a $100 billion deficit into the bill by mid-April. President Reagan's signature domestic initiative was sinking, and so was Packwood's reputation. He tried to start over, ordering the Joint Committee on Taxation's staff to write a new bill that would cap income-tax rates at 15 percent for the poor and 25 percent for most everyone else, but cynical committee members refused to even debate that.

When Reagan appeared to give up on the bill, Packwood denied paternity for his own baby. On 25 April he told a news conference the plan had been taxation committee director David Brockway's idea, not his. Packwood invited Brockway to step out of the audience to take credit for the failure, but Brockway refused, nervously shaking his head. Packwood then began motioning Brockway to come up to the stage, until finally the embarrassed staffer trudged to the microphones to answer reporters' questions.

Packwood had lost control of the most publicized tax measure in American history, and the media butchered him. A *New Republic* article labeled him "Senator Hackwood" for his special-interest pandering. A *New York Times* editorial concluded, "Vested interests die hard. But in the Senate Finance Committee, Chairman Packwood is simply surrendering to them."

After the Brockway debacle, a despondent Packwood left for lunch with committee tax expert Bill Diefenderfer. They dodged reporters by walking several blocks to Kelly's Irish Times, a Capitol Hill pub Packwood often visited when he drank heavily. As Packwood and Diefenderfer commiserated over a pitcher of Old Milwaukee, Packwood floated an idea: "Why not junk the whole thing and come up with a radical plan [to really stop loopholes] and cut the top income-tax rate in half—to 25 percent?"

As Diefenderfer tells it, "He looked at me and I looked at him and I said, 'Why not?'"

They left their half-empty pitcher and returned to work to restart the American tax reform debate. Packwood telephoned Bill Bradley that afternoon. The New Jersey Democrat had been openly disgusted at the way Packwood had turned tax revision into an interest-group fire sale. Now Packwood shocked him with a plea to compose a true reform bill.

Packwood spent Saturday and Sunday furiously working his forty-person Finance staff to write a measure before the historic opportunity for reform escaped them. The incentive had become very personal. Joe Lutz had ignited Oregon conservatives against Packwood, recruiting a small army of fundamentalist Christian volunteers equipped with canvass lists and lawn signs—the very weapons with which Packwood had begun his own political career.

Lutz expanded his appeal to secular conservatives by battering Packwood on "selling out" to special interests. The senator had already switched sides on tax reform six times; he might not survive a seventh. Packwood spent money like a desperate candidate, outadvertising Lutz by 50 to 1. Yet still Lutz gained on him.

Packwood's comeback began on 27 April with a dramatic reform that hit loophole-loving Wall Street like a slap in the face. The sweeping measure would affect the 99.6 million Americans and 3 million corporations paying federal taxes, and—more important—it would force those who had paid no taxes to cough up. The measure retained sacrosanct deductions for charitable contributions and home mortgage interest, but cut popular Individual Retirement Accounts, state and local sales tax deductions, and scores of other loopholes.

New York Senator Daniel Moynihan and Bradley enthusiastically endorsed it, along with other senators who feared the special-interest odor that voters now associated with them. "I think all of us wanted a second chance to say [to lobbyists], 'Hey, you guys in the $700 suits and Gucci shoes, you don't own us,'" one solon said.

———

Unseasonably hot weather brought Washington ninety-degree days and warm nights during the first week of May, and a forest of blossoming dogwoods greeted Packwood as he walked to the Dirksen Building each morning. While other lawmakers slipped away for warm-weather diversions, Packwood became more committed to his task than ever.

Fred Packwood had always loved performing surgery on tax bills so that they would appeal to greatly disparate groups, and Bob had been taught at his father's knee. One lesson he had learned is that such deals flower in the fertilizer of secrecy. U.S. Senate Rule XI forbade closing sessions to the public, but Packwood brazenly ordered Capitol guards to lock room 219's twelve-foot-tall maple doors. Packwood spent the next seven days sealed away, dealing for his political life. He ensured the indispensable backing of Dole and ranking Democratic Senator Russell Long of Louisiana by giving them the farm and oil interest loopholes, but Packwood insisted that any other tax breaks he wanted out would *stay* out.

At the end of the seventh day, Packwood pounded his gavel for a final up-or-down vote. Some of the senators did not even have printed copies of the bill. But at just after two o'clock in the morning, the weary Senate Finance Committee publicly approved Packwood's reform by a 20-to-0 vote—an unheard of mandate for a landmark tax bill. Packwood and Bradley spontaneously gripped each other in a bear hug. Special-interest lobbyists, feeling betrayed, hissed from the audience.

Individual senators rose to praise Packwood until everyone stood to applaud him, and an expression of joy swept across his face. The event was captured for posterity by a film crew Packwood had hired to record the historic moment for his future campaigns. The full Senate approved tax reform in an anticlimactic 97-to-3 vote on 24 June, and the Senate-House conference resoundingly ratified it in August. Packwood had snatched his career out of the flames.

Packwood called the victory a personal "catharsis" and wept. No one argued with the results. In the *Wall Street Journal,* Alan Murray described the Tax Reform Act of 1986 as "the single most sweeping change in the history of America's income tax. It marked the most significant achievement of the second Reagan administration. Indeed, in the history of the Republic, very few pieces of legislation have more profoundly affected so many Americans."

Packwood got everything he could have hoped for: a landmark national accomplishment and Senate reelection. The triumph enabled him to hold off Lutz by a 6 percent margin in one of the closest Senate primary elections that year.

How had he pulled it off? Packwood-watcher Brit Hume believed that the senator had always seen tax reform as a pie in the sky, operating on the cynical assumption that tax reform couldn't be done. Then, once reform got a breath of life and the public saw Packwood strangling it, he had to change. "I think the *New Republic* piece labeling him 'Senator Hackwood' affected him," said Hume. When Packwood saw "the momentum coming for reform [he] became the most articulate guy advocating it." Skeptics believed that Packwood's actions showed that one could achieve more without any core beliefs. But the senator could make doubters eat those words by adhering to his new reform principles.

In August *Time* wrote a flattering cover story on Reagan and Packwood's triumph. Although few politicians entering their general election campaign receive such national accolades, Packwood could not relax. Allegations of his love affair with Elaine Franklin—a taxpayer-financed employee—threatened to leak out. Her husband had filed for divorce, but when he tried to serve her with papers she managed to use the campaign as an excuse to dodge them. The last thing Packwood needed now was a scandal.

Andrew Franklin's attorney successfully petitioned Multnomah County Circuit Court Judge William Riggs on 12 August to sign an Order of Default against Elaine. When Packwood heard that, he exploded in rage. "Why couldn't Andy Franklin

182 have waited until after the November election?" he fumed to Georgie. Georgie pressed him about the rumors that he was having an affair with Elaine, but he denied them. When she asked why he usually traveled with attractive women aides, he replied that people would accuse him of being homosexual if he traveled only with male staff.

Meanwhile, Elaine spent the next six months stalling her husband. She hired attorney Garry McMurray, one of Packwood's former law partners, who told the judge in an affidavit that he had been unable to reach Elaine himself because of her campaign travels with Packwood in eastern Oregon.

"I am positive that Mrs. Elaine Franklin has not taken the knowledge of her husband's desire for dissolution of the marriage lightly, nor has she been flippant or forgetful," McMurray wrote. "To the contrary, she has been so emotionally and mentally distraught as to be unable to deal with this personal tragedy coupled with the enormous responsibilities and stress of her job as the senator's campaign manager."

She responded in an affidavit in September, explaining that recent months "have been extremely busy and stressful to say the least." She claimed that the withdrawal of Packwood's general election opponent, U.S. Representative Jim Weaver, and the entry of replacement candidate Rick Bauman had added to her duties.

The delay tactics worked. She stalled the legal notice of the divorce until after Packwood's reelection, signing the dissolution papers on 26 November.

In past election races, Packwood had taken Georgie on his trips back to Oregon. A natural campaigner, she enjoyed helping him work the crowds. But now Georgie began to fade out of the picture. Packwood encouraged gossip that she didn't care about her home state anymore, that she had contracted "Potomac fever." "The truth is," she told writer Tom Bates, "I was no longer invited."

Even before the campaign began, Packwood had begun to spend more time away on the fund-raising circuit, ignoring his wife and their children. Georgie was even discouraged from coming into the office, except for ceremonial appearances in her role as the senator's wife. "The primary responsibility for the children was mine; the primary responsibility for saving the world was Bob's," she recalls with some bitterness.

After Mindy Packwood died in 1988, Bob "went a little crazy," Georgie said. No one from his family of origin was alive. His wife tried to be supportive. "Bob was now alone, confronting his own mortality," she said, "and in his subconscious, he must have realized that he was now forever without the mothering he had missed as a child."

But Mindy's death also seemed to have released Bob. He wanted a way out of his marriage and shifted his emotional loyalty to a formidable woman who, ironically, reminded people of Mindy: Elaine Franklin.

Georgie hung on, still trying to make the marriage work. In 1989 she begged him to retire from office in 1992. "You'll only be sixty, you'll have had twenty-four successful years in the Senate. Why not quit while you're ahead?" she asked him. She tried to lure him into retirement, telling him, "You've got to realize that, from here on in, everybody who runs against you is going to be younger than you."

Franklin, meanwhile, was helping him do what Georgie had steadfastly opposed: test the water for a presidential bid. "She was a better enabler than I was," Georgie ruefully told a reporter.

Finally, Bob and Georgie began seeing a marriage counselor, but he acted as if the problems in the marriage were all hers. Later, trapped into agreeing to bring Elaine Franklin in on the discussions, he reneged at the last minute.

In late 1989 Bob called a family meeting to announce that he was moving out. According to Georgie, he also informed their two children, now ages twenty-three and twenty, that he no longer wished to have any financial responsibility for them, although Packwood later denied having made that statement.

"I don't want a wife, I don't want a house, I just want to be a senator," Georgie says he told them. "But Dad," his son, Bill, said, "someday you're going to get defeated, and we're the best friends you have."

On his son's birthday, 14 January 1990, Bob left Georgie, telling her that he should have done so years before. The news media, however, got another story. "I hope the trial separation

184 will allow the problems between Georgie and I to be worked out so that no divorce will occur," he told wire services. The senator "was disappointed" that a separation had become necessary, but hoped that having "more space between us" could lead to a reconciliation.

As Packwood left the family's home, Georgie asked if he was going to marry Elaine. "No," he responded, "she's too tough on me." Nonetheless Georgie blamed Franklin for the breakup of her marriage, saying she was "pure evil."

"I couldn't accept his relationship with Elaine Franklin," she told the *Oregonian*. "She never would have had influence with Bob if he hadn't been so sick. Because nobody in their right mind would give her the time of day." Franklin has repeatedly denied romantic involvement with the senator. "I rarely lie," she told the Portland newspaper. Then she amended her statement: "I never lie."

The Packwoods' divorce in June 1990 took two days in the Multnomah County Courthouse in downtown Portland. Circuit Court Judge Kathleen Nachtigall valued the couple's assets at about $1.2 million, including their $800,000 Bethesda home. The judge rejected Packwood's final request to have his alimony reduced to $500 per month, and instead ordered him to pay a monthly figure of $2,500.

Bob leafed through court documents, making notes as though it were another day at the office. When it was over he offered his ex-wife his hand as though concluding the successful drafting of a bill. "I was so numb with grief that I couldn't speak or think clearly," Georgie said, "but a little voice in the back of my head was saying, 'This is not the man I married. This man lost something on his way to the Senate.'"[12]

———

Throughout the 1980s Packwood remained the leading prochoice strategist in Congress. He defied Reagan by leading the opposition to antiabortion federal district judge Daniel Manion, and most important, to Supreme Court nominees Robert

12. Tom Bates. 11 April 1993, *Los Angeles Times Sunday Magazine.*

Bork and Antonin Scalia. Packwood became virtually the only Republican to challenge Reagan's chief justice nominee, Associate Justice William Rehnquist, to protest the fact that Rehnquist had voted against the Court's historic *Roe* v. *Wade* decision.

In January 1987 the Democratic takeover of the Senate reduced Packwood from chairman to ranking Republican on the Finance Committee. To compensate, he shifted his attention from tax reform to international trade, a topic in which his state had some interest.

Japan is a prime market for Oregon's timber and wheat exports. In fact, Oregon is one of the few states whose exports to Japan exceed its imports. Understandably, Packwood has been a free trader, opposing protectionist laws that might provoke Japan into retaliating against Oregon's goods. Packwood used his clout to help pass Reagan's U.S.-Canada free-trade accord, as well as a similar agreement with Mexico in 1988. He also supported that year's omnibus trade bill, but only after exempting Israel from any of the measure's penalties.

Packwood drew attention that year for his extraordinary efforts to defeat a bill to control campaign spending. As the Democrat-backed measure approached passage, Republicans tried to thwart approval by denying the Senate a quorum. Most GOP senators eventually straggled to the floor, but Packwood persisted in hiding out. Democratic majority leader Robert Byrd of West Virginia, a master parliamentarian, then invoked a seldom-used Senate rule allowing the sergeant at arms to arrest Packwood to compel his attendance, but the Oregon senator fled to his office, where he bolted the entrance and blocked another door with a heavy chair.

When deputies finally pushed their way in, the fifty-six-year-old Packwood reinjured a broken finger while resisting arrest. Once subdued, he tried passive resistance, forcing the lawmen to carry him to the Senate floor. Ultimately, of course, Packwood was grandstanding—President Reagan could easily veto any campaign finance bill, rendering the issue moot.

With his own presidential ambitions shelved for the time, the senator was pleased when the comparatively moderate George Bush dispatched Bob Dole and right-wing challenger

Pat Robertson to win the GOP nomination. The Bush campaign entrusted Packwood with a special assignment for the November race against Democratic presidential nominee Michael Dukakis: helping to prepare Senator Dan Quayle for his vice presidential debate against Senator Lloyd Bentsen.

Packwood, one of the Senate's best debaters, had watched Bentsen in Finance for years and probably knew more about him than any other Republican. The former high school and law school debate star threw himself into the job. But after the last dress rehearsal, Quayle feared Packwood might have been too easy on him. What if Bentsen tore into him?

"Don't worry," Packwood assured Quayle. "I know Lloyd Bentsen. He's a gentleman and won't attack you."

But during the debate, when Quayle made the mistake of comparing himself to John F. Kennedy, Bentsen shot back: "I knew Jack Kennedy. Jack Kennedy was a friend of mine. And senator, you're no Jack Kennedy."

Despite Quayle's poor showing, the Bush ticket had enough steam to beat Dukakis by 54 percent to 46 percent, and Packwood became an effective Bush ally. He carried the White House flag on the issue that Bush called his number one domestic priority: lowering the capital gains tax for business.

Tax reform supporters were furious. One of the hallmarks of the Packwood-led 1986 tax reform had been eliminating differential rates for capital gains, in return for a lower tax rate for overall income. Packwood's reversal rekindled cynicism that his conversion to tax reform had been self-serving and fleeting.

Packwood's strained relationship with the timber industry continued through the late 1980s. Several lobbyists even thought Packwood dropped pro-timber provisions from the 1986 Tax Reform Act because of old animosities about his father's firing. But Packwood could no longer afford that luxury as his reelection campaign approached. In 1990 and 1991, the spotted-owl issue dramatically widened the gulf between environmentalists and the timber industry, forcing Packwood to choose one or the other. He now became a reliable timber ally, and the industry would one day become virtually his only ally.

The senator opposed Bush on feminist issues but without the rancor that had marked his confrontations with Reagan. He contested the nomination of abortion critic David Souter to the Supreme Court, and helped organize the effort to reverse Bush's "gag rule" on abortion counseling at publicly funded clinics. He also fought the administration's ban on fetal-tissue research and the import of the French abortion pill RU-486. In 1990 he led efforts to override Bush's controversial veto of the Family and Medical Leave Act, which would have allowed workers as many as twelve weeks of unpaid leave to care for newborns.

But the conservative Oregon Citizens Alliance (OCA), the inheritor of the Joe Lutz constituency, bristled at their fellow Republican's liberal abortion views. Meanwhile, Bush's economic policies flopped in Oregon, and in the spring of 1991 Democrat Les AuCoin announced plans to challenge Packwood's reelection.

In October, Packwood, who had led the charge against Supreme Court nominees Bork and Rehnquist, was uncharacteristically low-key in voting against ardent abortion critic Clarence Thomas's confirmation. Packwood was one of only two Republicans to oppose Thomas, but he declined to speak out against him on the Senate floor.

While Packwood directed his energies toward his upcoming reelection, the impact of the Clarence Thomas–Anita Hill hearings on many of his former employees would change the course of his life.

Part IV

11

After the divorce, Georgie Packwood took a vacation in Denmark. When she got back to Washington after the November 1992 election, she found that all hell had broken loose. Penny Durenberger, her partner for several years in an antique business, and the estranged wife of Minnesota's Republican Senator David Durenberger, picked her up at the airport. "While you've been gone," Penny asked, "what have you heard?"

She had heard everything—a reporter had already filled her in on the impending *Post* story. She was not surprised about the disclosures, only saddened that her children would have to read about their father's philandering.

Georgie had not spoken with Bob since their divorce. When she caught her first glimpse of him on television in late January 1993, surrounded by screaming protestors in Eugene, Oregon, the change was startling. "I could see the fear in his eyes; he looked like a treed animal," she said. She turned the set off.

Packwood became the third senator that year to be publicly charged with sexual misconduct, but he was the only one to be investigated. Hawaii Democrat Daniel Inouye had been accused

192 of fondling a number of women, including his hairdresser, but the senator successfully repudiated the allegations and won re-election. Durenberger had been hit with a paternity suit, although he denied being the father of the baby.

In early 1993 the Senate Ethics Committee decided to expand the scope of its probe into the Packwood case, which had already become the biggest congressional investigation of sexual misconduct ever. Feminists were elated by the committee's decision to look into charges that Packwood had tried to discredit, intimidate, and smear witnesses.

This was a marked departure from the panel's perceived history of favoritism toward its own. During the Keating Five hearings of the early 1990s, the Ethics Committee had censured Senator Alan Cranston (D-California) but let the other four senators off with mild letters of admonishment. The committee had also suppressed a messy savings and loan case implicating Senator Phil Gramm, and dropped influence-peddling charges against Alfonse D'Amato. It refused to even examine sexual molestation charges against Brock Adams.

Only one member of the Ethics Committee remained from that era, but he was arguably the toughest—Democrat Richard Bryan of Nevada, according to *Roll Call*. Of more concern to Packwood, perhaps, was the fact that the jury for his case included, for the first time, a woman senator—Maryland Democrat Barbara Mikulski.

Mikulski has been described as "a burst of ferocity and intellect." When the Senate debated Clarence Thomas's Supreme Court confirmation in October 1991, Mikulski let loose with both barrels. Remarkable for her clarity amid the general befuddlement of ninety-eight male senators, she spelled out her views on the allegations: "I do not like the term 'sexual harassment' because it does not give the full impact of what that means to the person who must endure this type of abuse. And make no mistake, it is abuse. It is as abusive as a physical blow. I prefer the term 'sexual humiliation,' because that is what occurs when someone is subject to such treatment."

The other Ethics panel members included liberal Senator Tom Daschle (D-South Dakota), an eventual aspirant for Senate majority leader; committee vice chairman Mitch McConnell (R-Kentucky), a charter signatory to a feminist group's anti-sexual harassment policy; Senator Bob Smith (R-New Hampshire), who was too new to have fully absorbed the Senate's clubby values; and independent-minded conservative Senator Larry Craig (R-Idaho).

The committee could recommend three degrees of punishment: reprimand, censure (which might include stripping Packwood of seniority), or expulsion. Expulsion was unlikely; it had only been used to oust convicted felons or senators who were running guns for the Confederacy during the Civil War. Censure would be a cruel blow—after so many years in office, Packwood, who as a freshman senator had sought to take apart the seniority system, was now in a position to reap even more rewards. The best he could hope for, other than dismissal of the charges, was reprimand—and public humiliation.

The charges against Packwood were mushrooming rapidly, and people all over the country wondered how he had managed to approach so many women. "He couldn't seem to help himself," said a former Packwood aide who regularly refused his advances. "I cannot tell you how many people sat down with him and said, 'You are going to come to a bad end. All your career's work on women's issues and progressive issues is going to turn to dust.'"

That prediction was now coming to pass with a vengeance. In February 1993 the *Post's* second story by Florence Graves and Charles Shepard had brought the number of Packwood's accusers to twenty-three, and the *Oregonian* reported the stories of several more women, including:

- Former Packwood volunteer Susan Descamp visited Washington, D.C., in 1969 with her sister Anne Kelly Feeney and brother-in-law Richard Feeney, an aide to Representative Edith Green (D-Oregon). Descamp, then twenty-three, sat next to Packwood at a table in a popular bar with a group of about ten people. She was startled and appalled when Packwood put his hand up her skirt. Descamp quickly moved away from the senator, and told her sister and brother-in-law about the incident as soon as they left the bar.

- Gail Byler was a hostess at the Ramada Inn in downtown Portland in 1970. One night after closing, Packwood suddenly came up behind her in a dark dining room and ran his hand up the inside of her leg from her ankle to under her skirt. She told him to leave her alone.

  Drunkenly, Packwood replied, "Do you know who I am?"

  She responded that she did not care, and told him never to touch her again. He replied, "Well, you haven't heard the end of this." Byler thought he was threatening her job.

- A woman working on Packwood's 1986 reelection campaign reported that the senator "leered at her, pushed his body toward her, smacked his lips suggestively, and asked her to tell him her measurements." She said his actions made her feel like "some kind of beefsteak."

Stung into action by the new attacks, Packwood ordered his attorneys to take the offensive. Women who had hoped for a quick resolution of the problem were disappointed.

Packwood's Senate Republican colleagues, afraid his seat would be lost to a Democrat, stuck by him. Feminists feared he would ride out the storm, and several of his accusers became disheartened. Former aide Cathy Miles, who had first warned Packwood that the *Post* story was in the works, learned some hard lessons when she asked people to testify on her behalf. "I went through a very depressing time because people I thought were friends wouldn't testify for me," she said. Many people feared Packwood and Elaine Franklin had the power to hurt their careers.

Ethics Committee investigators crisscrossed the country to interview Packwood's accusers and supporters. In the spring of 1993, committee attorneys took Miles's deposition. Miles began by reading a prepared statement. "When I got to the part about how I saw [Packwood] as a mentor—I lost it, I started crying."

Three and a half hours later, when she broke down again, they let her take a brief break.

Linda Chapman, an outside attorney hired by the committee to question Miles, spent an hour grilling her on how the *Washington Post* reporters broke the story. Then she narrowed the focus to Miles's personal experience. One source summarized the following key dialogue:

Chapman: After this [the October 1990 incident in which she claimed the senator kissed her], were you ever alone with him?

Miles: I was still on his staff, so course I was. [Miles looked right at committee counsel Victor Baird and said, "When (your boss) Senator Bryan asks you to come into his office, do you go?" Baird gave an embarrassed smile.]

Chapman: Have you ever had wine with him?

Miles: Yes.

Chapman: How many times did you have wine with Packwood?

Miles: I can't remember.

Chapman: How many times would you estimate?

Miles: Maybe fifteen. [She became apprehensive, fearing that Packwood, a copious note-taker, probably had recorded whether it was exactly ten times or twenty times.]

Chapman: Do you have a drinking problem?

Miles: No.

Chapman: Why is he [Packwood] saying that you have a drinking problem?

Miles: I don't know.

Chapman: Why did [Packwood aides] Josie Martin, Lindy Paull, and Julia Brim-Edwards write [critical] statements about you?. . . Lindy Paull said you wore short skirts.

Miles: No, I didn't wear short skirts.

Chapman: For the record, what is your skirt length today?

Miles: A knee-length skirt. [Victor Baird, according to a source, now looked at Miles with eyes that said, "Sorry we have to do this."]

Paige Wagers had tried to forget about how Packwood made advances to her in 1976 and 1981, but she could not. Reluctantly, she stood by Packwood for years because she thought he was a "good senator," and she had "no right to interfere in his career." When the *Washington Post* contacted her, her attitude was changing. She cooperated with Florence Graves but still declined to talk on the record before the November general election, because she "did not want to be involved in party politics."

She decided to come forward after the election, however, when she discovered Packwood had contacted former staff members and persuaded her ex-boyfriend to submit derogatory statements about her. Feeling violated, she agreed to be interviewed by Senate Ethics Committee investigators.

"I want to make it easier for other women to speak out. I'd like to see sexual harassment taken very seriously. Kidding and joking with someone is one thing, but being touched is another. I choose who touches me," she told writer Linda Kramer.

"I don't feel vindictive," said Wagers. "I don't believe you can separate your public and private life to that extreme. If someone's character is so flawed in his private life, then it must affect his public life."

Satire is a lethal indicator for a politician. And a survey that year showed only President Clinton and Tonya Harding exceeding Packwood as the butt of comedians' humor, from *Saturday Night Live* to *Murphy Brown*.

"That's right," talk-show host Jay Leno says. "President Clinton wants to give vaccination shots to all kids. Not to be outdone, today Senator Robert Packwood promised free breast exams to all women—certainly good news."

"Boy, did you hear what happened to Packwood today?" Leno continues. "Broke three fingers when he tried to grab the rear end of a woman who used that Buns of Steel workout tape."

Meanwhile, the Senate Rules Committee was examining the charges lobbied by some women's groups that Packwood's preelection denials to the *Post* and the *Oregonian* constituted election fraud.

But late spring brought Packwood a respite from his troubles when the Rules Committee dismissed those charges. Freshman California Democratic Senator Dianne Feinstein surprised many feminists by declaring that probing the Packwood charges would open a "Pandora's box" that would affect all Senate races.

Packwood's comeback campaign picked up more conservative supporters. A friendly John McLaughlin, once the subject of sexual harassment complaints himself, held Packwood's hand during his "One on One" show in June. The senator told the television audience that his legal bills had exceeded $500,000. "When I pay my legal fees for my defense, I'll be broke."

But he had not dipped into his own pocket yet. Packwood benefited from the Senate law enabling members to spend excess campaign funds for their legal defense. He also formed a "Bob Packwood in 1998" political action committee, a handy accounting device to raise even more money for his lawyers.

Many women's groups feared that a Senate Ethics Committee verdict reached in secrecy would lack credibility and undoubtedly favor Packwood. NOW, the Women's Legal Defense Fund, and thirteen of Packwood's accusers, including Julie Myers Williamson, Paige Wagers, and Gena Hutton, officially requested the committee to hold public hearings on its final report.

Mikulski emphatically endorsed that idea. The women's attorneys pleaded to committee members that without public hearings the committee would have nothing but their own private reading of secret testimony with which to justify their conclusions to other senators and to the public.

The threat of televised hearings brought tremors to Capitol Hill, which was still reeling from the Thomas-Hill proceedings. "If [the sexual misconduct hearings] get on CNN, [Packwood] is dead," a top Senate source told *Newsweek*. The Rules Committee hearings now seemed of little consequence.

Some of the witnesses, however, *were* ready. Hutton said that "as scary as it seems, I'd like it public. That way nothing can slide by. It's not a secret. It's out in the open. I'm not hiding anything." The most frightened women were the ones who had

198   received threatening letters from Packwood—the accusers who had consequently talked to the *Post*. Julie Myers Williamson told reporters, "My concern is that there might be someone on the panel whose job is to try to destroy me in order to protect Senator Packwood. That worries me. . . . I just don't want to go through that kind of nightmare."

Both sides incurred casualties. Some of the women, like Paige Wagers, were afraid to tell loved ones of their predicament; some who did regretted doing so. Gena Hutton heard from a family member, "Oh, Gena, you've always been so outgoing, you probably gave him some mixed signals."

Packwood supporters took hits. Lawyer Peter Friedman of Washington, D.C., contributed to the senator's legal defense fund only to have critics complain to one of his key Portland clients. Former Packwood aide Timothy Lee angrily sent one reporter a video copy of *Absence of Malice,* the Paul Newman movie of media character assassination.

They weren't the only ones scorched from the magnifying glass of publicity. Ever since the scandal erupted, Packwood's relations with the state's news media had turned bitterly adversarial. The *Oregonian* editorial board, a longtime ally, now called for his resignation. Packwood stopped talking with the paper's reporters. The Associated Press's Capitol reporter Scott Sonner was one of the few reporters to whom he would still speak.

In early June 1993, Sonner called Packwood for some inside news on the Ethics Committee battle. As the senator deflected those questions, Sonner tried probing into another area.

"How are you coping with this ordeal?" he asked.

As Sonner waited for the response, he remembered that colleague Donald Rothberg had recently noticed a vehicle with the vanity plate "MASADA" parked in Packwood's home driveway. The senator now explained that he had selected the name to honor the heroic band of Jews who had killed themselves rather than surrender in the mountain fortress of Masada in southern Israel in A.D. 73.

Packwood insisted that his new plates were not a personal statement—they had nothing to do with the Senate Ethics Committee siege. He had wanted the Masada inscription ever since

he visited the historic site near Jerusalem in 1978. "I finally
called out to Oregon to see if [the plates] were available. I was
so admiring. I thought darn it, there are few acts in history I
admire more."

The senator began to soliloquize about Masada, his voice
drawing tight as he described how 960 Jews fought off a
Roman army for six years. Despite the Jewish soldiers' courage,
the Romans eventually built a ramp that would allow them to
storm the mountaintop. It soon became clear they would capture Masada.

To avoid capture and enslavement, the Jews began to prepare a mass suicide. They burned the fortress so the Romans
could not use it, and they left behind their food supply so the
victors would know they had died by choice, not starvation.
In meticulous detail, Packwood described how the Jewish soldiers gathered into groups of ten, and "one sliced the throat
of the other nine, and then the survivor committed suicide."

"By slicing the throat the same way Jewish butchers do for
kosher meat, it is painless. I know that is hard to believe, but
they say that," he explained.

As the senator continued, Sonner became worried that
Packwood might overidentify with the Masada suicides. He says
that when the interview ended, he "didn't know whether to call
[his] editor—or 911 to get Packwood help."

Before he had a chance to do either, he received a call from
Elaine Franklin, who demanded that he leave all embarrassing
references to Masada out of his story. Sonner wasn't sure if
Franklin had eavesdropped on the conversation, or if Packwood
had shared it with her. He ran the piece anyway.

Packwood did not turn to suicide. The career maverick now
became a born-again Republican loyalist. He knew that a united
Republican front might stop Democratic efforts for censure
or expulsion. As Packwood moved to the right looking for a
safer haven, he reversed his stand on several issues on which
his vote was needed by partisan Republicans, including GOP
leader Bob Dole. He voted against a job benefits extension and

a Democrat-sponsored bill that would allow people to register to vote when they registered their vehicles.

Republicans, furthermore, needed a strong Packwood on the Senate Finance Committee to shape or defeat President Bill Clinton's budget and health reform proposals. Finance Republican John Chafee of Rhode Island predicted they would need Packwood to challenge any Clinton budget-tinkering that might affect the 1986 Tax Reform Act, which Packwood had helped write. "This is clearly a burden on him, as it would be on anybody," Chafee told the *Oregonian*.

The Senate Ethics Committee expanded its search for witnesses in July by sending letters to nearly three hundred women who had worked for Packwood, asking them to come forward with any evidence they had supporting or refuting the allegations. The effort proved largely fruitless. "There aren't any guarantees that this case will break the hold of the old boys' network, but if people want to change it they have to step forward," Williamson said. "It's not good enough to say it's never changed before."

Jill Kleppe-McClelland, who had worked as Packwood's scheduler in the mid-1980s, came to the senator's defense. She said that she sat directly outside his door, and had never seen anything inappropriate. Kleppe-McClelland, who has since become a lawyer, claimed the investigation was baseless because none of the women had alleged that their jobs were threatened or that Packwood made repeated advances after being rebuffed. Alleging sexual harassment has become "the politically cool thing to do in the '90s," she told a Portland newspaper.

Post writer Charles Shepard had told Miles that some of the women seemed on a "crusade" against Packwood. And the senator's supporters emphasized that Roche, Williamson, and Heffernan had liberal Democratic connections. The women using former Oregon Supreme Court Justice Betty Roberts as a legal advisor strengthened Packwood's charges. The senator claimed Roberts held a grudge from their bitter 1974 Senate race.

It was also Packwood's misfortune that the *Post* revealed his problems while memories were raw from the Clarence Thomas

hearings. Women were incensed by the Senate narrowly con-
firming Thomas, and Packwood became the recipient of that
pent-up anger. That may have contributed to a degree of "pil-
ing on" of less serious allegations, such as Maura Roche's tepid
story accusing Packwood of reading a dirty joke to her.

And the ascendancy of Bill Clinton into the White House
in 1993 ended a twelve-year siege of Ronald Reagan and
George Bush veto power over women's issues. Feminists had
desperately needed Packwood during those years, but with a
pro-choice president, they no longer needed a pro-choice senator as much. At least some feminists decided that Packwood's
behavior was now more important—and more useful to the
cause—than his vote.

And now the Ethics Committee staff seemed to be gearing
up for a hearings showdown, asking women if they would be
willing to testify in public. On 16 September they announced
plans to complete the preliminary inquiry by late October, when
they would recommend a course of action to the committee.
They had interviewed or taken depositions from more than 150
people, but the most important deposition was yet to come:
from Packwood himself.

Packwood, accompanied by his lawyer, met for two days
with the committee's attorneys in a remote room on the Capitol's fourth floor, which is secured by a guard and reserved for
highly confidential matters, most often CIA and Defense Department briefings.

The committee later reported that "during depositions on
October 5 and 6, it became apparent that Senator Packwood's
diaries, covering years 1969 to the present . . . contained information relevant to the committee's inquiry."

Committee counsel had asked Packwood for any "exculpa-
tory" information on one of the complainants. As the senator
later told colleagues:

> I said, "Yes, a year later, this one [Cathy Miles] who had
> complained was drinking wine with me in the office one
> night. She stood up, approached me, put her arms around
> me, and gave me a great big kiss and said, 'You are wonder-
> ful.' I responded, 'Warts and all?' And she laughed, and she
> knew the reference."

Counsel then asked Packwood if he could corroborate that story. Packwood responded, "If I say no, I'm guilty of perjury. If I say yes, I have opened the diaries."

The statement shocked Ethics aides, who had asked Packwood in March and July for all documents regarding the misconduct and intimidation of witnesses charges. When he did not turn the diaries over, committee counsel Victor Baird, who was aware they existed, had concluded they contained nothing relevant.

Baird immediately halted the deposition, claiming that Packwood had failed to honor the documents request. Baird demanded to review the diaries. Packwood avoided a third day of depositions by calling in sick.

Attorneys for both sides spent several days negotiating an agreement by which Packwood would turn over all 8,200 diary pages except for those referring to legal, medical, and personal family matters. Under the guidelines, Packwood's lawyers covered the privileged sections with redacting tape.

Ethics attorneys began reviewing the diaries in mid-October, with the senator feeding them a few pages at a time. At the end of each day they told Packwood's lawyers which pages they wanted copied for further review. Over the next four days they examined 5,000 single-spaced pages covering the years 1969 to 1988.

But on Sunday, 17 October, they came across information that, although unrelated to the misconduct and intimidation issues, "raised questions about possible violation of one or more laws, including criminal laws." When informed that there was evidence of possible criminal wrongdoing, Packwood's attorneys refused to turn over the rest of the diary unless they could mask additional passages.

The committee rejected that request and proposed that an independent hearings examiner review the additional pages to ensure that only material covered by the original exemptions was masked.

But Packwood's attorney, James Fitzpatrick, wanted to cover any "collateral issues" unrelated to sexual misconduct, which the committee could see after completing its investigation and "in connection with any separate investigation it decides to initiate."

On 20 October the committee voted unanimously to subpoena the remaining pages of diaries covering 1989 to mid-
1993. An independent examiner, former Solicitor General
Kenneth W. Starr, would ensure that Packwood's attorneys had
masked only the entries covered by the original exemptions.

But Packwood refused to turn them over on the grounds
that the investigation was for sexual misconduct, not criminal
acts. The committee voted 6 to 0 to request the full Senate to
enforce the subpoena. Chairman Bryan introduced Senate Resolution 153 describing the subpoena, and making the matter
public for the first time.

Fitzpatrick accused the committee of scavenging through
the diaries for dirt unrelated to the investigation. He counter-
attacked their move in a press release that made many members of the Washington, D.C., establishment squirm. The vague
statement hinted that the diaries contained extensive "irrelevant" information, including:

- Conversations with a senator about that senator's extended
  affair with a staff member and the problems of his divorce.
- A description of an affair between a Senate staff member
  and a member of the Democratic congressional leadership.
- Private consensual personal relationships [between Packwood and] non-staff persons having absolutely nothing to
  do with the allegations of sexual misconduct by Senator
  Packwood, with no apparent [concern for the] rights of
  privacy of the women involved.

That weekend, Packwood realized that Fitzpatrick's statement had backfired. He took the Senate floor on 25 October
to deny threatening to divulge information about his colleagues'
personal lives. "This was not so-called gray mail," he said. "The
secrets in the diary are safe with me."

Nevertheless, he reiterated his decision to fight the subpoena, dishing up for his colleagues an unappealing choice: set
a precedent that would allow the Ethics Committee to paw
through their own personal journals in the future—or cast a
vote that could look like a cover-up for one of the old boys.

Each party huddled in caucuses. Packwood pleaded for Republican loyalty in what GOP Whip Alan Simpson called a

204 "poignant, personal meeting." In the Democratic caucus, Bryan explained how possible criminal wrongdoing had sparked the subpoena. That information became public when caucus members Tom Harkin and Bob Kerrey told reporters.

Senate GOP leader Robert Dole rose on the Senate floor to attack Bryan for the leak. The statement "ought to be followed by a charge, or it ought to be retracted," he said. But Majority Leader George Mitchell set a date of 1 November for the unprecedented subpoena debate. To drive home the gravity of the situation, Mitchell invoked a tactic usually reserved for impeachment proceedings: he shut down all other committee meetings scheduled that day to compel attendance.

There was more at stake in the looming battle than one senator's reputation. Many Americans scoffed at the Senate's ability to police itself after the Clarence Thomas confirmation. As much as they might sympathize with him, some senators said they dare not appear soft on Packwood.

Packwood arrived for the showdown in the Senate chamber shortly after noon. As other senators took their seats, one writer noticed how, "No one dropped by Packwood's desk to offer him support. There were no claps on the back, no sympathetic hands on the shoulder, no get-well cards. Everyone kept their distance. . ."[13]

With the nation watching on C-SPAN, Bryan opened the proceedings by laying out the case for the subpoena and criticizing Packwood's "disinformation campaign." He explained how when Packwood was informed of the possible criminal violations revealed in the diaries, his attorney dismissed them as "collateral issues."

Then Packwood took the floor and made the following statement:

> These diaries are as personal as anything you can write. They have 8,200 pages, maybe 8,400 pages now. I am not sure how many. And everything is in them: Lengthy descriptions of meetings with presidents, from President Nixon onward.

---

13. Steve Duin. 2 November 1993, *Oregonian.*

My first meeting with President Nixon by myself: He called me down, and I thought it was going to be in a group, and he called me down to lobby me on the appointment of Judge Haynsworth, and we went back and forth for forty-five minutes, I guess, the two of us, without even Bryce Harlow, who was his principal liaison in Congress. Meetings with President Reagan, President Bush. A wonderful description of the meeting with President Carter when Desert One failed.

These are all history and, I think, of marginal importance to some historian someday when they write. These books are left to the Oregon Historical Society, not to be opened until way after my death. And they may be footnote references; they may be more for others.

Are there personal things in there? Sure. Family heartaches. Disappointments. Irritation with the car repairman. They are all there.

No one had ever seen them except the woman who typed them, and it is the same woman who has typed them for as long as I have been keeping them. My former wife never saw them, my children, no other staff member. So they were very, very personal.

Is there humor in them? Sure. Are there nasty comments about some of you when I got mad or something? Sure. Are there warm comments about you? You bet. But personal beyond all measure.

It was very difficult to have the chairman brand me as a criminal last week, and there is no unringing this bell. I could bring the headlines in from all over the country. There is hardly a story—and I mean headlines—that does not contain the word "Packwood" and "criminal" in it.

Ethics Committee chairman Richard Bryan responded that "[the committee] did not put you in this position. We are merely doing our job as the Senate and the public deserve. This is the first time known to any of us that a United States senator failed to cooperate in an Ethics Committee proceeding."

Mitch McConnell, the Republican vice chairman, said that if Packwood's attorneys had responded properly to the committee's earlier requests, they would not have found themselves in this position. "As the old poem goes," he said, "'What a tangled web we weave . . .'"

The Kentucky Republican also harshly criticized Packwood's attorneys for "running rampant on the TV talk shows" and trying to portray the committee as "teenagers prowling around for pornography." He went on to say, "This debate is not about the secret sex life of the Senate—although that's bound to disappoint a lot of C-SPAN viewers out there."

Another Republican committee member, Senator Bob Smith of New Hampshire, asked rhetorically, Is there another way [besides the subpoena]? He had to answer no.

With that, Packwood dropped his head as if he had been hit. If Smith would not make a partisan defense, the chances were slight that many other Republicans would. Bob Dole sat in the second row during the debate, his face a study in bleakness.

That afternoon, newly elected Democratic Senator Patty Murray of Washington steered the attention away from the procedural debate—to the issue of sexual harassment itself:

> Two years ago I sat home in my living room like millions of other Americans and watched a strikingly similar debate in front of the Senate Judiciary Committee.
>
> And I remember thinking: "Why don't they get it? Why don't they understand that throughout this country women who have been victims of sexual misconduct are watching?"
>
> A vote for the resolution sends a message to citizens throughout the nation that sexual misconduct in this Senate will be investigated to the fullest possible extent.
>
> A vote against the resolution sends a clear message also to every woman in this country: If you are harassed, keep quiet. Say nothing. The cards are stacked against your ever winning. Procedures, rules, and other issues will obscure the allegations being investigated. . . .
>
> I am shocked and surprised that [the debate] appears to portray the senator from Oregon as the victim. I remind my colleagues more than two dozen women have brought their allegations to this body. Clearly, they see themselves as the victims.

The camaraderie of the new Democratic women in the Senate was evident when freshman California Democrat Barbara Boxer took the floor to praise Murray for bringing them "back to reality." California Democrat Dianne Feinstein said in an interview, "My own view is that the Senate's reputation is very much at stake."

_____

On the second day of the debate, the public learned just what the possible criminal charges were when the *Oregonian* disclosed that the disputed diary pages involved whether Packwood had made illegal quid pro quo promises to lobbyists in exchange for job offers for his then-estranged wife.

During their divorce proceedings in 1990, Georgie Packwood had received several unsolicited job offers. Her divorce attorney characterized them as the senator's attempt to reduce his alimony payments by showing evidence of his wife's earning potential.

The Associated Press obtained a letter from the courthouse divorce files that Packwood had written to Georgie on 14 June 1990, which said, "This business that I steer to you is not to be a gift to you nor a bribe to me." It was not clear what specific business he was referring to.

The Packwood associates who offered Georgie jobs were:

- Lester Pollack, a New York investment banker and former NYU Law School classmate of Packwood's. He was a long-time fund-raiser for the senator. Pollack told the Associated Press that after speaking with Packwood about his divorce proceedings, he offered Georgie a $5,000-a-year position on a corporate board. She turned it down.

- Timothy Lee, a Packwood aide in the mid-1970s, and now an Oregon political activist and trucking company owner. He offered Georgie assistance to set up an antique business in Oregon that would generate over $20,000 a year. She said that Lee told her that he had learned from the senator that the couple needed the money. She turned down the offer.

- Ronald Crawford, the husband of ex-Packwood aide Carol Crawford, who later served on the U.S. International Trade Commission. Ronald Crawford lobbied for a national cable television group, a Virgin Island firm, a drug company, and a bus association. All of those clients had business pending before either the Finance Committee, where Packwood is the senior Republican, or the Commerce Committee, where he is the top GOP member on the subcommittee dealing with cable television.

    Crawford offered Georgie Packwood a $7,500 annual fee as a political consultant. She said the offered puzzled her because Crawford knew much more about politics than she did. She refused the offer.

- Steven R. Saunders, a former Packwood aide and now a lobbyist for the Japanese embassy and two Japanese companies, including Mitsubishi Electric. He offered Georgie more than $20,000 annually to escort the wives of his clients on shopping trips to buy antiques and art. The *Oregonian* later reported that Packwood had asked questions at a 1989 Senate hearing on behalf of Mitsubishi Electric, which had been charged with unfair trade practices. Georgie told the *Post* she believed the Saunders offer was independent of her husband, but Saunders later dropped the offer.

Packwood acknowledged discussing jobs for his wife, but said he had not done anything wrong and had not initiated calls to the lobbyists.

After fifteen hours of debate the Senate voted 94 to 6 to force Packwood to comply with the subpoena, but still he refused. On 19 November, as committee lawyers prepared to ask the U.S. district court for the District of Columbia to enforce the subpoena, attorney James Fitzpatrick told reporters that his client might resign, making the misconduct case and subpoena moot, as the committee only has jurisdiction over incumbent senators.

That day, intense negotiations between Packwood and his colleagues climaxed in a tortured series of decisions and reversals. With an attorney waiting at the courthouse to file suit to force him to turn over his diaries, Packwood agreed to resign. But moments later, in Bob Dole's office, the FBI served him with a subpoena in connection with the "Jobs for Georgie" scandal, and Packwood changed his mind. Faced with a criminal investigation, he had little incentive to quit to avoid a misconduct probe.

Colleagues and others close to Packwood said that he was physically and emotionally shattered. They openly worried about the man who once said he hoped to die in the Senate. "It looks like I may have to quit," Packwood told a fellow senator. "I'm at the end of my rope."

"He's on the outer edge of the ledge," said Senator Arlen Specter, a longtime friend. "His whole life has been destroyed."

"It's tough, awful tough," said Wyoming Senator Alan Simpson. "Remember, there's a very tortured human being at the bottom of the pile."

After it became clear that he would not resign, the Ethics Committee went to court to enforce the subpoena. The case was assigned to Judge Thomas Penfield Jackson, a Reagan appointee. Packwood dismissed Fitzpatrick as his attorney and hired white-collar criminal defense specialist Jacob Stein.

Meanwhile, former Packwood secretary Cathy Wagner Cormack volunteered a two-page sworn statement amending an earlier deposition. Cormack, who had transcribed the senator's diaries since 1969, now stated that he had asked her to alter the tapes.

"Subsequent to the initiation of the Ethics Committee investigation, the senator took back some tapes in my possession which I had not yet transcribed," Cormack said in her statement. "At a later time, it appeared to me that he may have made some revisions to those tapes. Subsequently, he confirmed that he had." In response to the disclosures, Stein wrote the committee saying that "in discrete instances, transcripts depart inconsequentially from the original tapes."

Cormack had begun transcribing the diaries while she was working as a Senate aide. Later, Packwood paid her from Senate funds and, after that, from campaign funds. Because federal law prohibits the personal use of campaign funds, the committee asserted that Packwood could not argue that the diaries were his personal property.

On 8 December, Packwood invoked the Fifth Amendment against self-incrimination and the Fourth Amendment right to privacy in an effort to control his diaries. The ensuing debate eerily resembled Watergate-era arguments. In a statement defending the senator's stand, Stein cited a Supreme Court case in which Nixon won the right to keep his personal diaries.

Senate lawyers referred to the eighteen-and-a-half-minute gap in Nixon's Watergate tapes on 14 December, when they asked Judge Jackson to order Packwood to hand over all tapes and transcripts of his diaries for safekeeping by the court. Judge Jackson promptly issued an order that day, seizing all diary tapes and transcripts.

Like his father, Packwood loved history and dreamed of writing a comprehensive autobiography, just as his early political hero Winston Churchill had done. The twenty years of recording would immortalize his stands on abortion, health care, and Watergate.

Some ex-staffers, including Miles, suspected Packwood also used the diaries to keep tabs on people. The senator acknowledged as much when he alluded to diary references to colleagues' extramarital affairs. His ex-wife Georgie had long warned that the diaries would return to haunt him, but he had not listened.

In mid-December, pressure on Packwood increased from all directions. Another woman, Kerry Whitney of Dallas, surfaced to tell investigators that Packwood had kissed her against her will at least ten times when she worked as a Senate elevator operator. The *Post* also reported that nineteen more women had alleged unwanted sexual advances by Packwood but were not willing to testify before the Ethics Committee. The disclosure brought the number of his accusers to forty-eight.

After Packwood's personal showdown with resignation, he returned to the Old Testament to describe his situation. "Although I'm not a particularly religious man," he told Associated Press reporter Scott Sonner, "I take solace from time to time in reading the Book of Job. . . . Some people think they've got problems. That poor devil really had problems." The scriptural references were something new for this nonpracticing Unitarian who had long ridiculed colleagues for attributing divine purpose to their predicaments and positions.

12

In the weeks after the resignation scare, Packwood—who had once vowed to serve in the Senate longer than nonagenarian Strom Thurmond—seemed to change. Added to his legal woes, Packwood felt the sting of ostracism in the clubby Senate atmosphere. One reporter noticed at Finance Committee meetings that other senators stepped out of camera range whenever a news photographer began aiming Packwood's way. Glenn Simpson of *Roll Call* observed that as television cameras whirred, the Oregon senator often made erudite suggestions for advancing the legislation at hand, which died aborning because legislators did not want to associate themselves with him.

That political isolation deepened. After Packwood's misguided threat during the diary debates to reveal embarrassing sexual matters involving his colleagues, he reached a low point. That December he attended the annual White House Christmas party, hosted by President and Mrs. Clinton. As the power brokers of Washington reveled amid the East Room splendor, they assiduously walked right past Packwood, who sat forlornly in the corner with his date.

Finally, he buttonholed nearby Representative Al Swift, a Washington Democrat, and anxiously engaged him in conversation. The two had been testy adversaries over cable television deregulation issues and had never talked casually before. That he sought out Swift, of all people, to have a prolonged conversation underscored Packwood's desperation to make contact with his peers.

Over time, however, his depression seemed to lift, and he regained some of the fifteen pounds he had lost. Most important, he seemed to lose some of the fear of facing life without the armor of senatorial prestige, power, and perquisites.

On Packwood's return to Oregon that month, he claimed that the media held him to a double standard. "You would think the press might be interested in a fuller inquiry than they've made to date," Packwood told reporters. "But I understand that it is not [a] politically correct [line] to pursue."

The senator went after his accusers with renewed venom. He particularly singled out Gena Hutton. Yes, he admitted placing his tongue inside Hutton's mouth, but declared that was only half the story. After the incident, said Packwood, Hutton continued to volunteer for him. She attended his campaign functions and even dined with him and other staff members. "On a number of occasions, she kissed me. All of this happened," he remarked dryly, "after this traumatic evening where I kissed her." Packwood went on to say that in 1984 she had even asked him to invest in a business, but he declined.

Hutton denied ever asking him for investment money. She did ask for a letter of recommendation, and acknowledged that his staff wrote a "beautiful" one. Hutton admitted that although she did not remember kissing Packwood, it was possible—and not the issue. "I may have given him a kiss on the cheek in greeting," she said. "I do not think that's in the same ballpark as a tongue in the mouth." She kept working for him because of his stand on women's issues and abortion.

"It didn't ruin my life, but it spoke very strongly about power," Hutton explained to the *New Yorker*. "[It says] 'I'm the one on top, and you're the one that's not.'"

But why work for Packwood at all? "I think I responded pretty typically for a women of my generation," explained the forty-eight-year-old Hutton. "I took that incident and put it

214 away. . . . I thought it was important that I stay there and pretend that it didn't happen. "We women do that. It's humiliating to me that I did that, but I did it."

Hutton's explanation remained the most vulnerable part of the women's case. Anita Hill probably ensured Clarence Thomas's nomination when she admitted that she had cultivated him as a reference for years after the alleged harassment incidents. Similarly, former NARAL lobbyist Mary Heffernan had lobbied Packwood after he assaulted her and briefly considered taking an attractive job on his staff.

An unexpected public relations plum fell into Packwood's hands when conservative groups recruited an Arkansas woman, Paula Jones, to file a sexual harassment complaint against President Bill Clinton in May 1994. The senator quickly capitalized on that, writing a self-serving op-ed article titled "Bill and Me" for the *Wall Street Journal*. Packwood raised the ragged old bone that he—and now the president—were victims of changing mores.

> Fifteen or twenty or twenty-five years ago if a man made a pass at a woman and she accepted, it was okay. If a man made a pass and was rebuffed and that was the end of it, he may have been accused of boorish behavior, but he was not accused of "sexual misconduct." Attitudes change. Labels change.

Packwood's piece, however, omitted all the compelling differences between his situation and Clinton's. Packwood initially acknowledged being "just plain wrong" in his conduct with the women, whereas Clinton declared Jones's story to be a complete falsehood. At least thirteen of Packwood's accusers were his direct subordinates. Jones never worked for Clinton. A respected team of reporters, Florence Graves and Charles Shepard, had identified and corroborated the Packwood charges. At last count, the *Washington Post* reported the number of women accusing Packwood, including those afraid to come forth, totaled forty-eight, and many attorneys involved in the case believed the true figure to be much higher than that. In contrast, the national media had uncovered only one woman alleging one incident against Clinton, despite unprecedented efforts by some right-wing interest groups to find some.

Perhaps most important, Packwood had blatantly tried to intimidate the women, threatening to reveal their private sexual and personal histories. No other American politician had been accused of that.

Conservative Supreme Court Justice William Rehnquist, never a friend of Packwood's, was unimpressed with the senator's efforts at spin control. Packwood had gone all the way to the Supreme Court in a bid to stop lower federal court decisions upholding the Senate diary subpoena. On 2 March the chief justice slammed the door on Packwood's last-ditch effort to prevent the Senate from obtaining the diaries. Rehnquist wrote a sharp, three-page denial, saying that Packwood's argument that the subpoena violated his Fourth Amendment right to privacy and Fifth Amendment right against self-incrimination were "seriously undermined by the evidence . . . that his diary transcripts and tapes have been altered."

Packwood went on the offensive and brought his case to the national media. The producers of ABC-TV's *20/20* took his suggestion to investigate Julie Myers Williamson and Cathy Miles. Barbara Walters interviewed him for an April 1994 segment, in which former Packwood aide Carol Byrum was quoted as claiming that Williamson had "boasted" that the senator had made a pass at her and that Williamson didn't seem troubled by it.

The show gave Williamson's accusers a free ride. "The part that irritates me," Williamson told reporters "is they allowed that woman [Byrum] to say [that] if it happened I would have yelled and screamed and kicked him and told everyone about it. And I did do that," she said. "I would have given them *[20/20]* corroborating witnesses, but they weren't interested."

Barbara Walters also threatened to reveal Cathy Miles's true identity to boost the show's ratings. *20/20* producer Rob Wallace called Miles's husband to say that he intended to name her. "He said, 'We're doing a story, we're talking to Packwood, we're naming her, and you better get your licks in.'" Wallace even wrote a letter to Miles's attorney to say, "She is aware we are

216   proceeding with a report which may include information about her relationship with Senator Packwood."

Through her attorney, Miles sent a response that knocked *20/20* out of the water. Walters and Wallace withdrew their threat to publicly identify her.

While it is unclear whether Packwood encouraged *20/20* to undercut Miles, the senator certainly saw her as a lethal threat to political survival. First of all, her October 1991 incident is the most recent.* Moreover, Miles has testified under oath that on 22 April 1992 she personally informed Packwood of Florence Graves's impending article, flatly contradicting his subsequent denials of knowledge.

In the spring of 1994, as Miles boarded a flight at Portland International Airport for Washington, D.C., Packwood's former aide and admirer was stunned. "As I walked through the first-class section, I saw Packwood, and his eyes widened at the sight of me. He looked shocked."

Miles hurried to her seat to call her husband on the airplane telephone, and began crying. Awkward hours later, the plane landed for a stopover in Chicago. As Miles and Packwood warily eyed each other from across the lobby waiting area, she noticed a familiar habit. "At the Senate office, whenever Bob became worried he'd nervously pace back and forth." Now, as she watched the man who once intimidated her beating a path into the parquet floor of O'Hare Airport, Miles had a burst of illumination: she had challenged the bully and now saw the fear in his eyes. Miles stepped to the nearest pay phone and called her husband again.

"Bob Packwood is afraid of me!" she told him.

Her husband agreed happily, "That's right."

———

Packwood's media offensive included interviews with Larry King and *New Yorker* freelancer Peter Boyer, who largely saw

---

* Although the *Oregonian*'s Roberta Ulrich claims the senator kissed her as recently as March 1992, Ulrich has not filed a complaint with the Senate Ethics Committee.

matters his way. The senator explained to CNN host King that this conduct was excusable, or at least understandable, because much of it took place during a different era—when men "asked the girls out," bought the meals and corsages, and always took the first sexual step.

"And you're not a deviant," King said.

"I am not," replied Packwood. "I'm a man . . ."

"Who likes women," King finished for him.

Packwood used the *New Yorker* article to frame his defense: he was just an innocent social nerd whom feminists have scapegoated for many men's failures to abide by the rigid new rules of romance.

The senator explained the nerd defense: "I was such a shy guy growing up, I was a little afraid of women. I had no dates, and on the few occasions when I would try I was usually turned down. So I was hesitant to ask."

That calculatedly self-serving self-pity failed to jibe with what he himself had told others about his high school, college, and especially law school days. Packwood was not the most popular guy on campus, but he did date a high school debate team member and even transferred to Willamette University in part to be closer to her. Later, he almost married a woman he courted at NYU Law School. After law school, bathed in an aura of power and success, he had more opportunities that most men ever have in choosing to be respectful of women socially.

Yet despite the satyric bachelor and extramarital social life he lived through the 1970s and 1980s, Packwood claimed to be surprised to learn exactly what the social rules were. "I now realize that it is in the eye of the beholder," he says. "Therefore, you must not do anything now that might be conceived by the recipient as offensive, or misconduct, or whatever. You just mustn't." Then, with a hint of puzzlement, he added, "I don't know how you decide ahead of time what is going to be offensive. . . . If you don't try, how do you know?"

Many women would tell Packwood that a man's social behavior becomes unacceptable when it fails to recognize and respect a woman's personal boundaries, and legal experts concur. "Grabbing someone by surprise, pressing her against you,

218 pushing your tongue into her mouth, and putting your hands on her buttocks is not ambiguous conduct subject to different interpretation depending on a person's age and gender," said law professor Stephen Gillers. "Penal codes have names for these acts. They're called sexual assault in Washington, D.C., and sexual abuse in Oregon."

The senator who based much of his career on milking the women's movement for campaign funds now claimed that his erstwhile supporters were milking opportunities to find his victims. "If they were to take anybody in the journalism profession, or maybe any member of Congress, put out a 1-800 hot line, and say, 'Anybody who knows anything about Congressman Jones or Senator Smith, call in,' what would happen? And that is what happened to me." Of course, this isn't what happened to Packwood. They already had so much evidence they didn't need a toll-free line to get more.

Columnist William Safire, a longtime friend, entered the fight on Packwood's behalf:

> In a cynical attempt to make Sen. Bob Packwood, R-Ore., a scapegoat for generations of congressional sexism, the Senate Ethics Committee put Americans on notice: No private diary is safe from government investigators. . . .
>
> The scapegoaters are applying today's higher standards of behavior—deservedly higher than tolerated a generation ago—to accusations of yesterday's crude office gropings. That's ex post facto morality, which is neither ethical nor fair. . . .
>
> Packwood has been chosen to be harassment's celebrity villain. To some nervous colleagues, his ruination has become the ticket to forgiveness for all congressional sexist sins. . . .

Some Packwood supporters hoisted the changing-mores banner. "Not to say it's right, but there was a mind-set then that was totally different than today," said Ed Westerdahl, who served on Packwood's steering committee in his 1968 Senate race. "Twenty years ago at parties, I'd see people doing much more than he's being accused of, and nobody gave it a second thought. The touching, feeling was considered to be friendly, not harassing."

Other Packwood defenders, like Jeanette Slepian, retreated behind tightly defined legal walls. Slepian says that even "if every single [accusation] is true, it does not meet the legal definition of harassment." She claims his alleged actions did not threaten anyone's job or work environment, but concedes that the lawmaker does need "a talking to" regarding his behavior.

Westerdahl and Slepian apparently never asked any of the young Republican women who stumbled into Packwood's early campaigns how "friendly" or "threatening" they found the brazen leering and sexually suggestive hugging. It has never been acceptable for a man to maliciously humiliate, embarrass, and demean women. What Safire dismissed as "crude office gropings" was as unacceptable in the 1960s as it is in the 1990s, particularly when it involves a public figure whose wages are paid by the taxes of U.S. citizens.

The social standard hadn't changed, but women's realization of their own power had. Now they understood that they could fight back against those men who had always been able to violate the standards with impunity.

———

Packwood's explanations were becoming more sophisticated, but they didn't seem to speak of genuine reflection or remorse. He discussed these most personal allegations "in the same calm, dispassionate tones in which he discusses the nuances of the German health-care system; there is no averted glance, no embarrassed smile. It is as if, self-explanation being the cost of answering his public humiliation, he had fetched this pathetic inner narrative to the intellectual plane, where his footing is surest," Boyer wrote.

Packwood isn't alone among politicians in his inability to connect with his deeper motivations. According to University of California philosophy professor John Searle, who studies the semantics of accountability and apologies, finding a trace of heartfelt reflection among the tough men and women who inhabit the political and corporate hierarchy is harder than finding a spotted owl in one of Oregon's logged-out forests. Searle believes that some of this loathing to show remorse stems from

220 low self-esteem, hidden under a facade of vanity. "If you fear you'll lower yourself by saying you're sorry, you undoubtedly won't [say it]."

Personal inadequacies may also explain why a major American politician full of prestige and power—and with easy access to willing female sexual partners—would choose to bully and alienate women with malicious conduct. "Sexual harassment is a power play," says Mary Heffernan. "Beneath it is an animosity and lack of respect for women that is damaging to the women and the men. Packwood has low self-esteem, and one way he can feel better about himself is by making others feel worse."

The bottom line, she said, is simple: "If I can make you lower, I must be higher."

Williamson has an intriguing take on the question. "Bob's reputation as a philanderer was a great cover," she claims. So many people around him were trying to be "tolerant" of what they saw as his peccadilloes that they completely missed the real content of his behavior—emotional abuse and power plays.

And despite all the success and privileges that he has earned, Georgie believes that "Bob is not comfortable in his own skin. I think he still sees himself as the person behind the Coke-bottle lenses." Journalist Gail Sheehy has studied ambitious, cutthroat wunderkinds. Almost every one, she said, was:

> Afraid to let anyone come too close. Afraid to stop filling their time with external challenges they could probably surmount, for fear of glimpsing that vast and treacherous interior which seems insurmountable. Afraid that the moment they let down their guard, someone might ridicule them, expose them, move in on their weaknesses, and reduce them again to the powerlessness of a little boy. It is not their wives they are afraid of. It is themselves. That part of themselves I have called the inner custodian, which is derivative of parents and other figures from childhood.
>
> Somewhere, back in the dark recesses of boyhood, each wunderkind I studied recollected a figure who made him feel helpless or insecure. An overbearing mother, an alcoholic father, an absent father.

Even after after twenty-six years of marriage, says Georgie, **221** she and the children never really knew what was going on deep inside. "There's something else here that none of us know. . . . But there sure as hell was something. And it is scary as hell for him," Georgie says.

The question of whether Packwood's feelings toward women were rooted in resentment against a harshly critical mother or the wounds of teenage rejection is intriguing but unanswerable. His upbringing, certainly, seems to have been tense, driven, and emotionally barren. Perhaps springing from that was the relentless competitive drive to achieve, to be something besides someone who felt like a misfit. In the process he became an archetype of the American Dream—a senator at thirty-six, and a powerful national figure at fifty-six. But the problem with those who absorb the gospel of winning for winning's sake is that it leaves them in spiritual wreckage when they eventually lose the game.

The risk that his sexual misconduct would catch up with him was acceptably low when Packwood first entered politics. The maxim that a politician's private life was his own business prevailed, even though taxpayers foot the bill for the lawmakers and the female harems many accumulate on their staff. In the 1960s Packwood only had to look as far as President John F. Kennedy to see how a habitual womanizer's actions could be hidden from the voting public.

Midway through his career, the world began to change. Longtime rumors of philandering crippled Senator Ted Kennedy's bid for the presidency in 1980. Gary Hart, the front-runner for the Democratic presidential nomination in 1987, suffered the same fate. Similar scandal sank Packwood ally John Tower's bid to become defense secretary in 1989.

Packwood, however, continued on as he always had, arrogantly flaunting his disregard for women. Perhaps the most excessive moment came in 1990, during a Senate workshop on sexual assault. Two dozen female staffers attended the workshop to learn how to fend off attacks. The organizer, a newcomer to Capitol Hill, had naively asked a senator she had just met in the Finance Committee to act as the assailant in a series of demonstrations.

222   A chill went through the room when Bob Packwood walked through the door to play the assailant. Packwood happily fell into his role, grabbing women in the derriere and carrying out a mock assault. Unlike the workshop's leader, the participants were fully aware of the implications. One participant remarked nervously to some of the other women that Packwood "had a lot of experience for the role."

The Clarence Thomas and Anita Hill debate would have seemingly eliminated any last vestige of doubt from Packwood's mind that his behavior could ruin him. Yet six months after harassment allegations put Thomas through a purgatory from which his reputation will likely never recover, Packwood tried to sexually embarrass newspaper reporter Roberta Ulrich in front of a witness. Why would any senator, and especially one up for reelection, dance so close to the edge?

Former Packwood campaign aide Gary Eisler observes how "the very nature of sin is that it blinds people to the consequences on others. Packwood's position of power further shielded him from seeing the consequences and penalties for his actions. Being a senator enabled him to act that way with women and intimidate them from fighting back."

The senator failed to see that suppressing women only made them angry and likely to strike back some day. "And meanwhile," continued Eisler, "Packwood just got in deeper and deeper. He became like a mouse sitting on a dinosaur egg."

Packwood had a character flaw that was never treated. And in the Senate environment it grew like a flower in a hothouse. The Senate culture kept him from being accountable for twenty-five years.

"The public, the lobbyists, and their staff treat senators like gods," Heffernan says. "Some senators began to get confused. They wonder, 'Am I a mortal—or am I a god?' And if they choose the latter, they rationalize that since gods have power, that power must be acceptable. And gods don't get caught. Gods can hurt and destroy those who raise voices against them. And part of Bob Packwood convinced himself that he was like a god."

She drew a chilling parallel between Packwood and Icarus, the mythic figure who believed he could fly to the sun on wings made of wax: "And that burned him alive."

His former wife says much the same thing. He "is not evil," explains Georgie Packwood. "This is a decent man who is sick. His Senate seat is more important to him than anything in the world. He's fighting, as he sees it, for his life. . . . I keep hoping and praying that at some stage he will realize that he's lost his soul."

"We went to Washington together," Georgie remembers. "I thought we were going to make some improvements. To me that's why you acquire power, to improve the lot of people whose lot needs improving. But it's a corrupting system. Maybe not because you take money under the table, but ethically and morally it can be corrupting. It just seems that Bob lost something along the way."

———

Packwood's greatest impact may be the fact that all over the United States people are now debating issues that ten years ago were still smutty jokes. The Packwood story has focused awareness on the fact that nearly 50 percent of all women have been sexually harassed. The consequences of that will cost the nation nearly $100 billion over the next decade in lost productivity, litigation, job turnover, and absenteeism.

As a result of the Packwood case, the number of women fighting through the Equal Employment Opportunity Commission (EEOC) and the judiciary has swelled. And as the news of the controversy spreads around the world, the volume of women raising their voices in Great Britain, Canada, and Japan is also growing.

The Supreme Court continues to give support to women in sexual harassment cases. The same week that the Senate debated the Packwood diaries, the court ruled unanimously that a woman who contends she was sexually harassed on the job

224   need not prove she was psychologically injured to win monetary damages.

The case is also changing Congress. Packwood's predecessor, Wayne Morse, helped begin the congressional ethics movement in the late 1940s that a generation later led to the first Senate ethics panel. And the Packwood case is finally accelerating the glacial evolution of sexual misconduct investigations. Currently, Capitol Hill employees have only a short period of time in which to complain that they have been sexually harassed by their employer; after this time, they lose the right to make charges. Now, however, the Senate Ethics Committee is moving to change that rule. Senators are even considering legislation that would give female staff members who have been harassed legal redress against their lawmaker employers.

One of the biggest effects of the Packwood case has been on the women who have accused him of wrongdoing. In talking to the *Post* they risked losing their privacy and being ridiculed. But regardless of the final outcome of the case, their cause has raised consciousness on a formerly taboo issue. And they have also prevailed as people. "It's been difficult much of the time," says Gena Hutton, "but none of us regrets doing it."

Perhaps the most striking impact of the case has been on the very young voters of the future. Several months into the Senate investigation, one of Packwood's accusers invited Graves to speak to her college alumni audience in Philadelphia. There, Graves met the woman's daughter, Caitlin.

"She's one of these adorable, precocious four-year-olds," explained Graves. "You probably know one in your life or have known one in your life. And she marched right up to me and looked me right in the eye. She was on the staircase, so she could look me right in the eye. And she said—I'm going to say it in her voice, so listen carefully—'I called 911 and told powice to go awest Bob Packwood.'

"I said, 'Excuse me. You did what?'

"She said, 'I called 911 and told powice to go awest Bob Packwood.'

"I said, 'I can't wait. Why did you—what did you tell them?'

"'Well, he chased my mommy around a table and kissed her without her permission.'

"I said, 'What did they say?'

"And she said, 'They said they were on it.'

"So," Graves concluded, "there is hope."

Feminist champion Bob Packwood's journey has appeared to be one of the great ironies of American politics. But in reality, there was no inconsistency. Packwood never saw the feminist movement as anything more than a device to advance his own career. And just as he needed to control the political chessboard, he similarly needed to control people, particularly women. For decades his sexual behavior helped him do just that—until cultural changes enabled women to fight back. And that is where the real irony lies: the same cultural changes that empowered women and resulted in his downfall were underwritten by his own strong vocal and legislative support.

Ultimately, Packwood's future will not be resolved by the decisions of the Senate or the Justice Department. If more senators, congressmembers, or even a president are found guilty of sexual misconduct, Packwood will be remembered as the first, but not necessarily the worst, offender. But if he continues to stand alone, he will be locked into history alongside other symbols of tragic excess, like Fatty Arbuckle and Larry Flynt.

Packwood became the leading innovator at exploiting the legalese and loopholes of campaign finance laws and the vacuous technology of television advertising. His seminal leadership of the NRSC rewrote the book for raising special-interest money, and that contributed to the spiraling costs of Senate elections everywhere. Perhaps the most far-reaching effect of his legacy has been the influence on other candidates to believe that political survival depends on mastery of campaign science rather than possessing deeply held views on public policy.

As of this writing, midway through 1994, the Senate Ethics Committee appears likely to renew the public debate in 1995.

226   Packwood took advantage of that break in the action to marshall his resources—attacking Gena Hutton and waging his Barbara Walters/Larry King media campaign. He also benefited as
the Finance Committee debated the hottest issue in the country—Clinton's health-care reform. The committee's ranking Republican gained a reprieve as the White House and its insurance
industry foes furiously battled for his vote.

The White House especially coveted Packwood's support because he was a moderate Republican and had long supported
employer-mandated health care. Health and Human Services
Secretary Donna Shalala invited Packwood to a briefing for a
welcome opportunity to answer reporters' questions about
health care instead of the misconduct accusations.

The president even invited the ethics-beleaguered Packwood
to the White House for a dinner with Vice President Al Gore
and health-care leaders. "The White House was smart enough
to know that was a big favor to Bob," Scott Sonner said.

But to the president's frustration, Packwood—who had
helped pioneer the idea of employer mandates twenty years earlier and had been one of their articulate advocates—reversed his
support for employer mandates and solidly aligned himself with
Senate Republican leader Bob Dole in opposing any Clinton initiative on the health-care crisis. The embattled senator later told
Dole, "We've killed health-care reform. Now we've got to make
sure our fingerprints are not on it." Packwood had previously
aligned himself with Dole on almost all other GOP issues in what
observers perceived as an effort to ensure that fellow Republicans would protect him from harsh Ethics Committee charges.
Dole has even authorized his political action committee to give
a $10,000 contribution to Packwood's legal defense fund.

Sadly, in his ongoing struggle to retain power, Packwood
long ago lost sight of what was best for him. He can still leave
with a nice pension—up to $78,000 a year—but he has de-
stroyed much of his value in the private marketplace. "A year
ago, he could have quit and done well financially as a tax lobbyist. Now it's unclear whether any firm would want to have
him, so damaged is his reputation and his relationships with
his colleagues," reporter Jeff Mapes wrote.

If Packwood had sought his advice when the *Post* reporters contacted him, former aide Bob Witeck would have told him, "If just one charge is true, or has the appearance of truth, a public official or institution has the obligation to get out as much information as it can. You have to own up to it right away and right up front."

Witeck, who left Packwood's staff in 1989 to work for Hill and Knowlton, one of the nation's premier public relations and advertising agencies, thinks he knows why Packwood did not do this. While Packwood and Richard Nixon ended up as foes, they had a lot in common, Witeck says. "They were too interested in what their place in history would be." Packwood's fear of admitting any mistake caused the story to explode exponentially.

"We have a great need to reconcile grievances of all kinds in this country," Witeck continues. "The next several years are an opportunity for Packwood to do that. The ability of Americans to forgive is incredible. I hope Packwood realizes that."

What will be Packwood's place in political history? A lot will depend on what happens in the future. If there are worse scandals for other politicians, then the allegations against Packwood will pale in significance. But if most American politicians truly do "get it" now, history will remember Packwood harshly.

The danger for Packwood is if he deludes himself into thinking he can still beat the rap on the misconduct scandal, never truly confronting either it or his accusers. "He still hopes that history remembers him for his other achievements," says Scott Sonner.

Some time ago the Associated Press editors asked Sonner to update their prepared obituary file on Packwood. As a journalist writing the first draft of history, Sonner reflected on Packwood's career, and then basically typed out, "Senator Bob Packwood, whose accomplishments and career were irreversibly damaged by a sexual misconduct scandal, died xxx at the age of. . . ."

"If Packwood knew what obituaries will probably say," says Sonner, "I think he'd finally apologize to the women and put this behind him."

228   The senator, who claims to be fond of reading the Book of Job, might also take a turn at the letters of St. Paul. A. Robert Smith, whose critical book on Wayne Morse ultimately helped elect Packwood to the Senate, once challenged that senator to confront his weaknesses, writing: "'The Tiger of the old self,'" says St. Paul, 'never dies; but he who seeks atonement with man and God can drive it into the far hills of the soul.'"

Should Packwood venture to subdue his tiger within, he will challenge the toughest adversary of them all. But in that struggle he may yet achieve his most important victory.

NOTES ON SOURCES

Ambrose, Stephen E. *Nixon: Ruin and Recovery*. Simon and Schuster, 1991.

Baker, K. Ross. *Friend and Foe in the U.S. Senate*. Rutgers University, 1981.

Bates, Tom. *Los Angeles Times Sunday Magazine*, 11 April 1993.

Birnbaum, Jeffrey, and Alan Murray. *Showdown at Gucci Gulch: Lawmakers, Lobbyists and the Unlikely Triumph of Tax Reform*. Random House, 1987.

Boyer, Peter J. The *New Yorker*, 4 April 1994.

Brock, David. *The Real Anita Hill*. The Free Press, 1993.

Broder, David. *Changing of the Guard: Power and Leadership in America*. Simon and Schuster, 1980.

Douth, George. *Leaders Profiles: The U.S. Senate, 1975*. Speer and Douth.

Edsall, Thomas. *The New Politics of Inequality*. Norton, 1985.

———. *Power and Money*. Norton, 1989.

Ervin, Sam. *The Whole Truth: The Watergate Conspiracy*. Random House, 1981.

Gabriel, Trip. *New York Times Sunday Magazine*, 29 August 1993.

230 Graves, Florence, and Charles Shepard. *Washington Post,* 22 November 1992 and 7 February 1993.

Halberstam, David. *The Best and The Brightest.* Random House, 1972.

Kurtz, Howard. *The Trouble with Newspapers.* Random House, 1993.

Lasswell, Harold. *Power and Personality.* Viking, 1948.

Long, James O., and Steve Mayes. *Oregonian,* 13 December 1992.

Lukas, J. Anthony. *Nightmare: The Underside of the Nixon Years.* Viking, 1976.

MacKinnon, Catharine A. *Sexual Harassment of Working Women.* Yale University Press, 1979.

McCall, Tom, and Steve Neal. *Tom McCall: Maverick.* Binford & Mort, 1977.

Peabody, Robert L. *Leadership in Congress.* Little, Brown, 1976.

Phelps, Timothy, and Helen Winternitz. *Capitol Games.* Hyperion, 1992.

Sarasohn, David. *Oregonian,* 31 January 1993.

Seelye, Katharine. *New York Times,* 10 July 1994.

Shaffer, Sam. *On and Off the Floor.* Newsweek Books, 1980.

Simpson, Glenn. *Roll Call,* 6 December 1993 and 20 January 1994.

White, Theodore. *The Making of the President, 1964.* Atheneum, 1965; and *The Making of the President, 1972.* Atheneum, 1973.

Packwood entries in *Almanac of American Politics*; *Politics in America;* and *Current Biography* volumes; *Ralph Nader Congress Watch Project* by Jack Lyness. Grossman Publishers, 1972.

The Ronald Reagan presidential library and Richard Nixon presidential archives, White House central files.

Nestles Women's Forum, 13 September 1993.

Investigative Reporters and Editors conference transcript, June 1993, New York.

Kramer, Linda, Bill Donahue, and contributors. *People Magazine,* 14 December 1992.

Newsweek, 8 November 1993.

Congressional Quarterly, 13 March 1993 and 1994 cumulative sum- **231** mary on Packwood case.

Washington Post, 16 December 1993.

Los Angeles Times, Elizabeth Mertens, 1 November 1993 and 9 November 1993.

Dallas Morning News story on Kerry Whitney, December 1993.

Foster Church, 29 January 1993.

Steve Duin *Oregonian* columns 21 February 1993, 2 November 1993, and 12 December 1993.

Steve Mayes, Jim Long and Dee Lane 3 January 1993; 11 September 1993, Lane and Rose-Ellen O'Connor; 3 March 1994; ibid., 20 November 1993; ibid., O'Connor on National Republican Senatorial Committee; Gerry Frank, 11 March 1994; Ellen Emry Heltzel, 1994; *Oregonian* staff writers, 8 December 1992, 30 January 1993, 9 February 1993; Nancy McCarthy, 22 July 1992, Jeff Mapes, 8 September 1991; *Oregonian's Northwest* magazine, Lauren Cowen, 25 June 1989; *Register-Guard*, 13 February 1993, columnist Karen McCowan, and separate story, Paul Neville; *In These Times*, 26 December 1992.

Seattle Times 1986 profile, Terry McDermott; *Washingtonian* profile, Vera Glaser, 1986; The *Wall Street Journal* op-editorial, May 1986, Mark Kirchmeier; *Willamette Week*, 27 January 1993, ibid., and September 1985, Jim Redden Jr.; *People Magazine*, 22 March 1982; Steve Forrester columns 8 and 15 October, 1980 and *Northwest Newsletter* entries; columnist Mary McGrory, *The Downtowner*, 25 February 1981; the *Washington Post*, the *New Republic*, *New York Times* and the *Oregonian* tax reform coverage; *Jersulaem Post*, October 1979; *OREGON* magazine, October 1979, Tom Bates; *Vital Speeches* 1977; *Oregon Journal*, Doug Yocum, 7 October 1974; *Oregon Statesman*, Chris Carlson, 11 December 1972; *Newsweek* column by Kenneth Crawford, 1970; the *Oregonian's* Harry Bodine, 18 October 1968, and Joan Henniger, October 1968; and general coverage by The Associated Press, the *Washington Post*, the *Oregonian*, the *Register-Guard* and the former *Oregon Journal*, *Oregon Statesman*, Salem *Capitol Journal*, American, British, Japanese, Canadian and United Nations publications on sexual harassment laws in the workplace; unpublished notes of Associated Press writer Donald Rothberg's March 1982 Packwood interview; transcript of conference with Packwood and George Will at Center for the Study of Democratic Institutions, California, 1975; *Oregon Voter's Pamphlet* volumes; Senator Packwood's office biography of Georgie Packwood; Baker County, Oregon, historical society records; Mrs. Dolph Phipps and B. W. LeTourneau letters; and Margaret Moss Allen letter to the editor; *The Grantonian* and *Collegian* student newspapers; and New York University *Certiorari* yearbook.

Interviews included Irv Fletcher, Mary Heffernan, Julie Williamson, Theresa Riordan, Gladys (Mindy) Packwood, Opal Hamilton, Sharon Harbor, Mary Lou Oberson, Jack Benson Menashe, Arnold Cogan, George Marandas, Bill Watney, George Shaw, Frances DiGregorio, Roger Buchanan, Ronald Buel, Willamette University professors Ivan Lovell and Robert Gregg, Don Lieullan, Ruben Menashe, Harley Hoppe, Larry Standifer, Don Scarborough, Dolly Montag, New York University faculty Julian Marks, Bernard Schwartz, Howard Greenberger, and John Creedon; Jane Notson Gregg, Jack Lansing, Tom Doneca, Ken Rinke, Stan Church, Cecil Edwards, Pete Snedecor, Maurine Neuberger, Ed Armstrong, Marko Haggard, Don Balmer, William McClenaghan, Mike Katz, Bob Elliott, Sig Unander, Jr., Philip Roth, Lew Scott, Herb Legg, Bill Hamilton, Paul Ehrlich, Ted Hughes, Keith Skelton, F. F. (Monte) Montgomery, Howell Appling, Gena Hutton, Richard Kennedy, Connie McCready, Frank Roberts, Ed Whalen, Bill Stevenson, Stephen McCarthy, Peter Friedman, Mrs. Ladd Griffith, Tom Hatfield, Ted Hallock, Ron Abell, Bill Brown, Jeff Drumtra, M. Kenneth Bowler, Rob Leonard, John Nields, Jr., Paul Weyrich, Jo Blum, Marsha Dubrow, David Jory, Dan Lavey, Jeff Lewis, Betty Roberts, Linda McAlister Peters, Mary Ann Buchanan, Robin Shephard, Michael Salsgiver, Rob Gardner, Michael Bailey, Peter Friedman, Geoff Garin, Corrine Jennings, Gretchen Kafoury, Anne Greenfield, Jerry Weller, Nancy Roche, Gayle Rothrock, Joanne Rossoff, Mike Stern, Bob Van Brocklin, Carolyn Ossolinik, Wayne Thevenot, Charls Walker, former Senators Alan Cranston, William Proxmire, George McGovern, Eugene McCarthy, and Joseph Tydings; Paige Wagers, Bob

Witeck, Larry Swisher, and other women and men who could **233** not release their names for publication.

Interviews with journalists included Peter Boyer, Tom Bates, Lou Cannon, Glenn Simpson of *Roll Call;* Bob Cohn and Patricia King of *Newsweek;* Linda Kramer of *People Magazine;* Scott Sonner of The Associated Press; Philip Kuntz of the *Congressional Quarterly;* Trip Gabriel of the *New York Times;* Anne Swardson and the late Bill Peterson of the *Washington Post;* Chris Hanson of the *Seattle Post-Intelligencer;* Les Heintz of the Fisher Broadcasting Washington, D.C. bureau; Mark Hass of KATU-TV, Portland; Brent Walth of the *Register-Guard;* Jeffrey Birnbaum of the *Wall Street Journal;* Brit Hume of ABC News; John Dancy of NBC Nightly News; Steve Forrester of the *Daily Astorian;* Wolf Blitzer of the *Jerusalem Post;* Donald Rothberg, J. W. "Bud" Forrester, Win McCormack of *Oregon Business* magazine; Joe Berger, Paul W. Harvey, Floyd McKay, Doug Seymour, Jill Smith, John Armstrong, Mason Drukman, Kimbark MacColl; and former *Oregonian* reporters Gene Klare, A. Robert Smith, Jerry Tippens, Harold Hughes, and Bill Keller, the latter now of the *New York Times.*